LEARNING *to use*

PUBLISHER

2000

for Desktop Publishing Awards

SHARON SPENCER

Heinemann

Includes free
CD-ROM

Heinemann Educational Publishers,
Halley Court, Jordan Hill, Oxford OX2 8EJ
A division of Reed Educational & Professional Publishing Ltd

Heinemann is a registered trademark of Reed Educational & Professional Publishing Limited

OXFORD MELBOURNE AUCKLAND JOHANNESBURG BLANTYRE GABORONE IBADAN
PORTSMOUTH NH (USA) CHICAGO

First published 2001
2005 2004 2003 2002
10 9 8 7 6 5 4 3

A catalogue record for this book is available from the British Library on request.

ISBN 0 435 45410 2

Pages designed by Wendi Watson

Cover designed by Sarah Garbett

Typeset by TechType, Abingdon, Oxon

Printed and bound in Great Britain by Thomson Litho Ltd, East Kilbride, Scotland

Acknowledgements
I would like to thank my family for their support while writing this book and Pen Gresford and Rosalyn Bass for their endless patience and advice.

Sharon Spencer

The publishers would also like to thank Rosemary Wyatt at Abingdon College.

Screen shots reprinted with permission from Microsoft Corporation

To access the files on the accompanying CD-ROM, insert the CD into your CD-ROM drive and open them either from Windows Explorer or the appropriate software package as instructed.

Tel: 01865 888058 www.heinemann.co.uk

Contents

About this book

This book provides a simple step-by-step approach to learning desktop publishing using Publisher 2000, from the basic skills on how to set up a page to how to produce professional, accurate work.

The book is suitable for use in the classroom, in an open-learning workshop, at home or in the workplace. There are plenty of exercises throughout the book to practise your skills as well as consolidation exercises and mock examinations at the end of each section. Answers to all the exercises are also provided to enable you to check your own work.

There can be a few ways of performing a task using Publisher 2000 – using the keyboard, mouse or menu. The exercises throughout the book show one method. For example:

For keyboard Press: **Ctrl + S**
For mouse   Click on: the 💾 **Save** button
For menu   From the **File** menu, select: **Save**

A glossary of commands at the back of the book provides a comprehensive alphabetically-listed quick reference guide for all Publisher 2000 commands introduced in the book. The commands are shown using either keyboard, mouse or menu.

The disk accompanying the book contains files to be imported for the practice exercises, consolidation pieces and mock examinations.

The book is divided into three sections:

1 Introduction to Desktop Publishing

This section introduces you to the basics of desktop publishing. You will learn how to use the tools and menus in Publisher 2000, set up a basic page layout, import text and graphics and apply different text styles.

At the end of this section you will be ready to take the CLAIT (Desktop Publishing Application) assessment and two consolidation pieces and two mock assignments are included to practise the skills you have learnt to prepare you for CLAIT. A checklist is provided for you to keep a record of your progress.

2 Intermediate Desktop Publishing

This section teaches you how to work with larger blocks of text and produce documents that have a more professional look. It also looks at amending documents that have already been created. This is quite a different skill to creating your own documents.

At the end of Section 2 you will be ready to take the OCR Stage II DTP examination and two consolidation pieces and two mock examinations are included for practice.

3 Advanced Desktop Publishing

The final section gives you the opportunity to design your own page layouts within a specified design brief. You will also learn advanced copyfitting techniques, to help make your document look more professional.

This section also teaches you how to prepare colour documents ready for printing and you will also work on non-standard page sizes so that you can confidently produce business cards, leaflets and other documents.

At the end of Section 3 you will be ready to take the OCR Stage III DTP examination and two consolidation pieces and two mock examinations are included for practice.

Using the Mouse and Keyboard

Mouse

You will need to be familiar with using the mouse before you start using this book. The mouse is used to work with windows software programmes and as you move it a pointer ⟋ moves across the screen. The mouse has two buttons, a left and a right. The **left button** is used in a number of ways:

Point. As you move the mouse over an object, the pointer will change shape according to the object that is being highlighted. For example, if you are using the mouse within a text document, the pointer will change to a text pointer Ⅰ, if you move the mouse to outside the document, it will change back to a mouse pointer ⟋.

Click. Press the left button once and release. This is used to place the cursor in a certain position, for example if you wanted to change a character or word in a piece of text, or to select shortcut buttons to perform a task – for example, the ▣ **Save** button.

Double-click. Press the left button twice, in quick succession, and then release. This is used for opening folders and launching applications.

Drag. This is used for selecting items – for example, text or groups of objects.

For text: click at the beginning of the text you wish to select and, still holding down the mouse button, move the pointer to the end of the text then release the mouse button. The text will now be highlighted.

For groups of objects: click somewhere slightly above and to the left of the object that is furthest to the top/left and, still holding down the mouse button, move the mouse pointer diagonally to the opposite corner of the area you want to select, then release the mouse button. The objects you have selected will now be highlighted.

Drag and drop. If you want to move text from one place to another then you can use the drag and drop facility. First select the text (you can use the dragging method above), then click on the selected text and, still holding down the mouse button, move the pointer to where you want the text to go, then release the mouse button. The text will have moved to the new position.

The **right button** will, depending on what you are doing, provide alternative pop-up menus for common commands without having to go to the main toolbars or menus. See the appendix on page 199 for more information.

Keyboard

Use the keyboard to perform the following tasks:

The Enter key. When you are keying in text, use this key to insert a line break. It can also be used to accept commands, instead of clicking on **Yes** or **OK**. This is the large arrow key on the right of the main keyboard.

Cursor keys. These are the four arrow keys grouped at the bottom between the main keyboard and the key pad. These will easily move the insertion point (cursor) around the document.

The Delete key. This key can be found in the group of six keys at the top between the main keyboard and the keypad – it is the bottom, left key of the six. Use this to easily delete boxes and graphics. Select the item you wish to remove (by clicking on it) and then press the **Delete** key.

The Shift key. There are two shift keys on the keyboard, one immediately below the **Enter** key and the other directly underneath the **Caps Lock** key. Keep one of these pressed down to type a capital letter and also to carry out certain functions.

Many other tasks can be carried out using the keyboard and these are shown in the glossary at the back of the book on page 203.

PART 1

CLAIT

Introduction to Desktop Publishing

In Part 1 of the book you will learn about:

- creating a document
- importing text and images
- changing the appearance of text
- changing the appearance of graphic items.

You should make sure you learn everything in this section thoroughly as it provides the basis on which intermediate and advanced skills are built.

Chapter 1

Creating a document

In this chapter you will learn how to:
- ◼ load Publisher
- ◼ open a blank document
- ◼ set up a page layout
- ◼ use rulers and margin guides
- ◼ draw a text frame
- ◼ set up column guides
- ◼ set a space for a page-wide heading
- ◼ save your document
- ◼ close your document
- ◼ exit Publisher.

1.1 Loading Publisher

To open Publisher 2000 you will need to be in Windows. How you load Windows will depend on whether you are using a networked or stand-alone system.

Exercise 1.1

1 Find out whether you are using a networked or stand-alone system.
2 Find out how to load Windows on your system.
3 Load Windows.

Once you have loaded Windows you will see the 'desktop'. This is the main menu from which you move around in Windows. It will look something like Figure 1.1 but the icons may differ according to the programs installed and the set-up options that have been defined.

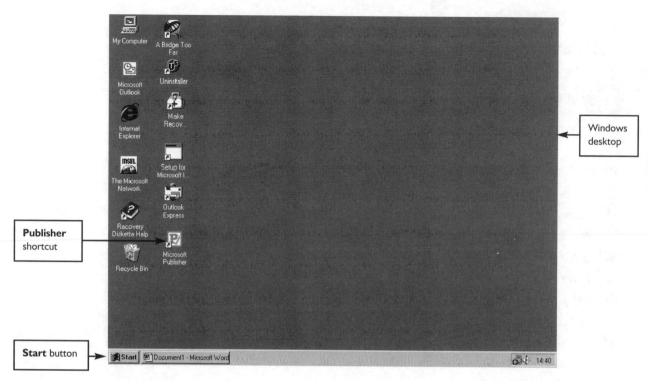

Figure 1.1 Windows desktop

Once you have reached the desktop you will be ready to open Publisher. You may see a short-cut icon on the desktop which will take you straight to the Publisher software. If the icon is not on the desktop then you will need to open Publisher from the Program menu, using the Start button.

 Load Publisher.

METHOD 1 1 Move the mouse cursor over the **Start** button and click the left mouse button – a pop-up menu will appear listing the various programs and applications installed on the computer (see Figure 1.2).

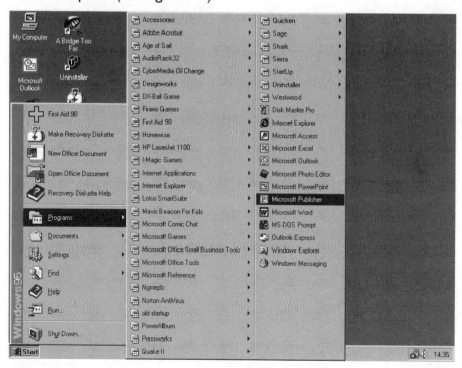

Figure 1.2 Loading Publisher using the Start button

2 Highlight **Programs** by moving the mouse over it – another menu will appear.

3 Drag the mouse across to **Microsoft Publisher** and click on it. Publisher will now begin to load.

METHOD 2

(Use if you have a shortcut icon to Publisher on your desktop.)

I Click on: the **Microsoft Publisher** shortcut icon (see Figure 1.3).

Figure 1.3 Publisher shortcut icon

1.2 Opening a blank document

Exercise 1.3 Set up a blank document.

Once Publisher has finished loading you may see the following catalogue on screen. If this does not appear, then you should see a blank page as shown in Figure 1.5 on page 6.

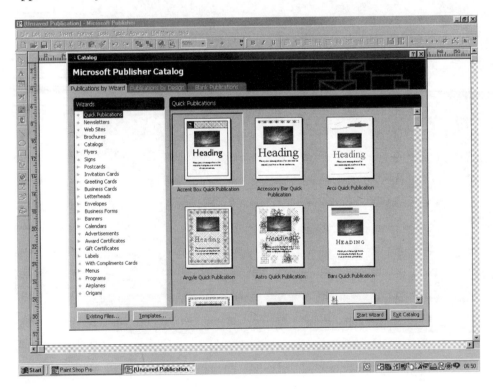

Figure 1.4 Microsoft Publisher Catalog

This catalogue gives you a choice of ready-prepared designs (known as wizards) that you can use as a basis for your design. However, in this book you will be learning how to set up your own pages, so you should close this menu:

METHOD 1 Click on: the ✖ **Close** button in the top right-hand corner of the catalogue window.

TIP

You might find it useful to switch off the catalogue so that it does not appear every time you load Publisher. To do this:

1 From the **Tools** menu, select: **Options**.

2 Select the **General** tab and click on the checkbox next to **Use Catalog at startup**. The tick should disappear from the checkbox.

The next time you load Publisher you will see a blank page straight away (as in Figure 1.5). If at a later point you want the catalogue to appear whenever you load Publisher, then:

1 Repeat steps 1–2 so that the tick reappears in the checkbox.

Your window should now look similar to the one in Figure 1.5 below – with a blank page in the centre. Your page may be displayed landscape instead of portrait and your toolbars (see below) may be in different positions.

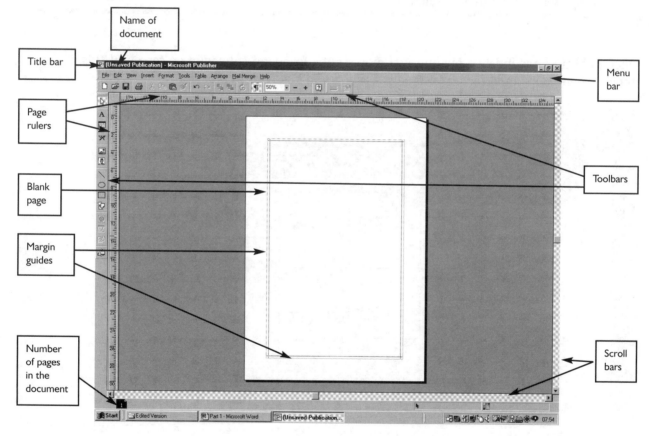

Figure 1.5 Blank page

TIP

Your screen may include a Quick Publication Wizard to the left of the blank page (see Figure 1.6).

Figure 1.6 Quick Publication Wizard

You can just click on the **Hide Wizard** button below it, or, if you prefer, you can switch this facility off, so that next time you open a blank document, the wizard is not there. To do this:

1   From the **Tools** menu, select: **Options**
2   Select the **User Assistance** tab and click on the checkbox next to **Use Quick Publication Wizard for blank publications**. The tick should disappear from the checkbox.

Parts of the document window

Title bar. This shows the name of the document and the application name (**Microsoft Publisher**). If you have not saved your publication the name displayed will be (**Unsaved Publication**).

Menu bar. This contains a number of menus that can be selected using the mouse or keyboard. When a menu has been selected a drop-down menu will be displayed containing a number of options that can be selected.

Toolbars. These contain buttons that can be clicked to access common functions. The positions of the toolbars on your screen may differ to that in Figure 1.5 – for example, all your toolbars might be displayed at the top or some may be displayed at the bottom of the window.

The Object Toolbar (Figure 1.7) contains tools for drawing objects – for example, the **A** **Text Frame Tool** button or the **Picture Frame Tool** button which are used for drawing text frames and picture frames respectively. The Object Toolbar will always be on screen.

Figure 1.7 Object Toolbar

The Standard Toolbar contains shortcut buttons for general document tasks – for example, the 🖫 **Save** button, and the 🖨 **Print** button, which are used to save the document and print the document respectively. The Standard Toolbar should be on screen, however, if it is not you can display it:

METHOD   1 From the **View** menu, select **Toolbars**.
2 From the drop-down menu, select **Standard**.

Figure 1.8 Standard Toolbar

The Formatting Toolbar (Figure 1.9) changes depending on what items are selected. Figure 1.9 is what it looks like when nothing is selected. See page 12 for the Formatting Toolbar when a text frame is selected and see page 24 for the Formatting Toolbar when a picture frame is selected. The Formatting Toolbar should be on screen, however, if it is not you can display it:

METHOD   1 From the **View** menu, select **Toolbars**.
2 From the drop-down menu, select **Formatting**.

Figure 1.9 Formatting Toolbar

You will find out about many of the buttons on the toolbars while going through this book. A number of them, however, are for specific purposes not covered in this book. If you want to find out about them, you should consult Publisher's **Help** files (click on: the ❓ **Microsoft Publisher Help** button).

Some commonly used buttons on the Object toolbar

 Use the **Text Frame Tool** to insert a text frame. Click on the button, then draw your text frame on the page.

 Use the **Clip Gallery Tool** to insert a piece of clip art. Click on the button, then draw your frame on the page. You can select the image you want to insert from the **Insert Clip Art** window.

 Use the **Line Tool** to draw lines. Click on the button, then draw your line on the page. If you want the lines to be perfectly straight (horizontally, vertically or diagonally), then hold down the **Shift** key while you draw.

 Use the **Oval Tool** to draw ovals or circles. Click on the button, then draw your oval on the page. If you want to draw a true circle (360°), then hold the **Shift** key while you draw.

Use the **Rectangle Tool** to draw rectangles or squares. Click on the button, then draw your rectangle on the page. If you want to draw a true square, then hold down the **Shift** key while you draw.

 Use the **Picture Frame Tool** to insert picture files or scanned images. Click on the button, then draw your picture frame on the page. You will learn how to insert a picture into the frame later (page 24).

1.3 Set up a page layout

Once the design catalogue has been closed you will be left with a blank screen as shown in Figure 1.5. The default page layout in Publisher is usually A4 size and either landscape or portrait orientation, the measurements of which are shown in Figures 1.10 and 1.11. The default layout may change depending on the type of publication you were using previously.

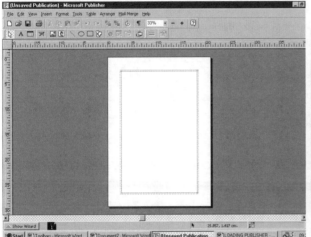

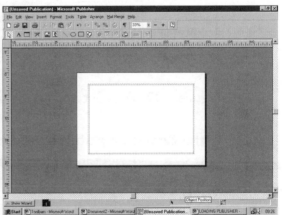

Figure 1.10 A4 Portrait (29.7 cm x 21 cm) The page is displayed with the shorter edge at the top.

Figure 1.11 A4 Landscape (21 cm x 29.7 cm) The page is displayed with the longer edge at the top.

Exercise 1.4   Check that your page is set up as A4 portrait.

METHOD 1 From the **File** menu, select **Page Setup**. The **Page Setup** dialogue box will appear:

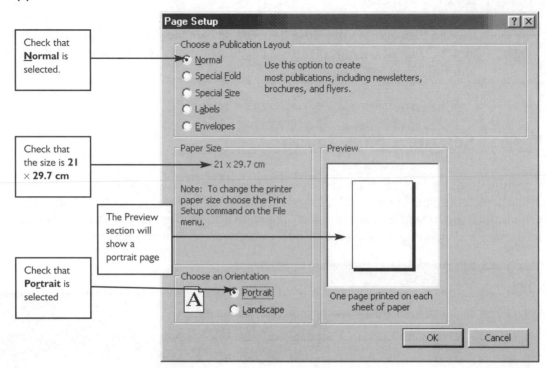

Check that **Normal** is selected.

Check that the size is **21 × 29.7 cm**

The Preview section will show a portrait page

Check that **Portrait** is selected

Figure 1.12 Page Setup dialogue box

2 In the **Choose a Publication Layout** section, check that the **Normal** radio button is selected (and select it if not).

3 In the **Paper Size** section, check that the dimensions **29.7 × 21 cm** are shown.

4 In the **Choose an Orientation** section, check that the **Portrait** radio button is selected (and select it if not).

5 Click on: **OK**.

You can also create non-standard page sizes (**Special Size**) which will be looked at in Part 3 (page 130).

1.4 Use rulers and margin guides

Publisher has rulers and guides that help you lay out items on the page (see Figure 1.13).

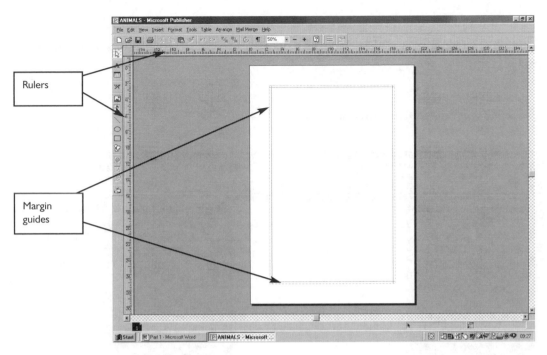

Figure 1.13 Rulers and margin guides

Rulers

The rulers are at the top and left-hand side of the page. They will help you line up items on the page with a high degree of accuracy.

Margin Guides

In desktop publishing software, the margin guides are in fact only guides and you can place text and graphics outside of these lines. This is different to most word processing software packages where you cannot place anything outside of the margins.

If you decide to place text or graphics outside of the margin boundaries you should check that your printer is able to print close to the edge of the paper. Some printers have a default setting of 5 mm and may not be able to print closer to the edge of the page.

The default margins for Publisher are set at 2.5 cm all round. These are suitable for the pages that are to be created in this part of the book. Changing the margins is covered in Part 2 (page 51).

1.5 Draw a text frame

It is usual practice in the workplace for text files to be created in word-processing software and then inserted (imported) into the desktop publishing software. In order to do this in Publisher, text frames need to be drawn on the page before the text files can be inserted.

Exercise 1.5 Draw a text frame to fill the space between the margin guides.

METHOD I Click on: the **A Text Frame Tool** button.

2 Move the cursor to the top left-hand corner of the margin guides.

3 Click and drag down and to the right to the bottom right-hand corner of the margin guides.

You should now see a one-column text frame on screen:

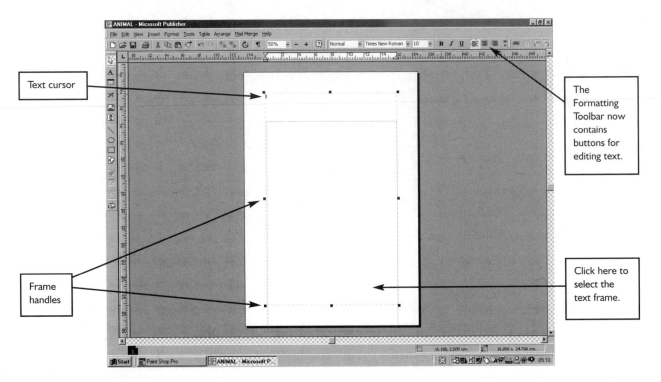

Figure 1.14 Text frame

You can see that the handles of the text frame are displayed and that the text frame fills the spaces between the margin guides. Notice also that the Formatting Toolbar has changed so that it now contains buttons for editing text:

Figure 1.15 Formatting Toolbar when a text frame is selected

1.6 Set up column guides

Exercise 1.6 Set up your text frame to contain two columns with gutter space of 5 mm.

METHOD 1 Select the text frame (by clicking anywhere within it).

2 From the **Format** menu, select: **Text Frame Properties** (it is important that you have selected the text frame otherwise the **Text Frame Properties** option will not show on the **Format** menu).

The **Text Frame Properties** dialogue box will appear:

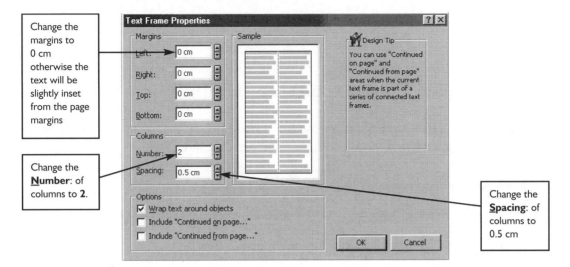

Change the margins to 0 cm otherwise the text will be slightly inset from the page margins

Change the **Number**: of columns to **2**.

Change the **Spacing**: of columns to 0.5 cm

Figure 1.16 Text Frame Properties dialogue box

3 Change all the margins to 0 cm (so that the text is not inset from the main page margins) by clicking on the ⊠ down arrows.

4 Change the **Number** of columns to 2 by clicking on the ⊠ up arrow.

5 Change the **Spacing of columns** to 0.5 cm by selecting the number (double-clicking) and keying in **0.5 cm**.

6 Click on: **OK**.

Your text frame will now be shown with two columns:

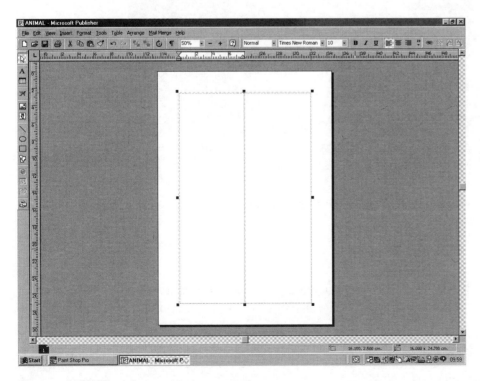

Figure 1.17 Text frame with two columns

TIP
In the CLAIT assignment the gutter space is not specified. If you keep to 5 mm this will be acceptable.

1.7   Set a space for a page-wide heading

If you want to have a heading that spans across the width of the page, you will need to draw a text frame at the top of the page where the heading can be inserted later.

Exercise 1.7   Set a space for a page-wide heading.

METHOD **1** Click on: the **A Text Frame Tool** button.

2 Click in the top left-hand corner of your text frame and drag down and to the right to the right margin.

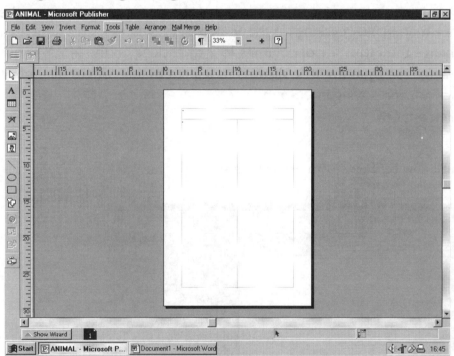

Figure 1.18 Drawing a text frame for the heading

1.8   Save your document

It is a good idea to get into the habit of saving your work early on and frequently while you are working. When you first save a document you will have to give it a name and decide where to save it.

Exercise 1.8   Save your document as **ANIMAL**.

METHOD 1 From the **File** menu, select: **Save As**.

The Save As dialogue box will appear:

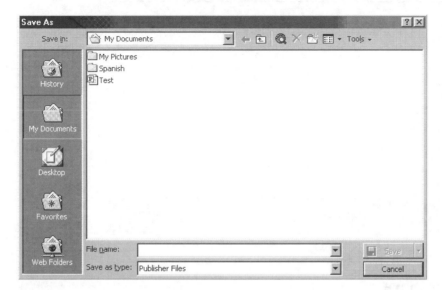

Figure 1.19 Save As dialogue box

2 Click on: the ▼ down arrow at the right of the **Save**: box to display a drop-down menu of locations on your computer:

Figure 1.20 Selecting a drive

3 Select the drive you are going to save to.
(You may need to check with your tutor which drive to use. For example, you may need to save to a floppy disk – see Figure 1.20 – or you may have space on your college or school's network.)

In order to save the document in the correct place, such as your personal work folder, you may need to open a number of folders:

4 Double-click: on a ▢ folder icon to open it.

When you have opened the folder in which you want to save the document, you can then key in the name of the file:

5 In the **File name**: box, key in: **ANIMAL**:

Figure 1.21 Save as **ANIMAL**

6 Click on: **Save**.

Your document has now been saved. (*Notice that the Title Bar now reads* **ANIMAL - Microsoft Publisher**.)

You should remember to save your document regularly (Publisher may remind you to do so at certain intervals) to ensure that you do not lose any changes you have made. Now that you have named your file, saving is much easier:

METHOD 1 Click on: the ⊟ **Save** button (on the Standard Toolbar).

METHOD 2 Press: **Ctrl + S**

1.9 Close your document

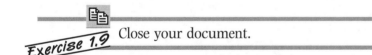

Exercise 1.9 Close your document.

METHOD 1 From the **File** menu, select: **Close**.

A prompt box may appear asking if you want to save the changes you have made:

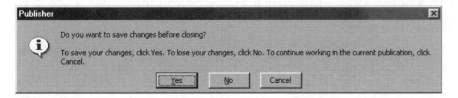

Figure 1.22 Save prompt box

2   Click on: **Yes**.

A new blank page will appear on screen.

1.10   Exit Publisher

Exercise 1.10   Exit Publisher.

METHOD 1	From the **File** menu, select: **Exit**.
METHOD 2	Click on: the ☒ **Close** button in the top right-hand corner of the window.

You should now have exited Publisher and your screen should have returned to the Windows desktop that you saw at the beginning of the chapter (Fig 1.1, page 4).

Exercise 2

1   Launch Windows (if you are not already in Windows).
2   Launch Publisher.
3   Set up a blank document. Leave the margins as default.
4   Check that your page is set up as A4 portrait.
5   Draw a text frame that fills the page to each margin.
6   Set up your text frame to contain three columns with a gutter space of 3 mm (0.3 cm).
7   Draw a text frame for a page-wide heading.
8   Save your document as **ANTIQUE**.
9   Close your document.
10 Exit Publisher.

Chapter 2

Importing text and images

In this chapter you will learn how to:
- ■ open a Publisher document
- ■ import text
- ■ save using a different filename
- ■ key in a heading
- ■ draw a picture frame
- ■ import a picture
- ■ move a picture
- ■ print a document.

2.1   Open a Publisher document

Exercise 3.1   Open the document **ANIMAL**. (Launch Publisher first if necessary.)

METHOD   I   **Either**: Click on: the 🗁 **Open** button.
Or: From the **File** menu, select: **Open**.

The Open Publication dialogue box will appear:

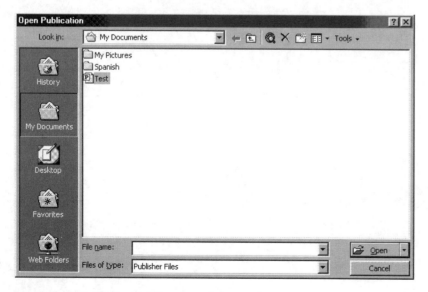

Figure 2.1 Open Publication dialogue box

You will need to select the location of your file (if your documents are on a floppy disk, remember to put in the disk drive).

2 Click on: the ▼ down button to the right of the Look in: box.

3 Select the drive you require (for example, **3¹/₂ Floppy (A:)**).

4 Double-click on the ⬜ folder icons until you are in the folder you require.

5 **Either**:
- Double-click on the file you want to open (**ANIMAL**)

Or:
- Click on: the file you want to open to select it (see Figure 2.2).
- Click on: the 🗁 **Open** button.

Figure 2.2 Select the file you want to open

Your document should now be on screen:

Figure 2.3 ANIMAL document opened

2.2 Import text

It is usual practice to create text files in a word-processing application and then import it into the desktop publishing document. In Publisher, text needs to be imported into a text frame. In Chapter 1 you drew two text frames on your page – one for the main text and one for the heading.

Exercise 3.2

Import the text file **ANIMALS** into your main text frame.

METHOD 1 Click anywhere within the main (large) text frame.
2 From the **Insert** menu, select: **Text File**.

The **Insert Text** dialogue box will appear on screen:

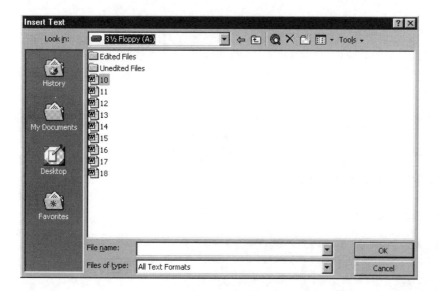

Figure 2.4 Insert Text dialogue box

Notice that this looks just like the **Open Publication** dialogue box (see Figure 2.2, page 19). It also works in the same way.

3 Select the drive you require.
4 Double-click on the folder icons until you find the file you require.
5 Select the file you want to insert (see Figure 2.5).

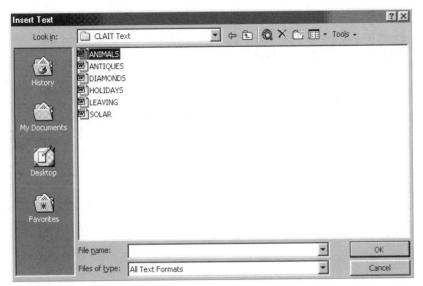

Figure 2.5 Select the file you want to insert

6 Click on: **OK**.

The text will be imported into your document:

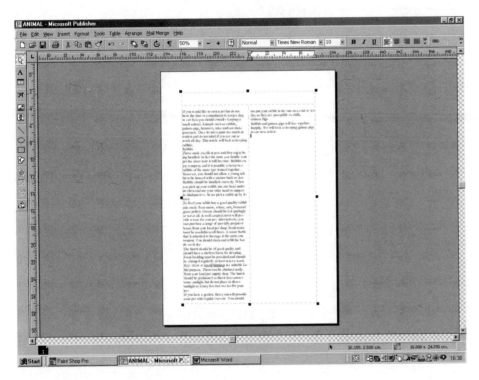

Figure 2.6 Text imported into document

Notice that the text has automatically flowed into the second column because the text box has been split into two columns. If you only had a few lines of text, then it would not need to flow into the second column. If you had more text than would fit into the two columns you would need to make some changes to the text size. This is covered later (page 29).

2.3 Save using a different filename

You may need to keep different versions of your publications. This is useful in the workplace as you may want to look back at previous versions to check when changes have been made or you may need to produce different versions of a document for different purposes. It is a good idea to save your new version early on (for example, as soon as you have made the first change) otherwise you may accidentally save the changes in your original document.

Save your document as **ANIMAL1**.

METHOD | From the **File** menu, select: **Save As**.

The Save As dialogue box should open with the folder where files that are already open have been saved. (If not, double-click on the ⬜ folder icons until you reach the correct folder.)

2   In the **File name**: box, key in: **ANIMAL1**.
3   Click on: **Save**.

2.4 Key in a heading

You will need to key a heading into the heading text frame you prepared earlier.

Remember that when you are keying in text, the words wrap automatically from line to line – you do not need to press the return key at the end of each line.

Key in the heading: **KEEPING SMALL ANIMALS**.

So that you can see what you are keying in, you may find it helpful to zoom in to the 100% (actual size):

METHOD 1 | 1 From the **View** menu, select: **Zoom**.
         2 From the drop-down menu that appears, select **100%**.

METHOD 2 | 1 Click on: the ▾ down button next to the ⎡50% ▾⎤ **Zoom** box.
         2 From the drop-down menu that appears, select **100%.**

You may need to use the scroll bars to move up to the top of the page so you can see the heading text frame:

METHOD | 1 Click: anywhere in the heading text frame
         2 Key in: **KEEPING SMALL ANIMALS**.

2.5 Draw a picture frame

If you are going to place a picture into your document, then you will need to draw a picture frame and then insert (import) the picture.

There are a number of different types of pictures that can be inserted. You can insert picture files that have been saved on disk. You should also have a selection of images in the clipart files which are attached to Publisher. Alternatively, you may be given images to scan into the document. You might also want to draw your own pictures in a package such as Paintbox or Freehand and then insert these in your documents.

Exercise 3.5 Draw a picture frame in the top left-hand corner (below the heading box).

When you are given a layout to follow, make sure you place the picture frame exactly as specified.

METHOD
1 Click on: the 🖼 **Picture Frame Tool** button.
2 Press: the **Shift** key and keep holding it down.
3 Click and drag (still holding down the **Shift** key) from the left-hand margin at the top of the text, down and right to the edge of the text in the first column:

By holding down the Shift key, you are ensuring that the picture frame is a true square. If you do not require a true square or do not have sufficient room, then you can draw the picture frame without holding down the shift key.

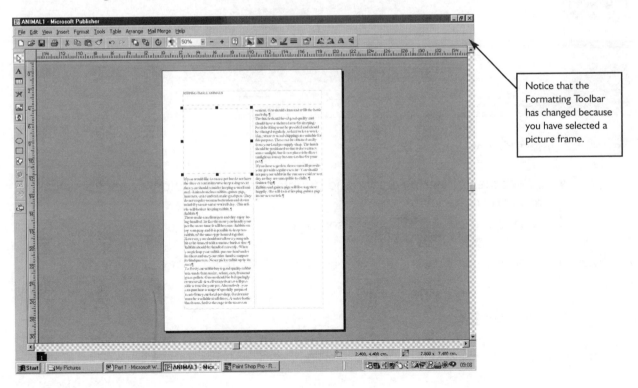

Figure 2.7 Picture frame

Notice that the text has moved out of the way of the picture frame, this happens automatically so you don't need to worry about the text being hidden underneath the picture. (If, for some reason, this has not happened in your document, look at page 68 to find out how to set text wrap.)

2.6   Import a picture

Now you have your picture frame positioned, you are ready to import an image file.

Import the picture file **RABBIT** into the picture frame.

Exercise 3.6

METHOD 1 Click anywhere within the picture frame to select it.
2 From the **Insert** menu, select: **Picture**
3 From the drop-down menu that appears, select: **From File**.

The **Insert Picture** dialogue box will appear on screen:

Figure 2.8 Insert Picture dialogue box

4 Select the correct directory and double-click on the folders until you are in the correct folder.
5 Click on: the **RABBIT** file to select it.

A preview of the picture may appear – this enables you to check that you are inserting the correct picture.

6 Click on: **Insert**.

Your picture will now be inserted in your picture frame:

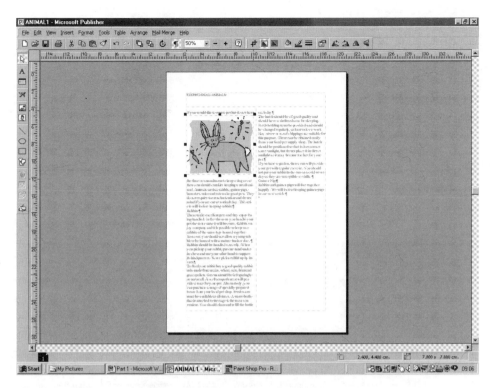

Figure 2.9 RABBIT file inserted in picture frame

Notice that the picture frame has changed size to fit the picture: it has kept the same width, but the height has changed (it is no longer square). As you can see, there is now one line of text above the picture. If this has happened, this looks very unprofessional and as you have been told to put the picture at the top left-hand corner of the document, it will need to be moved up.

2.7   Move a picture

Exercise 3.7   Ensure your picture is still in the correct place.

METHOD   I   Click anywhere in the picture frame and drag the picture upwards until it is in the correct place.

Notice that while you were doing this the cursor icon changed. If you accidentally moved the picture to the left or right while moving it, you can nudge it a small amount at a time in the direction you need to bring it back into line:

METHOD   I   Click on: the picture to select it.
          2   Press and hold down: the **Alt** key and use the cursor keys to nudge your picture in the required direction.

2.8   Print a document

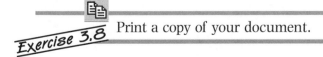

Exercise 3.8   Print a copy of your document.

METHOD 1   Click on: the 🖨 Print button.

The document will be sent straight to the default printer.

METHOD 2   **Either**:
From the **File** menu, select: **Print**.
Or:
Press: **Ctrl + P**.

The **Print** dialogue box will appear:

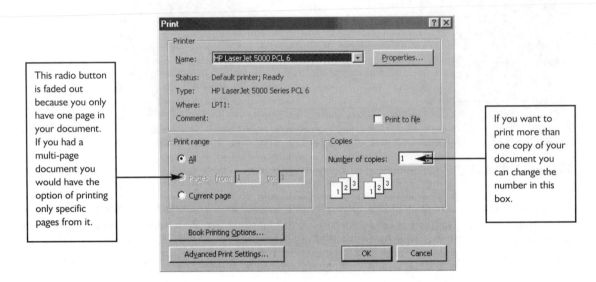

This radio button is faded out because you only have one page in your document. If you had a multi-page document you would have the option of printing only specific pages from it.

If you want to print more than one copy of your document you can change the number in this box.

Figure 2.10 Print dialogue box

> **2** Check that the printer in the **Name**: box is the one you want to print to (and if not, change it by clicking on: the ▾ down arrow and selecting the correct one).
>
> **3** Click on: **OK**.

Exercise 3.9   Close your document. (Look back at page 16 if you cannot remember how to do this.)

Exercise 4
   1   Open the document **ANTIQUE**.
   2   Import the text file **ANTIQUES** into your main text frame.
   3   Save your document as **ANTIQUE1**.
   4   Draw a picture frame at the bottom of the third column.
   5   Import the picture file **JUG** into the picture frame.
   6   Ensure your picture is still in the correct place.
   7   Key in the heading **AFFORDABLE ANTIQUES**.
   8   Print a copy of your document.
   9   Close your document.

Chapter 3

Changing the appearance of the text

In this chapter you will learn how to:
- change the alignment of text
- set up indents
- change the size of text
- change the font style
- add emphasis to text.

Once you have imported the text into your document you can then alter its appearance in a number of ways. You will learn about five of these in this chapter.

3.1 Change the alignment of text

There are five main ways to align text:

- Justify
- Left align
- Right align
- Centre
- Force justify

Look at the examples below:

> The text in this box has been justified. It stretches from margin to margin and gives a neat effect. This alignment is often used in reports, magazines, and newspapers where there are a number of narrow columns. However, it is not the best alignment for long lines of text – for example the full width of an A4 page – as it can be difficult for the eye to follow.

> The text in this box has been left aligned. This is usually the default alignment. The lines end naturally and are easy to read.

> This text is right aligned.
> Note that the lines end in the same place on the right hand side and extend to the left.
> If a document were keyed in in this style it would be difficult to read.

> This text is centred within the box.
> In order to centre text in the middle of a page, you must ensure that your text box runs from margin to margin.

This piece of text has been force justified. Unlike plain justification it justifies the last line of the paragraph as well – even if there is only one word, which can make it very difficult to read. Force justification can sometimes be useful if you are trying to fit a piece of text into a limited space. Ordinary justification, however, will probably be sufficient   for   your   examination   work.

TIP

If you want to force justify a paragraph, then do the following:
- Highlight the paragraph you want to justify.
- Click on: the **Justify** button.
- Position the insertion point (cursor) at the very end of the paragraph.
- Press: **Shift + Enter**.

The alignment buttons are visible on the Formatting Toolbar when you have selected a text frame:

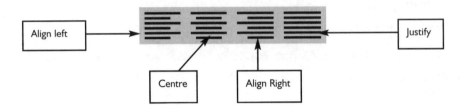

Align left

Justify

Centre

Align Right

Exercise 5.1   Open the document **ANIMAL1** and save it as **ANIMAL2**. (If you have forgotten how to do this, then look back at page 22.)

Exercise 5.2   Centre the heading across the page.

In order to centre text in the middle of the page, you need to ensure that the text frame runs from margin to margin and is a single-column text frame. If you centred the main text of the document then it would centre within each of the two columns and not across the page.

METHOD 1 Highlight the heading.
           2 Click on: the ≣ **Center** button.

The heading will now be centred:

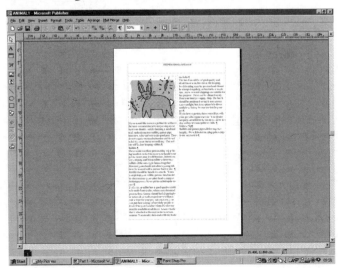

Figure 3.1 Heading centred

3.2   Set up indents

In desktop publishing, it is usual to leave only one space after a full stop. It is also common for the first line of each paragraph to be indented instead of a line space between paragraphs (as you would use in a letter). When setting the indent, choose a small value, such as 0.25 cm.

Exercise 5.3   Give the body text a first-line indent of 0.25 cm.

The body text is the main text that fills your main text frame except for the subheadings (in this case **Rabbit** and **Guinea Pigs**). You need to change it paragraph by paragraph so that you don't change the subheadings as well.

METHOD 1   Highlight the first paragraph (**If you need…keeping rabbits**.)
    2   From the **Format** menu, select: **Indents and Lists**.

The **Indents and Lists** dialogue will appear on screen:

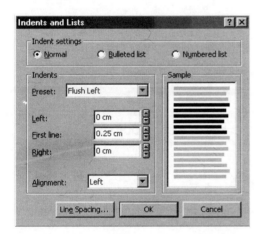

Figure 3.2 Indents and Lists dialogue box

    3   In the **Firstline**: box, key in: **0.25 cm**.
    4   Click on: **OK**.
    5   Repeat steps 1–4 for the other paragraphs, remembering not to change the subheadings.

The body text will now be indented.

3.3   Change the size of text

You may want to make each of the three different parts of the text – heading, subheadings and body text – a different size in order to give emphasis to your document:

■   Heading (or headline) – this is placed at the top of a document
■   Subheadings – these are headings within the main text
■   Body text – this is the main text of the document

Text sizes are measured in points. The text sizes for the different types of text should be sufficiently different to show up on the printed version of your publication. For example, if you used point sizes of 9, 10 and 11, the differences between the three are so slight it would be difficult to distinguish between them.

Some suggested combinations for the three are shown in Figure 3.3:

Heading — 18 or 16
Subheading — 16 or 14
Body text — 12 or 10

Figure 3.3 Sizes of text

In Figure 3.3 the heading is in a point size of 18, the subheading is in a point size of 16 and the body text is in a point size of 12. You can easily see the difference between the three sizes.

Try to ensure that you have at least two point sizes between each type of text.

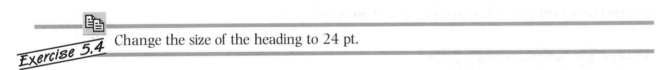

Exercise 5.4   Change the size of the heading to 24 pt.

METHOD 1 Highlight the heading.
2 **Either**:
  • Click in the [12 ▼] **Font Size** box (on the Formatting Toolbar)
  • Key in: **24**.
  • Press: **Enter**.
  Or:
  • From the **Format** menu, select **Font**.

The **Font** dialogue box will appear:

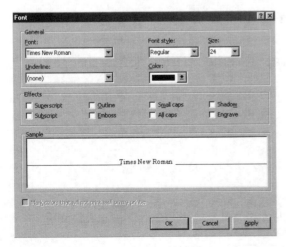

Figure 3.4 Font dialogue box

- Double-click in the **Size**: box.
- Key in: **24**.
- Click on: **OK**.

The heading will now be much larger.

Exercise 5.5 Change the subheading size to 18.

The subheadings are the words **Rabbit** and **Guinea Pigs**.

METHOD 1 Highlight the word **Rabbits**.
2 Click in the 12 ▾ **Font Size** box.
3 Key in: **18**.
4 Press: **Enter**.
5 Repeat the process for the **Guinea Pigs** subheading.

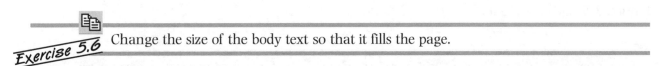

Exercise 5.6 Change the size of the body text so that it fills the page.

When filling the page, the text should not go over the bottom margin guide. If the text finishes slightly above the margin guide this will be acceptable. You may need to try a number of different sizes before you find one that will fill the page. For a page of A4 text, the size of the body text is usually in the range of 8-14 points. If you are having trouble making the text fit the page using the values 10 and 12 points, you can select a point size of 11 or key in a point size of 13 in the Font Size box, even though it is not displayed.

3.4 Change the font style

There are two types of font – serif and sans-serif. You will need to know the difference between these fonts (also known as typefaces).

Serif fonts have small strokes (serifs) at the top and/or bottom of some letters that help guide the reader's eye across the page. The text you are reading now is in a serif font. One of the most common serif fonts is **Times New Roman**.

Sans-serif fonts are 'without' serifs – the strokes at the top or bottom of certain letters. These fonts are best used for headings and points of emphasis, as large blocks of sans-serif text can be difficult to read. The text for the method instructions in this book is set in a sans-serif font. A common sans-serif font is **Arial**.

This is a serif font – look at the strokes at the bottom of the letters, **l**, **m** and **k**.

This is a sans-serif font – there are no strokes at the bottom of any letters.

There are many different fonts, both serif and sans-serif. It is important to be able to tell the difference between serif and sans-serif fonts. A selection of fonts is given in Figure 3.5.

> This is Book Antiqua, - it is a serif font.
> This is Europa – it is sans-serif font
> This is Poor Richard – it is a serif font.
> This is Gill Sans – it is a sans-serif font.
> This is Sage - it is a serif font.
> This is Tahmoa – it is a sans-serif font.
>
> **This is Toujours – it is a serif font.**

Figure 3.5 Different fonts

Proportional and monospaced fonts

The fonts you use will probably be proportional fonts. This means that each letter will take up only the amount of space it requires. For example, the letter **l** will take up less space on a line than the letter **w**.

There are some fonts, such as **Courier New**, that are monospaced. This means that each letter takes up the same amount of space on a line regardless of its size. These fonts imitate the typewriter, where letters always take up the same amount of space on a line. The monospaced font does not look as professional as other fonts.

```
This is an example of a monospaced font, COURIER NEW. Note that all
the letters are the same width.
```

Change the heading to a sans-serif font.

Exercise 5.7

We are going to use Arial as the sans-serif font as this is one of the most common ones.

METHOD I Highlight the heading.

2 **Either**:
   - Click in the `Times New Roman ▾` **Font** box (on the Formatting Toolbar).
   - Key in: **Arial**.
   - Press: **Enter**.
   Or:
   - From the **Format** menu, select **Font**.

The **Font** dialogue box will appear on screen:

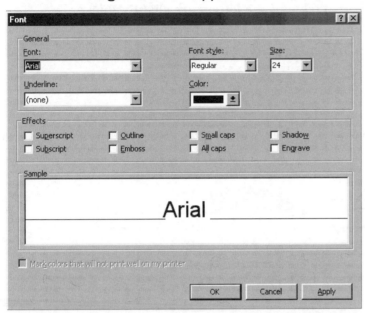

Figure 3.6 Font dialogue box

- Highlight the font in the **Font** box.
- Key in: **Arial**.
- Click on: **OK**.
   Or:
- Click on: the arrow to the right of the **Font**: box.
- From the drop-down menu, select: **Arial**.

Your heading will now be in Arial.

Exercise 5.8 Change the subheadings to a sans-serif font.

METHOD   Follow the same method as above – still using Arial.

Exercise 5.9 Change the body text to a serif font.

METHOD   The body text should already be in a serif font (Times New Roman) as this is usually the default font in Publisher. However, if your body text is not in

Times New Roman, then change it following the above method but selecting **Times New Roman** instead.

3.5 Add emphasis to text

You may wish to emphasise your text in some way, particularly headings and subheadings. Using the **bold** and/or changing text to italic can be very effective. It can change the appearance of a font quite considerably. Figure 3.7 shows examples of bold and italic text using the same font.

This is bold text – it looks very dark and the letters are slightly thicker.
This is italic text – it slants to the right.
This is bold italic text – it is dark and thick and also slants to the right.

Figure 3.7 Text emphasis

The text emphasis buttons can be found on the Formatting Toolbar (when you are in a text frame).

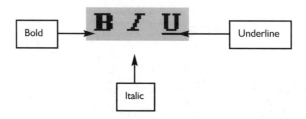

 Embolden the heading.

Exercise 5.10

METHOD   1   Highlight the heading.
            2   **Either**:
                • Click on: the **B** **Bold** button.
                Or:
                • Press: **Ctrl + B**.
                Or:
                • From the **Format** menu, select **Font**.

The **Font** dialogue box will appear on screen.

                • Click on: the arrow to the right of the **Font Style** box.
                • From the drop-down menu, select: **Bold**.
                • Click on: **OK**.

Embolden and italicise the subheadings.

Exercise 5.11

METHOD Use the method outlined above to embolden the subheadings. Then italicise them in the following way:

I Highlight the subheadings.

2 **Either**:
 • Click on: the *I* **Italic** button.
 Or:
 • Press: **Ctrl + I**.

Exercise 5.12 Check that the text still fills the page and adjust the body text size if necessary

Exercise 5.13 Print one copy of your document. (Look back at page 25 if you have forgotten how to do this.)

Exercise 5.14 Close your document.

Exercise 6

1 Open the document **ANTIQUE1** and save it as **ANTIQUE2**.
2 Change the alignment of the heading to centred and of the subheadings (**Modern Collectables** and **Restoration**) to right aligned and of the body text to justified.
3 Give the body text a first-line indent of 0.5 cm.
4 Change the size of the heading to 22 pt.
5 Change the size of the subheadings to 16 pt.
6 Change the size of the body text so that it fills the page.
7 Ensure the heading is in a serif font.
8 Ensure the subheadings are in a serif font.
9 Change the body text to a sans-serif font.
10 Embolden the heading.
11 Embolden the subheadings.
12 Check that the text still fills the page and change the body text size if necessary.
13 Print one copy of your document.
14 Close your document.

Chapter 4

Changing the appearance of graphic items

In this chapter you will learn how to:

- resize images
- draw lines
- change the weight of lines
- draw boxes.

Exercise 7.1 Open the document **ANIMAL2** and save as **ANIMAL3**.

4.1 Resize an image

In order to make the document look neat and tidy, or if the image you import is the wrong size, you may need to resize an image.

Exercise 7.2 Move the rabbit image to the bottom of the page and resize it so that it stretches across both columns.

METHOD
1. Move the image to the bottom of the first column. (Look back at page 25 if you have forgotten how to move images.)
2. Click on: the image to select it.
3. Click on: the top right-hand corner handle.
4. Drag: the handle up and to the right until it reaches the far right margin guide.

You should make sure you always resize images in proportion so as to avoid distorting them too much. It can be very difficult to resize an image in proportion, because in order to keep the correct dimensions, the image may take up too much space. Generally, if you ensure that both the length and height of the image are increased (or decreased) equally, without any noticeable distortion, this will be acceptable for OCR examinations.

TIP
If you use any of the centre handles, your image will be resized in only one direction and will therefore distort. Avoid doing this unless you are specifically instructed to distort the image.

Notice that the image is now very large and a lot of your text has disappeared. You will need to change the body text size so that it fills the available space.

4.2 Draw a line

The appearance of a document can often be improved by adding lines to separate the different parts of the document.

Draw a line under the heading ensuring that it does not touch any of the text.

METHOD I Click on: the ◥ **Line Tool** button (on the Object Toolbar). (Notice that the cursor changes to a cross.)

2 Press and hold down: the **Shift** key and, still holding down the **Shift** key, click and drag from the left-hand margin to the right-hand margin.

(Holding down the **Shift** key allows you to draw a straight line – if you wanted to draw a diagonal line, you would not hold down the **Shift** key.)

4.3 Change the weight of lines

The term used to describe the thickness of a line is **weight** and there are a number of different weights you can use. If the line weight is not specified, you should choose the weight to suit your document.

Although there are many different line designs, such as dotted, dashed, etc, it is much neater to use a plain line.

_____ 1 pt

━━━━━━━━━━━━━━━━━━━━━━━━━━━ 3 pt

━━━━━━━━━━━━━━━━━━━━━━━━━━━ 6 pt

Change the weight of the line below the heading to 4 pt.

METHOD I Double-click on the line.

The **Line** dialogue box will appear on screen:

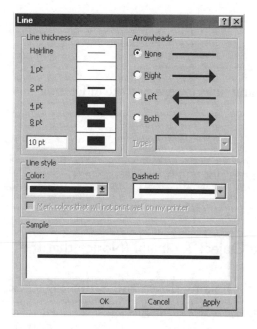

Figure 4.1 Line dialogue box

2 Click on: the line next to **4 pt**.

3 Click on: **OK**.

4 If you want to move the line so that it appears in the middle of the heading and the body text:

- Hold down the **Alt** key.
- At the same time, press the down cursor key to move the line.
- Keep pressing the down cursor key until the line is in the correct place.

If you move the line too far, then you can adjust the position by repeating the above method but holding down the up cursor key instead.

4.4 Draw boxes

It can also be useful to emphasise images or sections of text by drawing boxes round them.

Exercise 7.5 Draw a box with a line weight of 2 pt around the image ensuring that it doesn't touch any of the text or the image.

To draw a box around an image, you just change the frame – you don't actually need to draw a box.

METHOD 1 Click on: the image to select it.

2 **Either**:
- Click on: the ☰ **Line/Border Style** button (on the Formatting Toolbar when an image is selected).
- From the drop-down menu, select: **More Styles**.

Or:
- From the **Format** menu, select: **Line/Border Style**.
- From the drop-down menu, select: **More Styles**.

3 Click on: the line next to **2 pt**.

4 Click on: **OK**.

A frame will be drawn around the image.

Notice that the image is touching the frame – it is important that the image is inset from the frame so that it does not touch it at all:

METHOD 1 Click on: the image to select it.

2 **Either**:
   • Click on: the 🖼 **Picture Frame Properties** button (on the Formatting Toolbar)

   Or:

   From the **Format** menu, select: **Picture Frame Properties**.

The **Picture Frame Properties** dialogue box will appear on screen:

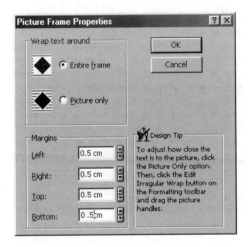

Figure 4.2 Picture Frame Properties dialogue box

3 In the **Wrap text** around section, ensure that the **Entire frame** radio button is selected.

4 In the **Margins** section, key in **0.5 cm** in all four boxes to inset the picture 0.5 cm from the frame.

5 Click on: **OK**.

The image will now be reduced so that it is not touching the frame. You must ensure that the frame is not touching the text above it. If it is:

METHOD 1 Hold down: the **Alt** key.

2 At the same time, press the down cursor key to move the frame.

3 Keep pressing the down cursor key until the frame is in the correct place i.e. clear of any text.

If you move the frame too far, then you can adjust the position by repeating the above method but holding down the up cursor key instead.

Exercise 7.6 Draw a box around the heading ensuring it does not touch any of the text or the line below the heading.

METHOD 1 Click on: the ☐ **Rectangle Tool** button (on the Object Toolbar).
2 Click and drag: from slightly above the text until you are clear of the text on the right-hand side. Then drag down the cursor until you are clear of the bottom of the text.

Try to keep the box an even space from the text on all sides. If you haven't, then you can adjust the box slightly using the corner handles until it is in the correct place.

Now change the line weight of the box to 2 pt:

METHOD 1 Double-click on: the box.

The **Border Style** box will appear on screen.

2 Click on: the **2 pt** option.
3 Click on: **OK**.

TIP
It is extremely important that in examinations you do not alter the text or add lines or boxes unless it is specified in the examination paper.

Exercise 7.7 Ensure that the body text still fills the space available (and adjust the body text size if not).

Exercise 7.8 Print one copy of your document.

Exercise 7.9 Close your document.

Exercise 8 1 Open the document **ANTIQUE2** and save it as **ANTIQUE3**.
2 Move the graphic **JUG** to the end of the **Modern Collectables** section and reduce the size of the image.
3 Draw a box around the graphic ensuring that it does not touch either the graphic or any text.
4 Draw a box around the headline text. Ensure that it does not touch any text.
5 Change the weight of the box around the heading to 2 pt.
6 Ensure that the body text still fits the available space.
7 Print one copy of the document.
8 Close the document

Consolidation 1

You will need to do the following:

Choose a serif font and a sans-serif font for this document

Ensure that you have access to the text file **SOLAR** and the graphic file **PLANET**.

Choose three type sizes, one for each of the following:

- Heading (large)
- Subheading (medium)
- Body text (small)

1 Set up a page layout for your document. You will need a page-wide space for a heading and two columns.

2 Import the previously prepared text file: **SOLAR** and place it in the two columns.

3 Import the previously prepared graphic file: **PLANET** and place it at the bottom of the second column below all text. Ensure no text is obscured by the image or lost off the page.

4 In the prepared space, using a serif font and a heading type size, key in a heading **THE SOLAR SYSTEM**. Ensure the heading is left aligned and emboldened.

5 Ensure that the rest of the text is in the body text size, a serif font and left aligned.

6 Save your work as **SOLAR** and print one copy.

7 Increase the size of the image and move it to the top of the two columns, below the headline. Ensure that it stretches across both columns. Ensure that no text is obscured by the image or lost off the page.

8 Change the subheadings **PLUTO** and **MERCURY** to a sans-serif font and the subheading size.

9 Change the body text type size so that it fits in the two columns.

10 Draw a line between the image and the headline, ensuring that it stretches across both columns.

12 Save your work as **SOLAR1**

13 Print one copy of your work.

14 Exit from Publisher.

Consolidation 2

You will need to do the following:

Choose a serif font and a sans-serif font for this document

Ensure that you have access to the text file **HOLIDAYS** and the graphic file **PARIS**.

Choose three type sizes, one for each of the following:

- Heading (large)
- Subheading (medium)
- Body text (small)

1   Set up a page layout for your document. You will need a page-wide space for a heading and three columns.

2   Import the previously prepared text file: **HOLIDAYS** and place it in the three columns.

3   Import the previously prepared graphic file: **PARIS** and place it at the bottom of the middle column below all text. Ensure no text is obscured by the image or lost off the page.

4   In the prepared space, using a serif font and a heading type size, key in a heading **SHORT BREAK HOLIDAYS**. Ensure the heading is right aligned and emboldened.

5   Ensure that the rest of the text is in the body text size, a sans-serif font and left aligned.

6   Save your work as **BREAKS** and print one copy.

7   Increase the size of the image and move it to the top of the three columns, below the headline. Ensure that it stretches across the first and second columns. Ensure that no text is obscured by the image or lost off the page.

8   Change the subheadings **Day One, Day Two** and **Day Three** to a serif font and the subheading size. Embolden the subheadings and ensure they are left aligned.

9   Change the body text type size if necessary so that it fits in the three columns. Set a first line indent of 0.25 cm.

10   Draw a box around the image, ensuring that it does not touch any text.

12   Save your work as **BREAKS1**

13   Print one copy of your work.

14   Exit from Publisher.

Exam Practice 1

OCR CLAIT (DTP Application)

You will need:

- A desktop publishing application
- Previously prepared text file: **LEAVING**
- Previously prepared graphic file: **STAIRS**
- A serif type face (font)
- A sans-serif type face (font)
- Three type sizes, one for each of the following:
  - Heading (large)
  - Subheading (medium)
  - Body text (small)

Assessment Objectives

5.1.1	Load the desktop publishing application.
5.1.2	Set up a page layout for your document. You will need a page-wide space for a heading and two columns.
5.1.3	Import the previously prepared text file: **LEAVING** and place it in the two columns.
5.1.4	Import the previously prepared graphic file: **STAIRS** and place it at the bottom of the second column below all text. Ensure no text is obscured by the image or lost off the page.
5.2.1, 5.2.4, 5.2.5	In the prepared space, using a sans-serif font and a heading type size, key in a heading **LEAVING HOME**.
5.2.2	Centre the heading, ensuring that it is on one line and clearly centred across the two columns. Embolden and italicise the heading.
5.2.3, 5.2.4, 5.2.5	Ensure the rest of the text is in the body text size, a serif font and a justified right margin.
5.2.4, 5.2.5	Ensure the subheadings are in a serif font and change to a subheading type size. Apply emboldening and italics.
5.2.6	Draw a line between the heading and the text. Ensure that no text is obscured.
5.4.1, 5.4.2	Save your work as **HOME** and print one copy.
5.3.2	Reduce the size of the image and move it to the middle of the first column. Ensure that no text is obscured by the image or lost off the page.
5.3.1	Change the size of the body text so that it fills the two columns.
5.4.1, 5.4.2	Save your work as **HOME1** and print one copy.
5.4.3	Exit from the desktop publishing application.

Exam Practice 2

OCR CLAIT (DTP Application)

You will need:

- A desktop publishing application
- Previously prepared text file: **DIAMONDS**
- Previously prepared graphic file: **DIAMOND**
- A serif type face (font)
- A sans-serif type face (font)
- Three type sizes, one for each of the following:
  - Heading (large)
  - Subheading (medium)
  - Body Text (small)

Assessment Objectives

5.1.1	Load the desktop publishing application.
5.1.2	Set up a page layout for your document. You will need a page-wide space for a heading and three columns.
5.1.3	Import the previously prepared text file: **DIAMONDS** and place it in the three columns.
5.1.4	Import the previously prepared graphic file: **DIAMOND** and place it at the top of the first column above all text. Ensure no text is obscured by the image or lost off the page.
5.2.1, 5.2.4, 5.2.5	In the prepared space, using a sans-serif font and a heading type size, key in a heading **Romancing the Stone**.
5.2.2	Centre the heading ensuring that it is on one line and clearly centred across the three columns. Ensure the heading is emboldened.
5.2.4, 5.2.5	Ensure the subheadings are in a serif font and change to a subheading type size.
5.2.3, 5.2.4, 5.2.5	Ensure the rest of the text is in the body text size, a serif font and fully justified.
5.4.1, 5.4.2	Save your work as **STONE** and print one copy.
5.3.2	Increase the size of the image and move it to the top of the second and third columns. Ensure that no text is obscured by the image or lost off the page.
5.3.1	Change the size of the body text so that it fills the three columns.
5.2.6	Draw a box around the graphic ensuring it does not touch the graphic or any text.
5.4.1, 5.4.2	Save your work as **STONE1** and print one copy.
5.4.3	Exit from the desktop publishing application.

CLAIT Checklist

Did you remember to	Assessment Objective	Con 1	Con 2	Exam 1	Exam 2
...set up the required number of columns and leave a space for the heading?	5.1.2				
...import the text and graphic files and place where specified?	5.1.3 5.1.4				
...check that no text was lost or obscured when you placed the graphic images?	5.1.3 5.1.4				
...key in the heading, using the correct font and size with 100% accuracy?	5.2.1 5.2.4 5.2.5				
...centre the heading making sure that it fitted across the page?	5.2.2				
...correctly apply the body text and subheading styles, fonts and alignments?	5.2.3 5.2.4 5.2.5				
...save your work and print as specified?	5.4.1 5.4.2				
...reduce, or increase and move the image as specified without losing or obscuring any text?	5.3.2				
...change the text sizes, fonts and styles as specified?	5.3.1 5.2.4 5.2.5				
...draw the line and/or box as specified without touching any text?	5.2.6				
...save and print a second copy of your work?	5.4.1 5.4.2				
...exit correctly from Publisher?	5.4.3				

2

STAGE II
Intermediate Desktop
Publishing

Part 1 of this book showed you how to set up a page layout and import one short text file and one graphic image. In Part 2 we will be dealing with larger blocks of text and two or more graphic files.

Working with large blocks of text can be quite time-consuming, especially when changing point sizes or type styles. There are a number of tools available in Publisher 2000 that can help you work with large blocks of text quickly and easily.

Before you start Part 2 make sure you can:

- load Publisher 2000
- create a new document
- open an existing file
- save and print documents
- set up page layouts

- draw text frames
- draw picture frames
- import text and images
- change text appearance
- insert lines and boxes.

In Part 2 of the book you will learn about:

- setting up master pages
- resizing images and copyfitting
- working with images and drawing objects.

- applying text styles and text wrap
- amending an existing publication

Chapter 5

Setting up Master Pages

In this chapter you will learn how to:
- work on two or more pages
- set accurate margins
- move to background
- prepare style sheets
- set up headers and footers
- set up automatic page numbering
- move to foreground
- set up column guides
- save master pages.

What are master pages?

Most desktop publishing applications have a facility to set items which are to be repeated throughout a document in the background. For example, if you were setting out a magazine, you might want to have a page number, the title of the magazine and the logo on every page. Instead of having to place these items individually on every page, you can set them in the background so that they are automatically repeated. You can have two different master pages, one for right-hand pages and one for left-hand pages. In some desktop publishing applications this background is referred to as the *master page* or *master pages*, in Publisher, however, it is referred to as the **Background**.

> **TIP**
>
> The terminology can be a little confusing. Master pages can either mean a template file or the background pages where you set up items to be repeated throughout the document. In the OCR Stage II Desktop Publishing exam, master pages means a template file which contains the specified number of pages, correct margins, column guides, style sheets and headers and footers set up. In the exam this *must* be saved as a separate file before you start importing any text or images.
>
> This whole chapter deals with the process of setting up this template and looks at setting up items (such as guides, headers and footers) on the background. From now on, when the term *master page(s)* is used, this will mean the template file and the term *background* will refer to the area where you place items which you want to be repeated on every page.

5.1 Work on two or more pages

If you know that you are going to be working on two or more pages it is much easier if you set them up before starting work on your document. This will make it easier for you when inserting the text into your document as it will flow from page to page automatically.

Exercise 9.1 Load Publisher and create an A4 document with portrait orientation. Insert a new page so that you have a two-page document. Save it as **HOLIDAYS**. These are your master pages.

NB Ensure that your document is A4 and portrait.

METHOD 1

1 From the **Insert** menu, select: **Page**.
The **Insert Page** dialogue box will appear on screen:

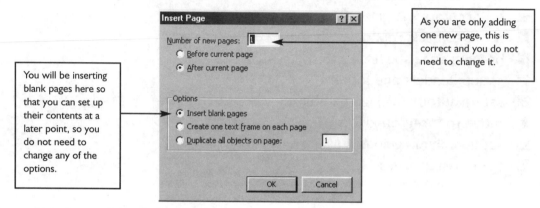

You will be inserting blank pages here so that you can set up their contents at a later point, so you do not need to change any of the options.

As you are only adding one new page, this is correct and you do not need to change it.

Figure 5.1 Insert Page dialogue box

2 Check that the **Number of new pages:** box says 1.
3 In the **Options** section, check that the **Insert blank pages** radio button is selected.
4 Click on: **OK**.

METHOD 2

1 Press: **Ctrl + Shift + N**. (This will add one blank page – if you wanted to add more, you would need to use Method 1.)

You will now have two pages in your document:

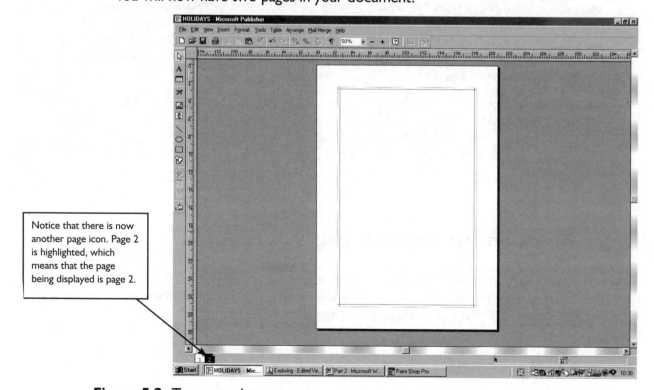

Notice that there is now another page icon. Page 2 is highlighted, which means that the page being displayed is page 2.

Figure 5.2 Two-page document

TIP

You will see in the Insert Page dialogue box that there are options for adding pages **before** and **after** the current page. Ensure you place your new page in the correct position for your document.

5.2 Set accurate margins

When you set up your master pages, you should specify the margins required before you start to place text and images in the document.

Exercise 9.2 Set up margins of 2.5cm for the left and right of your document and 2.75cm for the top and bottom of your document.

METHOD

1 From the **A̲rrange** menu, select: **Layout Guides**.
The **Layout Guides** dialogue box will appear on screen:

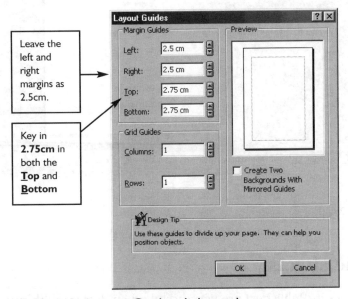

Figure 5.3 Layout Guides dialogue box

2 In the **Margin Guides** section, leave the **Le̲ft** and **R̲ight** boxes the same (2.5cm) and in the **T̲op** and **B̲ottom** boxes key in **2.75cm**.
3 Click on: **OK**.

TIP

If you are given specific margin measurements then it is important that you keep to them. In an examination you will incur penalties if you do not. If you are given specific measurements in the workplace this could be because your document is going to fit into a larger publication and needs to be consistent, or it may be because of the printing process.

5.3 Move to background

The background is where you will set up layout guides and items such as headers and footers, that you want to appear on every page.

Move to the background of your document.

METHOD 1 From the **View** menu, select: **Go to background**.

METHOD 2 Press: **Ctrl + M**.
Your screen will now display the background of your document:

The way to tell that you are on the background is the page icon at the bottom of the window. This will show the letter **R** instead of the page number.

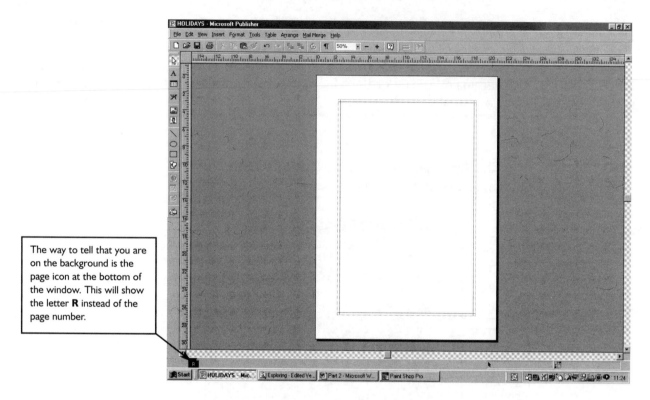

Figure 5.4 Background displayed

5.4 Prepare style sheets

Style sheets (known as text styles in Publisher) are very useful when dealing with multi-page documents. You can set different styles for each part of the text such as headings, subheadings and the main text. When you have imported the text, you just need to select the specific parts of text and change them to the relevant style. For example, if you wanted to have all your main headings in bold, closed capitals and centred, you could set this up and call the style **Main Heading**. Each time you came across a main heading all you would need to do is highlight the words and select the correct style. The text you had highlighted would then change to bold, closed capitals and centred.

It is useful to set the style sheet when you are preparing the master pages. Then, as soon as you have imported the text, you can assign the correct styles.

Set up the following text styles for your document:

Name	Font	Size	Alignment
Headline	Serif, bold, italic	18	Centred
Subheading	Serif, italic	14	Centred
Body Text	Sans serif	12	Left, with first-line indent

METHOD   I   From the **Format** menu, select: **Text Style**.
The **Text Style** dialogue box will appear on screen:

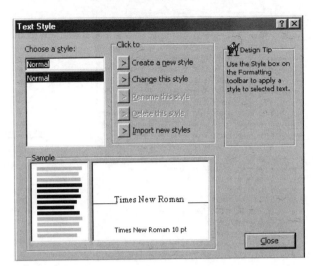

Figure 5.5 Text Style dialogue box

You need to create three new styles.

> **TIP**
>
> If a number of styles have already been set, it is a good idea to delete them at this point. This will ensure that you do not get them mixed up and that the styles you use in your document are those that you have created. This is particularly important in examination work, as if you use the wrong size or type of font, you will incur penalties. (You should note that the **Normal** style in Publisher cannot be deleted.)

2   Click on the ⎡>⎤ arrow button next to **Create a new style**.
The **Create New Style** dialogue box will appear on screen:

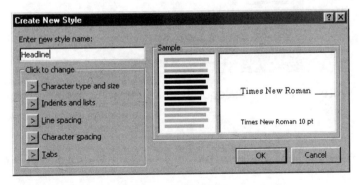

Figure 5.6 Create New Style dialogue box

Start by creating the **Headline** style.

3   In the **Enter new style name:** box, key in **Headline**.

Now set the font, font size and text emphasis. You will need to use the **Font** dialogue box.

4   Click on: the ⎡>⎤ arrow button next to **Character type and size**.
The **Font** dialogue box will appear on screen:

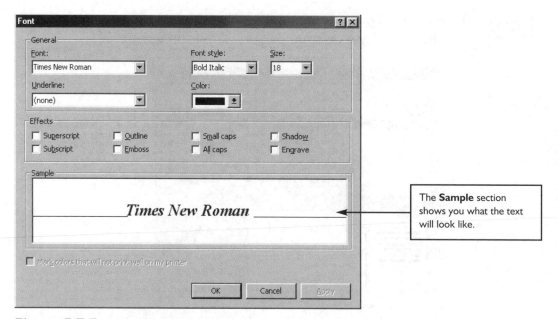

The **Sample** section shows you what the text will look like.

Figure 5.7 Font dialogue box

5 From the **Font** drop-down menu (display this by clicking on: the ⏷ arrow to the right of the **Font** box), select: **Times New Roman**.

6 From the **Font style** drop-down menu, select: **Bold Italic**.

7 From the **Size** drop-down menu, select 18 (or key in 18 in the box).

8 Click on: **OK**.

Your screen will now show the **Create New Style** dialogue box again:

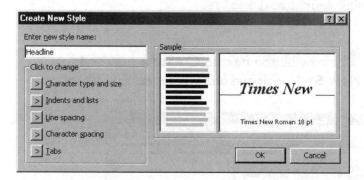

Figure 5.8 Create New Style dialogue box – font, font size and text emphasis changed

Notice that the text in the **Sample** section has changed (look back at Figure 5.6, if you cannot remember what it looked like before).

TIP

Although you may only want to change the font style and size, it is a good idea to get into the habit of checking the other options to ensure that all the elements of the style are correct. This is particularly important in examinations as, if you were to have a default setting of, for example, double-line spacing, you might incur penalties if you did not change your style correctly.

Now set the text alignment. This can be found in the **Indents and lists** dialogue box.

9 Click on: the ⏵ arrow button next to **Indents and lists**.

The **Indents and Lists** dialogue box will appear on screen:

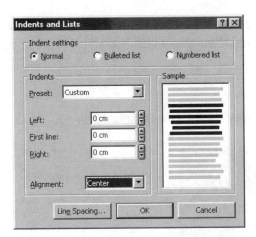

Figure 5.9 Indents and Lists dialogue box

10 From the **Alignment** drop-down menu, select: **Center**.
11 Click on: **OK**.

The **Create New Style** dialogue will appear on screen again:

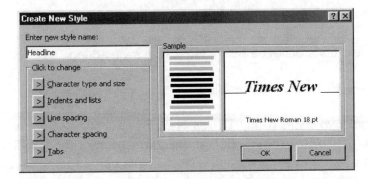

Figure 5.10 Create New Style dialogue box – alignment changed

Notice that the **Sample** section has changed again – in the left-hand box the black lines are now centred instead of left-aligned (compare Figure 5.10 with the earlier Figure 5.8 to see the difference).

Now check the **Line Spacing** option.

12 Click on: the ≥ arrow button next to **Line spacing**.

The **Line Spacing** dialogue box will appear on screen:

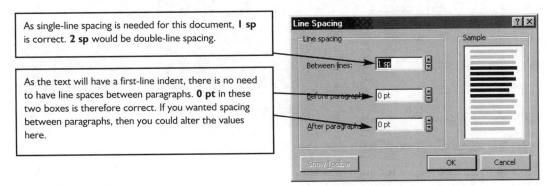

Figure 5.11 Line Spacing dialogue box

13 There are no changes to be made so you can just click on: **OK**.

You will be returned to the **Create New Style** dialogue box. (As you have not made any changes to the line spacing, then this will still look like Figure 5.13.)

14 Click on: **OK**.

The **Text Style** dialogue box will now be on screen again:

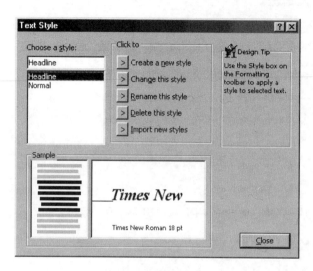

Figure 5.12 Text Style dialogue box – **Headline** style added

Notice that there is now a new style in the list (Headline).

15 Set up the other two styles (using **Times New Roman** for serif fonts and **Arial** for sans-serif fonts), following the method above. (Don't forget the first-line indent for the Body Text is set in the Indents and Lists dialogue box – look back at page 54 if you have forgotten how to do this.) You should end up with the **Text Style** dialogue box looking like this:

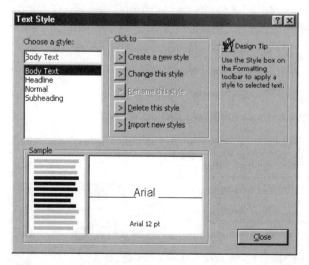

Figure 5.13 Text Style dialogue box – all styles added

16 Click on: **Close**.

5.5 Set up headers and footers

Headers are placed at the top of a document, outside the normal margins. Footers are placed at the bottom of a document, again outside the normal margins. They are useful for placing page numbers, the date, initials, copyright symbol, etc.

It is advisable to set headers and footers on the master page(s).

Set up the following header and footer using the **Body Text** text style:

Header Article (left aligned)
Footer Holiday Feature   Your name
            (left aligned)   (centred)

You need to ensure that there is a clear space between the main text and the headers and footers. To make this easier you can set up some guidelines and then draw the text frames to put the headers and footers in and then align the text to the guidelines.

Horizontal and vertical guidelines

As well as the margin guides which appear automatically when you open a blank document, you can also place horizontal and vertical guidelines. These are useful if you need to place items with a high degree of accuracy. When they are placed on your document they are coloured green, but they are not printed.

To place a horizontal guideline on your page:

 METHOD
1 Point the cursor at the ruler directly above the page.
2 Hold down the **Shift** key. Note that the cursor changes shape.
3 Drag the cursor to where you want the guide to appear.

To place a vertical guideline:

 METHOD
1 Point the cursor at the ruler to the left of the page.
2 Hold down the **Shift** key. Note that the cursor changes shape.
3 Drag the cursor to where you want the guide to appear.

If at any time you want to move the guidelines to a new position, or remove them from the page altogether:

 METHOD
1 Point the cursor on the guideline, note that it changes shape.
2 Move the guideline to the new position. If you wish to remove the guideline, drag it off the page, it will then disappear.

To set up the header and footer for Exercise 9.5:

METHOD

1 Drag a horizontal guideline to approximately 1 cm above the top margin.
2 Drag a horizontal guideline to approximately 1 cm below the bottom margin.
3 Draw a text frame 1 cm high to stretch from left to right margin (look back at page 11 if you have forgotten how to do this) and make sure its internal margins are set at **0 cm** (look back at page 13 if you have forgotten how to do this).
4 Make sure the text frame is selected (by clicking on it) and then copy the text frame:

   Either:
   • From the **Edit** menu, select **Copy**
   • From the **Edit** menu, select **Paste**.
   Or:
   • Press: **Ctrl +C**
   • Press: **Ctrl + V**.
   Or:
   • Click on: the 📋 **Copy** button.
   • Click on: the 📋 **Paste** button

5 Move one of the text frames to the top of the page (above the guideline you placed) and one of them to the bottom of the page (below the guideline you placed). In order to move the text frame, click anywhere in the text frame and drag.
6 In the header text frame (the top one), key in: **Article** and change it to the **Body Text** text style:
   • Press: **Ctrl +A** (to select all the text in the header text frame)
   • From the **Style** drop-down menu, select: **Body Text** (see Figure 5.14).

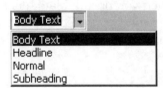

Figure 5.14 Style drop-down menu (on the Formatting toolbar)

7 In the footer text frame (the bottom one), key in: **Holiday Feature**, press: the **Tab** key, then key in: **Your name**. Change it all to the **Body Text** text style using the method above.

Now you need to align your name so that it is centred. You do this by setting a tab.

8 Highlight all the text in the footer text frame. Look at the horizontal ruler, you will notice that it has a white section – this is the individual ruler section for your text frame:

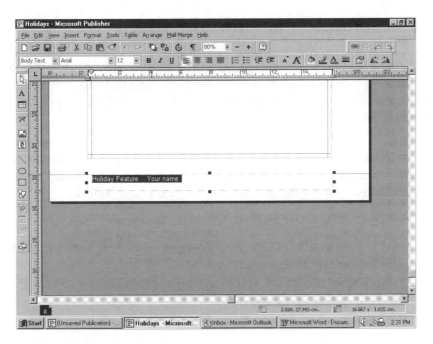

Figure 5.15 Footer ruler

9   Click on the ⌊ **Tab** button at the far left of the main ruler until it changes to a ⊥ **Centre Tab** button.

10 Click in the centre of the footer ruler (this is at about the 8 cm mark).

Notice that **Your name** has moved to the centre:

Now you need to align your header and footer more accurately, using the guidelines you drew earlier.

11 Click on: the header text frame to select it, then, holding down the **Alt** key, press the down cursor until the bottom of the text aligns with the guideline.

12 Do the same for the footer text frame except align the top of the text with the guideline instead of the bottom.

13 Zoom out to **Whole Page**. (Look back at page 22 if you cannot remember how to zoom.)

Your background page should now look like this:

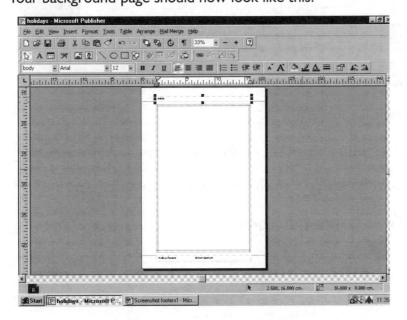

Figure 5.16 Headers and Footers inserted on background

5.6 Set up automatic page numbering

Publisher has a facility for numbering your pages for you automatically, so that you do not have to key each one in individually. It is therefore best to set up your page numbering on the background so that it appears in the same place on every page. You can set up an automatic page numbering option on your master pages.

Exercise 9.6 Insert a page number in the footer (right aligned). Page numbering should start from 3. You must ensure you are still working on background.

METHOD

1 Select all the text in the footer text frame, and put a ◢ **Right align** tab at the very end of the footer ruler.
2 Click at the end of the **Your name** and press the **Tab** key so that the text cursor is at the far right of the text frame.
3 From the **Insert** menu, select: **Page Numbers**.

A page number sign will appear at the far right of the text frame as follows #:

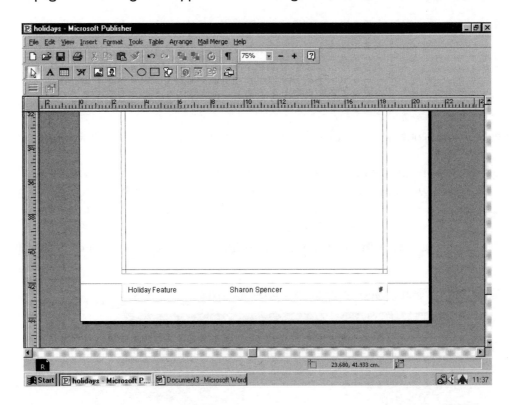

Figure 5.17 Page number sign

This means that the correct page number will be displayed at that point in the document.

The page numbering is to start from page 3, so you will need to change the page numbering options.

4 From the **Tools** menu, select: **Options**.

The **Options** dialogue box will appear on screen:

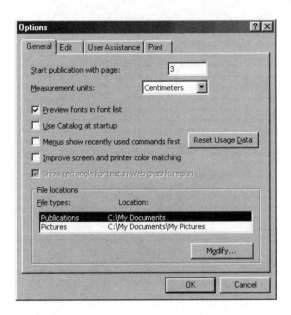

Figure 5.18 Options dialogue box

5 Click on: the **General** tab.
6 In the **Start publication with page** box key in **3**.
7 Click on: **OK.**

Your page numbering will now start from page 3.

5.7   Move to foreground

Now you have set up the background pages you can return to the foreground and check that everything is appearing where you want it to. (If it's not, then you can go back to the background and make changes until it's correct.)

Move to the foreground of your document.

Exercise 9.7

METHOD 1   From the **View** menu, select: **Go to foreground**.

METHOD 2   Press: **Ctrl + M**.
Your screen will now display the foreground of your document. It should look something like this:

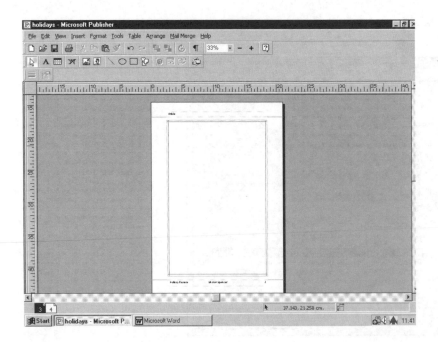

Figure 5.19 Foreground of document after background has been set up

Notice that the page icons in the bottom left-hand corner of the window now read **3** and **4** and also that the page number in your footer has changed to the correct page number.

5.8 Set up column guides

Exercise 9.8

Set up guides for three columns with a gutter space of 0.45cm.

Follow the method given in Part 1 (see pages 12–14). You will need to draw a text box on both pages and then link the two boxes so that your text will flow from the first to the second page.

METHOD

1 Draw a text frame on page 3 and set up three columns with a gutter space of 0.45 cm.
2 Move to page 4, by clicking on the page 4 icon at the bottom left-hand corner.
3 Draw a text frame and set up three columns with a gutter space of 0.45 cm.
4 Move back to page 3.
5 Click on the text frame to select it.
6 Click on: the 🔗 **Connect Text Frames** button. (Notice how the cursor changes.)
7 Move to page 4.
8 Click on: the text frame.

Your text frames are now linked. If you click on a text frame you will see special buttons attached to it at the top and bottom which indicate that it is linked to another text frame (or more).

If you click on the ⬅ **Go to Previous Frame** button you will go to the previous frame in the link. If you click on the ➡ **Go to Next Frame** button you will go to the next frame in the link.

Exercise 9.9 Save and close your master pages.

METHOD You should save your master pages in the usual way.

Exercise 10

1 Load Publisher if necessary and create an A4 document with landscape orientation.
2 Insert a new page so that you have a two-page document.
3 Set up margins of 2.75cm for the left, right, top and bottom of your document. Save it as **TEA**. These are your master pages.
4 Move to the background of your document.
5 Set up the following text styles for your document:

Name	Font	Size	Alignment
Headline	Sans serif, bold	18	Left
Subheading	Sans serif, bold, italic	14	Left
Body Text	Serif	11	Justified, with first-line indent

6 Set up the following header and footer using the Body Text text style:

Header	Feature (centred)
Footer	Your name
	(left aligned)

7 Insert a page number in the footer (right aligned). Page numbering should start from 6.
8 Move to the foreground of your document.
9 Draw text frames and set up three columns with a gutter space of 4.5 mm (0.45 cm) on each of the two pages of your document and link them so that the text will flow from page to page.
10 Save and close your master pages.

Extra information

Facing or mirrored pages
When you are designing a document you can set up as many blank pages as you need before you actually place anything on them.

In a book or magazine the inside margin of the pages has to take into account the binding. This means that the inside margin is generally wider than the outside margin. These are called 'facing' or 'mirrored' pages. Look at Figure 5.20

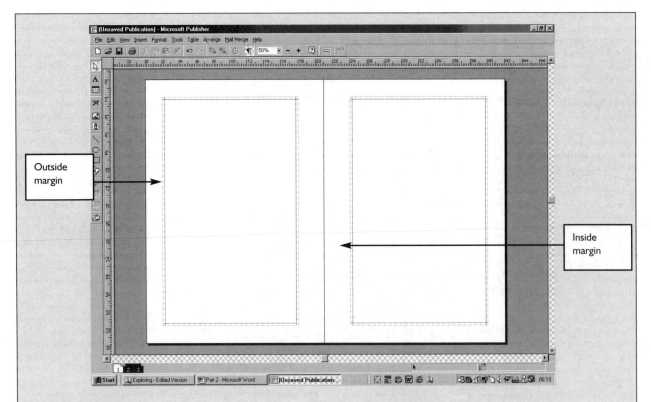

Figure 5.20 Facing/mirror pages

When setting multiple pages you will see that the left-hand pages are always even-numbered pages and the right-hand pages are always odd-numbered pages. This means that if we were to set up a three-page document you would see the pages on screen in the order shown in Figure 5.21 below.

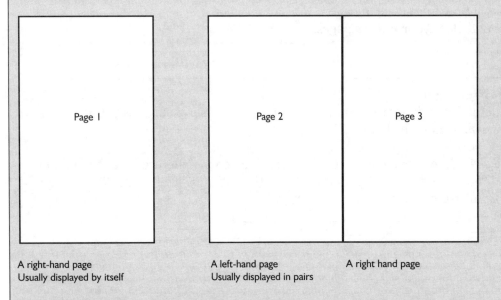

A right-hand page
Usually displayed by itself

A left-hand page
Usually displayed in pairs

A right hand page

Figure 5.21 Three-page document with facing pages

Publisher gives you the option of having mirrored pages or single pages. The margin options on the **layout guides** will change accordingly. For example, if you are using mirrored pages then the options are top, bottom, inside and outside margins – for single pages you will have top, bottom, left and right options.

The default setting in Publisher 2000 is for single pages. To change the format to mirrored pages do the following:

I From the **Arrange** menu, select: **Layout Guides**.

The **Layout Guides** dialogue box will appear on screen:

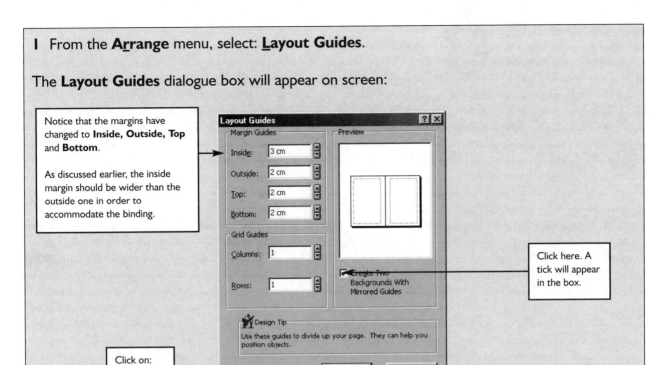

Notice that the margins have changed to **Inside, Outside, Top** and **Bottom**.

As discussed earlier, the inside margin should be wider than the outside one in order to accommodate the binding.

Click here. A tick will appear in the box.

Click on:
OK

Figure 5.22 Layout Guides dialogue box

2 In the **Preview** section, click on: **Create Two Backgrounds with Mirrored Guides**. A tick will appear in the box.
3 Click on: **OK**.

TIP

There are two important points to remember when working on background.

• You must remember to move back to the 'real' or working pages when importing text or images otherwise the same text or image will print on every page.
• If you wish to amend anything on the master page you must go to background. You cannot amend these items from your working pages.

Chapter 6

Applying Text Styles and Text Wrap

In this chapter you will learn how to:
- apply text styles
- apply text wrap.

Now that your master pages are ready you can start putting things on them. The first thing to do is import your text.

Exercise 11.1 Load Publisher (if necessary) and open the document **HOLIDAYS** (your master page). Save it as **HOLIDAYS1** to ensure your master pages are blank. Import the text file **HOLS** into your document.

It is very important that, before you add text or graphics to your master pages, you save it using a different filename (in this case as **HOLIDAYS1**). This will ensure that the master pages (filename: **HOLIDAYS**) remain unaltered. This is important for examination purposes as your tutor will ask you to show him or her the blank master pages and will verify this on your examination answer book.

METHOD

1 Make sure you are on the foreground and not the background and on the first page (page 3).
2 Click in the text frame on the far left.
3 Import the text file **HOLS**. (Look back at page 20 if you cannot remember how to do this.)

Notice how the text flows through the columns on to the second page:

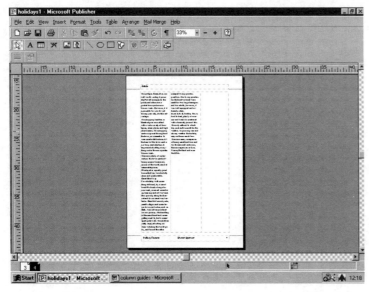

Figure 6.1 Text flowed on to second page

6.1 Apply text styles

You now need to apply the text styles that you set up in Chapter 5 to the text that you have just imported.

 Exercise 11.2 Apply the three text styles to the appropriate parts of the imported text.

You must ensure that the text styles are applied correctly. Change the headline first, then go through the text and identify the subheadings and apply the subheading style to them. Finally, change the remaining text to body text style, including the header and footer.

METHOD

1 Highlight the first heading **Holidays in the UK**.
2 From the **Style** drop-down menu, select: **Headline** (see Figure 6.2)

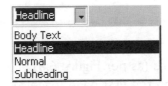

Figure 6.2 Style drop-down menu (on the Formatting toolbar)

Now you need to apply the Subheading and Body Text styles.

3 Ensure you are on the first page (page 3).
4 Click at the top of the left-hand text frame.
5 Zoom in to **100%**.
6 Scroll down until you see the subheading **Self-Catering in Pembrokeshire**.
7 Highlight the subheading and apply the **Subheading** style to it.
8 Do the same with **Weekend Break in Cambridge** and **Canal Boat Trip**.
9 Now go back to the first page. Highlight all the body text from under the headline **Holidays in the UK** down to **Self-Catering in Pembrokeshire** and apply the **Body Text** style to it.
10 Do the same for the text between **Self-Catering in Pembrokeshire** and **Weekend Break in Cambridge**; between **Weekend Break in Cambridge** and **Canal Boat Trip**; and finally, the text after **Canal Boat Trip**.

Checking your work

It is important that you check your text styles once you have applied them. If you are able to print out your document, you may find it easier to check the styles have been applied on a printed copy. If you can't print it out, or prefer to check it on screen, then ensure that the page view is at a size where the text can be read easily (at least 100% if not 150%) and check each heading, subheading and paragraph. You can click in each section individually and then check in the **Style** box that the correct style is showing. Remember also to check that you have actually set up the styles correctly!

The images now need to be imported into the document.

Exercise 11.3 Import the two graphic files **CAR** (Image 1) and **FAMILY** (Image 2). Place Image 1 in the middle of the first column on the first page immediately prior to the subheading *Self-Catering in Pembrokeshire*. Place Image 2 at the top of the first column on the second page. Figure 6.3 shows the correct placement.

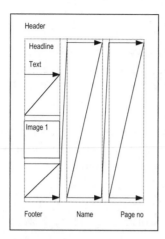 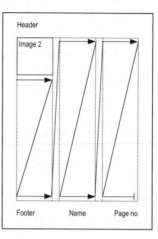

Figure 6.3 Layout for Exercise 11.3

METHOD
1 Draw the picture frames in the correct places (as per Figure 6.3).
2 Insert Image 1 (**CAR**) in the picture frame on the first page (page 3).
3 Insert Image 2 (**FAMILY**) in the picture frame on the second page (page 4).
4 Make sure the pictures are still where they are supposed to be – and move them if not.

6.2 Apply text wrap

Exercise 11.4 Check that none of the images are overlapping the text or visa versa.

Publisher automatically sets text to wrap around pictures unless you tell it otherwise. Therefore, your pictures should not be overlapping or hiding any text. However, if they are, then you can change it in the following way:

METHOD
1 Select all the text frames on a page (by holding down the **Shift** key and clicking on each text frame in turn – keeping the **Shift** key held down throughout).
2 Click on: the 📰 **Text Frame Properties** button.
3 In the **Options** section of the **Text Frame Properties** dialogue box make sure that the **Wrap text around objects** box is ticked (and click on it if not).

You can also change the margins within the picture frames – so that the pictures are inset from the edges of the frames.

Exercise 11.5 Print one copy and close the document.

1 Load Publisher (if necessary) and open the document **TEA**. Save it as **TEA1**. Import the text file **TEA** into your document.

2 Apply the three typestyles to the appropriate parts of the imported text.

3 Import the two graphic files **TEA** (Image 1) and **SIGN** (Image 2). Place Image 1 at the bottom of the third column on the first page. Place Image 2 at the bottom of the first column on the second page. Figure 6.4 shows the correct placement.

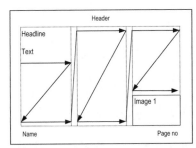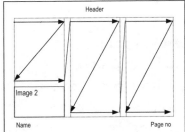

Figure 6.4 Layout for Exercise 12

4 Check that none of the images are overlapping the text or visa versa.

5 Print one copy and close the document.

Chapter 7

Copyfitting

In this chapter you will learn how to:
- ensure images are resized in proportion
- ensure headings and related text are together
- ensure there are no widows or orphans
- ensure images are not superimposed on text
- ensure paragraph spacing is consistent
- make a final check to ensure your document looks professional.

You will often want to make changes to your document to make it look neater. For example, you might want to resize one or more images and check that there are no words on their own at the top of columns. The skills you learn in this chapter will make your work look much more professional.

7.1 Ensure images are resized in proportion

Exercise 13.1

- Open the document **HOLIDAYS1** and save it as **HOLIDAYS2**.
- Resize, in proportion, Image 2 on the second page to extend across the first and second columns as in Figure 7.1

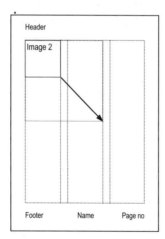

Figure 7.1 Layout for Exercise 13.1

You should always make sure that you resize images in proportion. Remember to resize images using the **Corner** handles and *not* the centre handles. This way your image will not be distorted.

However, some graphics become very large when resized in proportion and may not fit the columns as specified. If this is the case, then ensure that the image has increased or decreased in both width and height. This will be acceptable in an OCR Stage II examination. In fact, if the graphic will not fit the specified space when resized proportionally, then you must resize to the specified space, as if you go over then you will incur penalties. In the workplace, however, this would probably not be acceptable as the image might be distorted.

METHOD

1 Zoom in to 200% so that you can see more clearly (and scroll across if necessary so that the first two columns are visible.
2 Click on: the picture to select it.
3 Select the bottom right-hand corner handle.
4 Drag down and to the right until the right edge of the image is aligned with the right-hand column guide of the middle column.

If you zoom back out to **Whole Page** your document should look like this:

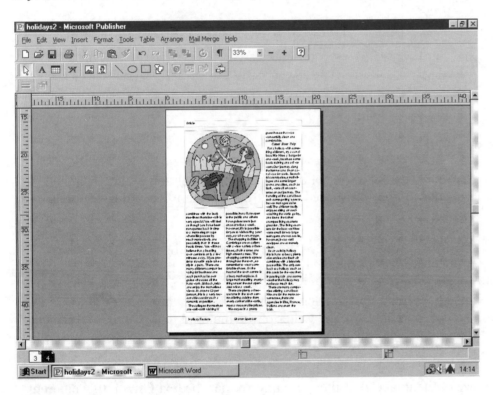

Figure 7.2 Picture resized

TIP

For images and clipart, Publisher will automatically resize the image proportionally if you use a **corner** handle.

However, if you are resizing a text frame or a drawing object such as a box, you need to hold down the **Shift** key while resizing in order to keep it in proportion.

7.2 Ensure headings and related text are together

Ensure that, in your document, all headings and related text are kept together.

Exercise 13.2

You should ensure that a heading and at least **two** lines of text are always in the same column. Look at Figure 7.3.

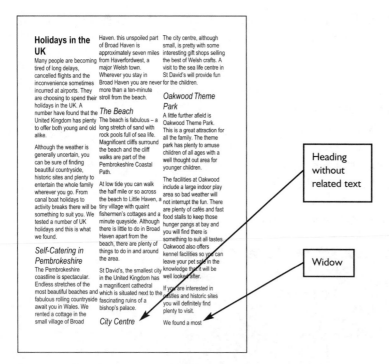

Figure 7.3 Headings and related text

In Figure 7.3 you can see that the heading at the bottom of the second column has no related text with it. However, all the other subheadings are placed correctly. Also, there is a widow at the bottom of the third column (see below).

To resolve the problems in Figure 7.3, you could move the subheading to the next column (by pressing: the **Return** key at the beginning of the subheading or by rolling the text box up – dragging the bottom, centre handle up). This would also fix the widow. This would mean that the bottom of your columns would not end at the same place, but this is acceptable in OCR examinations. (In the workplace, you might ask the writer of the material to add some text to some of the paragraphs so that the columns did still end in the same place.) You must however, ensure your margins are of the specified size.

You could also adjust the size of the image(s), if there are any, so that the text flows into a different position. This is not a particularly technical method and can therefore be unreliable. If you do this you must ensure that you have not moved any other text out of line. You must also ensure that the image still fits the columns as specified.

7.3　Ensure there are no widows and orphans

One line (or word) that appears at either the top or bottom of a column or page is classed as a widow or orphan. Widow is the name given to a line or word that appears on its own at the bottom of a page, orphan for words/line at the top.

Exercise 13.3 Ensure that, in your document, there are no widow or orphans.

As with keeping headings and related text together, probably the best way to correct widows and orphans is to take over the relevant line to the next column, using one of the above methods. Make sure you do not lose any text or alter the margins.

7.4 Ensure images are not superimposed on text

Ensure that, in your document, no images are superimposed on text (or vice versa).

You have already looked, in Chapter 6, at the use of text wrap to ensure text and images are not superimposed. However, when you are making changes in order to copyfit, it is easy for the text or images to move out of line. Before you print your work, you must check very carefully that the text and images are not touching. If necessary, zoom to a reasonably large size so that the borders of the images can be seen clearly.

7.5 Ensure paragraph spacing is consistent

Ensure that the paragraph spacing in your document is consistent.

The paragraph spacing of your text should be consistent throughout the document. Traditionally, when a clear space is not left between paragraphs, the first line of each paragraph is indented to make the distinction.

If your imported text has clear spaces between each paragraph, this is perfectly acceptable; there is no need to go through the document altering each paragraph. However, you must ensure that the space is equal. If, for example, you have several paragraphs with a clear space between and several without, your work will look untidy.

It is perfectly acceptable to have both a first line indent amd paragraph spacing.

If you want to set spacing between paragraphs:

METHOD
1 From the **Format** menu, select: **Text Style**.
2 Select: the style you want to change (you will need to change all of them).
3 Click on: the > arrow button next to **Change this style**.
4 Click on: the > arrow button next to **Line spacing**.
5 In the **After paragraphs** box, key in **10 pt**. This point size will give a reasonable space after each paragraph.

7.6 Hyphenation

Publisher will add hyphens to words at the end of lines in order to make the lines fit neatly. You may want to turn the hyphenation off as this can make your document look tidier. You need to do this for each text frame as you cannot do it for the whole document at once.

Ensure that hyphenation is removed.

METHOD
1 From the **Tools** menu, select: **Language** and then **Hyphenation**.

The **Hyphenation** dialogue box will appear on screen.

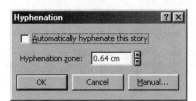

Figure 7.4 Hyphenation dialogue box

2 Click on **Automatically hyphenate this story** to remove the tick from the check box.

3 Click on: **OK**.

Note

If you do switch off hyphenation it will not remove the hyphen from words that have been keyed in with a hyphen, such as **first-class** or **full-time**.

7.7 Make a final check to ensure your document looks professional

Exercise 13.7

Do a final check on your document to make sure everything is still copyfitted and then print one copy.

You need to check your work carefully on screen before printing as, when you are manipulating text and images, it is easy to add extra spaces or delete them or for text to reflow so that it no longer copyfits.

TIP

Have a look at a variety of posters, magazines, newspapers etc. How neat is the work, are there headings left without text or widows and orphans appearing? Does the work look professional and if not, how would you change it?

Exercise 14

1 Open the document **TEA1** and save it as **TEA2**.

2 Resize, in proportion, Image 1 on the first page to extend across the second and third columns as in Figure 7.5.

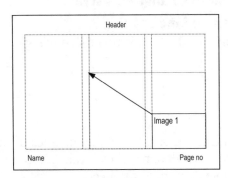

Figure 7.5 Layout for Exercise 14

3 Copyfit your publication to ensure:
  • headings and related text are grouped together
  • one line or less of text is grouped with the rest of the related text
  • text/graphics are adjusted so that they are not superimposed on other text or images
  • paragraph spacing is consistent
  • hyphenation is removed.

4 When you are sure your document is correct, print one copy.

Chapter 8

Amending an Existing Publication

In this chapter you will learn how to:

■ amend style sheets
■ use correction signs
■ use bullets
■ use spell check.

You may find that there are times when you have to amend a document that has been created by someone else. You will need to know about correction signs and be able to make amendments to the text following these.

8.1 Amend style sheets

Exercise 15.1

Load Publisher (if necessary) and open the Publisher file **BEAUTY** which you will find on the accompanying disk. Save it as **BEAUTY1**. Ensure the following **text styles** are applied.

Style Name	Typeface	Point Size	Alignment
Headline	Bold	18	Centred
Subheading	Serif	14	
Bullet text	Italic		Justified
Body text			

If you are working on a previously-prepared document and need to change the text styles, there is a great temptation to highlight the individual parts of the text to make the necessary changes, particularly if you are feeling rushed for time. However, although this may seem the easy option, it is not as reliable as changing the text styles and can actually be more time consuming (even if your document is only two pages long).

METHOD
1 From the **Format** menu, select: **Text Styles**.
2 Select the **Headline** style.
3 Click on: the > arrow button next to **Change this style**.
4 Click on: the > arrow button next to **Character type and size**.
5 From the **Font style** drop-down menu, select: **Bold**.
6 From the **Size** drop-down menu, select: 18.

7 Click on: **OK**.

8 Click on: the > arrow button next to **Indents and Lists**.

9 From the **Alignment** drop-down menu, select: **Center**.

10 Click on: **OK**.

11 Make the changes to the other styles in the same way.

Note: Publisher does not always change all the text as specified. So you need to double-check that all the subheadings, headlines, etc have been changed as you wanted.

8.2 Use correction signs

Exercise 15.2

Make the amendments as indicated on the proof copy on page 82. (Ignore the spelling mistakes that are not marked for the moment – these will be corrected using the spell check facility in Exercise 15.4).

Each proof correction should be marked both in the text and in the margin. Follow the instructions given very carefully. Make sure you are confident that you know the meaning of each correction sign.

TIP

When you are amending documents, it may be helpful to cross off each correction sign on the paper copy once you have made the correction.

METHOD

1 To change a word or letter, select it and then key in the correct version.

2 To move a word, select it then drag it to the correct position.

3 To add a space, click where the space is to go and press: the **Space** bar.

4 To add a new paragraph, click where the paragraph is to go and press: the **Return** key.

Given below is a list of common correction signs. Make sure that you know what each means.

Instruction	Mark in Text	Mark in Margin
Instruction	**Mark in Text**	**Mark in Margin**
Insert new copy	Please let me know/if you agree.	⌐ as soon as ⌐ possible
Correct version:	Please let me know as soon as possible if you agree.	
Delete (Remove)	John would ~~very much~~ like to pass this exam.	℮
Correct version:	John would like to pass this exam.	
Insert space	Judith|s excellent at geography.	#
Correct version:	Judith is excellent at geography.	
Start new paragraph	.....end of sentence. ⌐This sign means start a new paragraph.	⊏
	Or	
	...end of sentence. ‖This sign means start a new paragraph.	‖
Correct version (either sign)	...end of sentence. This sign means start a new paragraph.	
Close up	This sign means c‿lose up a space.	(close up)
Correct version:	This sign means close up a space.	
Stet	~~Change~~ Amend the word to the one with the dashes under it.	(Stet)
Correct version:	Change the word to the one with the dashes under it.	
Set in caps	<u>this</u> means use a capital letter.	☰
Correct version:	This means use a capital letter.	
Transpose	Put the words in the order⌐correct.	∼
Correct version:	Put the words in the correct order.	
Align (Left)	⌐The text should be neatly aligned to the left. It should not be indented at all.	⌐
Correct version:	The text should be neatly aligned to the left. It should not be indented at all.	

8.3 Use bullets

Bullet points can be used in place of numbers to give emphasis to points. Look at Figure 8.1.

> • The traditional bullet is slightly larger than a full stop and sits vertically in the middle of the typing line.
> • The bullet should be in line with the left-hand margin.
> • The text should be indented on each line to give a neat appearance.
> • You can have a clear line space between each bullet point to separate the text.

Figure 8.1 Bullets

There are a number of different bullets you can use, but for examination work it is neater to use a plain bullet as in Figure 8.1, above.

Exercise 15.3
In the **Hair** story (this is the bottom section of text, which begins with the subheading **Hair**), insert a bullet character at the beginning of the following three paragraphs:
There ...
Hair ....
The ...
Ensure all bullet text is indented from the bullet point.

As the document has been set up with a text style for bullet text, it would be best to change the text style rather than highlighting the text and changing it individually.

METHOD
1 From the **Format** menu, select: **Text Style**.
2 Select the **Bullet text** style.
3 Click on: the ⏵ arrow button next to **Change this style**.
4 Click on: the ⏵ arrow button next to **Indents and Lists**.
5 Click on: the **Bulleted list** radio button.

The **Indents and Lists** dialogue box will now show the options for bullets:

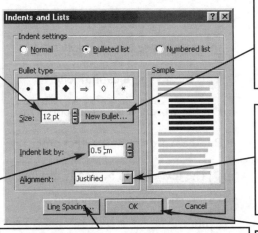

You can change the size of the bullet. The default size for this bullet is **12 pt** which is sufficient for most purposes. However, if your text was much larger – e.g. **16 pt** – you would probably want to change the bullet to **16 pt** as well. To do this, either key in the new value or use the up and down arrows to change the size.

This is the amount of space between the bullet and the list. The default is 1 cm, which can sometimes look a bit too big. **0.5 cm** is better. You can change this by keying in the new amount or using the up and down arrows to change the size.

If you click on: **New Bullet** you will be given a choice of symbols to use as a bullet point. Click on your choice and you will return to this menu. Your new bullet point will now be listed in the **Bullet type** section.

This allows you to change the alignment of the bulleted list. You should keep the alignment the same as the body text unless you are instructed otherwise. To change the alignment, click on the down arrow, and select from the drop-down menu.

If you want to change the line spacing of the bulleted list, click here. However, for exam purposes you should keep the line spacing the same as for the rest of the text.

Click on: **OK** when you have finished making your changes.

Figure 8.2 Indents and Lists dialogue box – Bulleted list selected

6   Click on: the slightly larger bullet (second from left).
7   In the **Indent list by** box, key in 0.5 cm. (This will indent all of the bulleted text 5 mm from the bullet points.)
8   Click on: **OK**.
9   You will be returned to the **Change Style** box, click on **OK**.
10 Close the Text Style menu.

Your Hair story should now look like this:

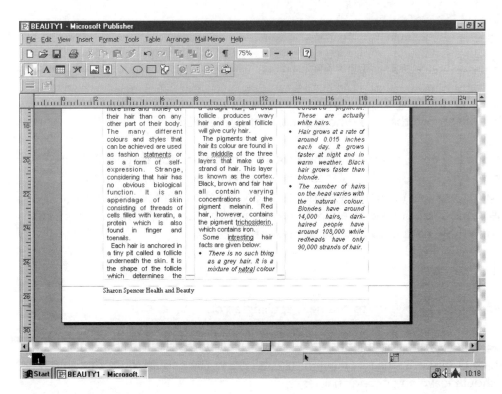

Figure 8.3 Bulleted text

8.4 Use spell check

Once you have finished correcting your work, you should run it through the spell check facility to make sure there are no spelling errors. *There are deliberate errors in the proof copy that must be corrected. These are not marked.*

Exercise 15.4 Check the spelling of the document (starting at the beginning) and print one copy.

METHOD
1   Click in one of the columns of text to select the story.
2   From the **Tools** menu, select: **Spelling**, then: **Check Spelling**.
    The **Check Spelling** dialogue box will appear on screen:

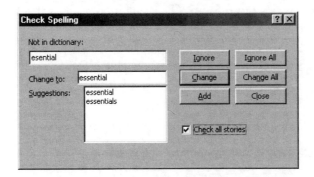

Figure 8.4 Check Spelling dialogue box

3   Make sure that the **Check all stories** check box has a tick in it (and click on it if not). This will ensure that the whole document is checked.

The first spelling error is shown in the **Not in dictionary** box (esential). In the **Change to** box, Publisher has placed the most likely suggestion and in the **Suggestions** box are further suggestions as to what the correct version might be. You must always read these carefully to decide which is the right one. In this case, the word in the **Change to** box is the correct one.

4   Click on: **Change**.

Publisher will then move on to the next spelling error.

5   Continue making your corrections until you get to **trichosiderin**. This is a scientific term which Publisher does not have in its dictionary. You should leave this as it is (as you should leave any proper names):
    • Click on: **Ignore**.

6   Continue making your corrections.

When Publisher has checked the whole document a box will appear telling you that it has finished:

Figure 8.5 Spelling check complete

TIP

If the spell check offers more than one alternative to a spelling error, look very carefully to see which option you should choose. Do not be tempted to take the first option without reading the text. Many errors are caused by careless use of the spell check.

Print a copy of your document, save it as **Beauty1** and close.

1 Load Publisher (if necessary) and open the Publisher file **DOGS** which you will find on the accompanying disk. Save it as **DOGS1** and ensure the following text styles are applied.

Style Name	Typeface	Point Size	Alignment
Heading	Serif		Centred
Subheading	Serif	16	
Bullet text	Sans serif		Justified
Body text	Sans serif		

2 Make the amendments as indicated on the proof copy on page 83.

3 In the **Choosing a Breed** story, insert a bullet character at the beginning of the following four paragraphs:

Labrador ...

Cairn Terrier ...

Cocker ...

Mongrels ...

Ensure all bullet text is indented from the bullet point.

4 Check the spelling of your document and print one copy.

Proof copy for Exercise 15.2

LOOKING GOOD

Cleansing

In order to look good you need to spend some time on your cleansing and moisturising regime. Clean, fresh skin will automatically make you feel and look years younger. Here are a few of our top tips.

If you wear make-up it is esential that all traces are removed before you go to bed. Leaving make-up on overnight will block the pores, preventing skin from breatheing. Spots and blackheads may also appear.

Your first step to wonderful looking skin is to remove your make-up. There are many differrent make-up removers avalable and you should choose one that will suit your skin type. Using cotton wool and a good quality cleanser, ensure that all traces of make-up and grime have been removed.

The second step is to clean your face. There are many types of cleanser on the market, ranging from face

scrubs, which contain tiny particles that exfoliate the skin, to cleansing milks which are heavier and creamier in consistency. Some well-known brands sell special types of soap that are designed especially for use on the face. A sales advisor will be able to help you determine the best cleanser for your skin type.

The last step is to apply a good quality moisturiser. Again, you should find one that suits your skin type. Gently apply to your face and neck every night. Within a few months you should be able to see the difference this 5-minute routine makes. Hopefully others will notice as well.

Hair

People probably spend more time and money on their hair than on any other part of their body. The many different styles and colours that can be achieved are used as fashion statments or as a form of self-expression. Strange, considering that hair has no obvious biological function. It is an appendage of skin consisting of threads of cells filled with keratin, a protein which is also found in finger and toenails.

Each hair is anchored in a pit called a follicle underneath the skin. It is the shape of the follicle which determines the appearance of the hair. A round follicle will produce a straight hair, an oval follicle produces wavy hair and a spiral follicle will give curly hair.

the pigments that give hair its colour are found in the midddle of the three layers that make up a strand of hair. This layer is known as the cortex. Black, brown and fair hair all contain varying concentrations of the pigment melanin. Red hair, however, contains the pigment trichosiderin, which contains iron.

Some intresting hair facts are given below:
There is no such thing as a grey hair. It is a mixture of natral colour hair and strands that no longer contain the coloured pigment. These are actually white hairs.
Hair grows at a rate of around 0.015 inches each day. It grows faster at night and in warm weather. Black hair grows faster than blonde.
The number of hairs on the head varies with the natural colour. Blondes have around 14,000 hairs, dark-haired people have around 108,000 while redheads have only 90,000 strands of hair.

Insert your name

Health and Beauty

Proof copy for Exercise 16

DOGS

OWNING A DOG

Dogs make great pets and can soon become a much-loved member of the family. They provide companonship, are fun to be with and give you a good excuse to take regular exercise. Howver, they do require time, money and commitment from their owners.

Dogs are very social animals and do not enjoy being left on their own for long periods of time. If you work full time and are thinking of getting a dog you may consider taking on an older rescue dog that does not need constant attention.

Think carefully before choosing a dog. There are many aspects of dog ownership that need to be taken into consideration before you make a final choice. Firstly, you should consider your home enviroment. For example, if you live in a flat or house with no garden, then a small dog would probably be the most suitable. If you must have a larger dog then you need to consider where you will be able to exercise it.

Most dogs need regular, outdoor exercise. Some breeds require much more exercise than others. Be realistic about how much time you can spare to walk your pet.

Cost is another important consideration. large dogs can eat a great deal of food and this can cost a considerable sum over a few weeks. If you add to the cost of food, vet bills, kennel fees, bedding, leads, toys and other accessories you can see the bills mount up to a very large sum indeed.

If you do decide to have a pet dog you will soon find the advantages far outweigh the setbacks. *disadvantages*

CHOOSING A BREED

As mentioned, there are some general considerations that have to be taken into account before you decide to own a dog. However, once the decision has been made, you need to choose which breed to own. Some breeds make much better family pets than others. You may wish to own a particular type of dog such as a gundog or toy dog. You also need to consider whether you are interested in showing your animal.

Some of the most popular breeds are given below.

Labrador Retriever. These make excellent family pets. They are usually even-tempered, intelligent animals and are good with children. They can also make good guard dogs.

Cairn Terrier. These are very friendly small dogs. They make excellent companions as they are intelligent and loyal. Cairn terriers do however require regular grooming.

Cocker Spaniel. These medium-sized dogs make excellent companions. They require regular grooming and lots of exercise. This is very important as they do have a tendency to put on weight.

Mongrels. Usually very hardy dogs, they make excellent family pets. Depending on the type, they may not require much grooming *but do enjoy regular exercise.*

Chapter 9

Working with Images and Drawing Objects

In this chapter you will learn how to:

- layer items
- draw boxes with rounded corners
- use drawing tools.

9.1 Layer items

You can place items on top of each other to give various effects. In Figure 9.1, the image has been brought to the front and in Figure 9.2, the text has been brought to the front. Placing items to front or back is much easier than it sounds.

In this le you
should b to see both
the text ar grap
This is cal
objects. d to
fr nd 'send k'.
This element may d a
little practice to e re
success.

Figure 9.1 Image in front

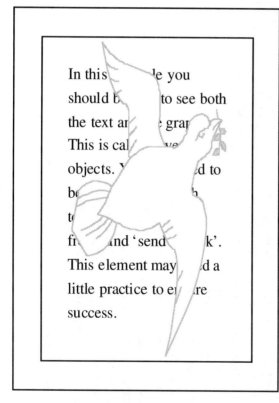

In this example you
should be able to see both
the text and the graphic.
This is called layering
objects. You will need to
become familiar with
terms such as 'bring to
front' and 'send to back'.
This element may need a
little practice to ensure
success.

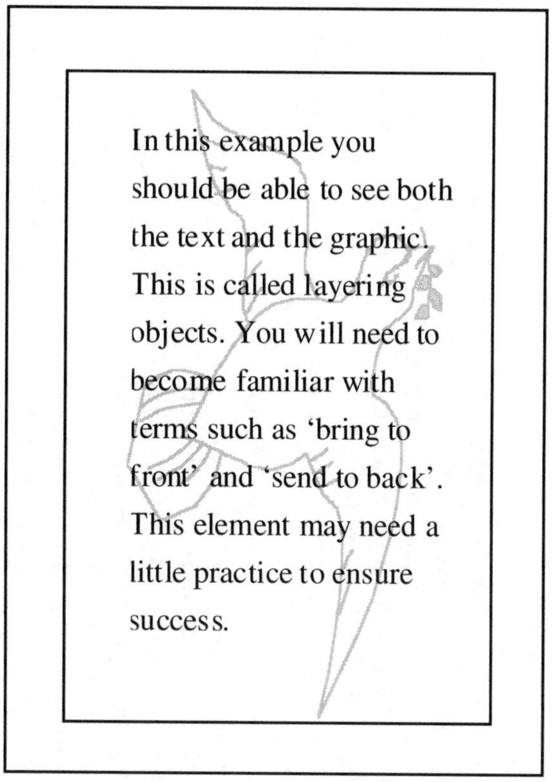

Figure 9.2 Text in front

Exercise 17.1

- Open the file **BEAUTY1** and save it as **BEAUTY2**.
- In the **Cleansing** story, overlay the text so that it is superimposed over the **COSMETICS** image. Ensure that the text is at the front and that the image can be seen in the background.

You must be able to see both the text and the graphic when layering items. In Figure 9.2 on the previous page, the graphic is very light which enables us to clearly read the text. If the graphic was dark or of a high density, then the text would be slightly obscured. In Figure 9.1 the bird is in front of the text box and therefore obscures some of the text.

METHOD

First of all, you need to take the fill off the picture frame so that it has a transparent background.

1 Click on the picture to select it.
2 **Either:**
   - From the **Format** menu, select: **Fill Color**.
   Or:
   - Click on: the 🖌 **Fill Color** button (on the Formatting toolbar).
3 From the drop-down menu that appears, select: **No Fill**.

You now need to bring the text to the front.

4 Click on the text frame to select it.
5 **Either:**
   - From the **Arrange** menu, select: **Bring to Front**.
   Or:
   - Press: **F6**.
   Or:
   - Click on: the 🔲 **Bring to Front** button.

The text will now be at the front:

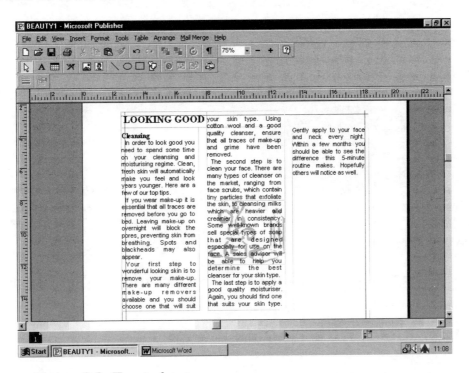

Figure 9.3 Text in front

Notice, however, that the heading box has now been obscured by the text frame. You now need to bring the heading text frame to the front.

6 Click on: the heading text frame to select it.

7 Either:

• From the **A̱rrange** menu, select: **Bring to Front̲**.

Or:

• Press: **F6**.

Or:

• Click on: the 🔲 **Bring to Front** button.

The heading text frame will no longer be obscured:

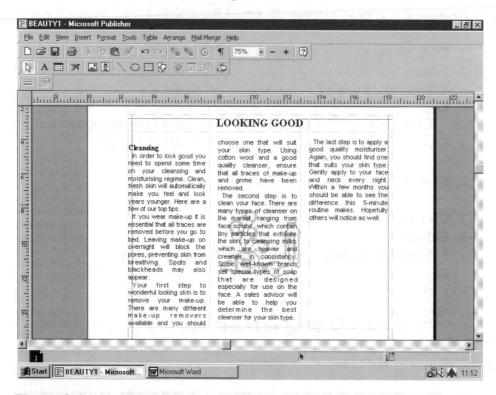

Figure 9.4 Heading in front

Bring to Front/Send to Back

These features also allow you to show different parts of the same diagram. Look at the examples below.

In this example the box has been sent to the back. In order to do this the box was selected and then the 'send to back' option was used.

In this example the box has been brought to the front. The box was selected and 'bring to the front' option was used.

Figure 9.5 Box to back

Figure 9.6 Box to front

The effects would have been the same had the ellipse been sent to back or brought forward.

9.2   Draw a box with rounded corners

You may need to draw a box with rounded corners for examination or display work. Look at Figure 9.7.

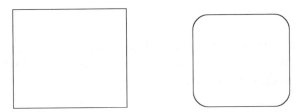

This is a box with square corners   This is a box with rounded corners

Figure 9.7 Square and rounded corners

Exercise 17.2   Place a box with rounded corners around the headline text, ensuring that the edges of the box do not touch any text. Ensure that the text remains centred between the margins.

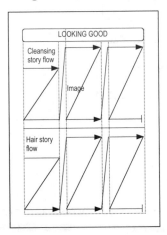

Figure 9.8 Layout for Exercise 17.2

METHOD

1 Click on: the  **Custom Shapes** button (on the **Object** toolbar).

2 From the drop-down menu (see Figure 9.9), select: the ⬭ rounded box button.

Figure 9.9 Custom Shapes drop-down menu

3 Draw your box as you would an ordinary box. (Look back at page 38 if you cannot remember how to do this.)

TIP

If your box completely obscures the graphic or text, it is possible that it has a white or paper fill colour. This means that the box will blank out anything that is underneath it. In order to solve this problem, you need to set the fill colour of the box to none.

9.3 Use drawing tools

You may decide to draw a line or box to enhance your text or image. You have already looked at this in chapter 4. You have also covered setting text wrap around objects. Look back at pages 39–40 and page 68 if you cannot remember how to do these tasks.

As you can see in Figure 9.10, space needs to be left between the graphic or text and the box.

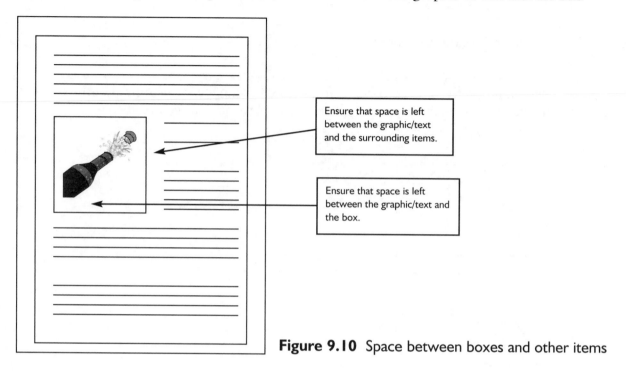

Ensure that space is left between the graphic/text and the surrounding items.

Ensure that space is left between the graphic/text and the box.

Figure 9.10 Space between boxes and other items

Exercise 17.3 Draw a horizontal line across the page below the **CLEANSING** story to separate it from the **HAIR** story. The line should be between 1 and 3 pt rule weight. Ensure the line does not touch the text or image.

You covered drawing lines and changing the weight of lines in Part 1. Look back at page 37 if you cannot remember how to do this.

Exercise 17.4 Save the finished publication and print one copy.

1 Open the file **DOGS1** and save it as **DOGS2**.

2 In the **Choosing a Breed** story, overlay the text so that it is superimposed over the **DOG** image. Ensure that the text is at the front and that the image can be seen in the background.

3 Place a box with rounded corners around the headline text, ensuring that the edges of the box do not touch any text. Ensure that the text remains centred between the margins.

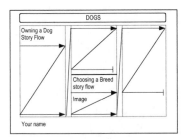

Figure 9.11 Layout for Exercise 18

4 Draw a horizontal line across the middle column below the **Owning a Dog** story to separate it from the **Choosing a Breed** story. The line should be between 3 and 5 pt rule weight. Ensure the line does not touch the text or image.

5 Save the finished publication and print one copy.

Consolidation 3

Part 1

1   Load Publisher 2000 and set up a two-page document. The paper size should be A4 and the orientation set to landscape. Specify four equal columns with a 4.5 mm (0.45 cm) gutter. Margins should be as follows:

Top   25 mm (2.5 cm)
Bottom   25 mm (2.5 cm)
Left   25 mm (2.5 cm)
Right   25 mm (2.5 cm)

2   Set up a style sheet with the following styles:

Style Name	Typeface	Point Size	Alignment
Body text	Serif	12	Justified
Subheading	Sans serif, bold	14	Centred
Headline	Sans serif, bold	18	Left

3   Set a header and footer as follows, using the body text typestyle:

Header	INTERNET FEATURE (Right aligned)	
Footer	Your name (left aligned)	Page Number (centred)

Page numbering should start from page 4.

4   Save the file as a master page using the following filename: **SHOPPING**.

5   Load the master page **SHOPPING**. Import the text file called **NET**. The text should start in the left-hand column of your first page. It will fill the columns on your first page and flow onto a second page.

6   Select and apply the three different styles, prepared in Step 2, to the three appropriate areas of the text.

7   Import the supplied images called **MARKET** (Image 1) and **NET** (Image 2) and display them as shown in Figure C3.1. Place Image 1 in the middle of the third column of the first page and Image 2 at the bottom of the second column on the second page.

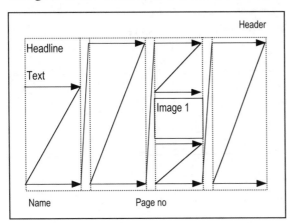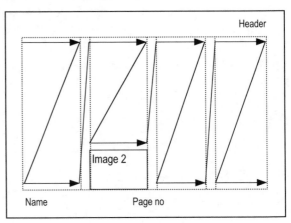

Figure C3.1 Page layout for Consolidation 3 Part 1

8   Save your document as **SHOPPING1** and print one copy.

9   Image 2 on the second page at the bottom of the third column should be resized to extend across the full width of columns 2 and 3. The image *must* be kept in proportion. Ensure that the finished publication takes no more than 2 pages. If necessary, Image 1 may also be resized to achieve this.

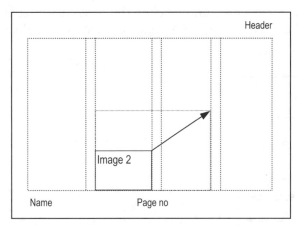

Figure C3.2 Resize Image 2

10 Copyfit your publication to ensure that:

- headings and related text are grouped together
- one line or less of text is grouped with the rest of the related text (ie there are no widows or orphans)
- text/graphics are adjusted so that they are not superimposed on other text or images
- paragraph spacing is consistent.

11 Save your document as **SHOPPING2** and print one copy.

Part 2

1 Load the document **PARTY**.

2 Amendments to the publication need to be made. The instructions for the amendments are indicated on the proof copy on page 93.

3 Changes to the style sheet need to be made as follows:

Style Name	Typeface	Point Size	Alignment
Headline	Bold		
Subheading	Italic	18	
Body text	Serif	14	
Bullet text	Serif		Justified

4 In the **THEMED PARTIES** story, insert a bullet character at the beginning of the following three paragraphs:

Teddy Bears' Picnic
Pirate Party
Disco Party

Ensure that all bullet text is indented from the bullet point.

5 In the **Children's Parties** story, overlay the text so that it is superimposed on the **CAKE** image. Ensure that the text is at the front and that the image can be seen in the background.

6 Place a box with **square** corners around the story **Themed Parties**, ensuring that the edges of the box do not touch the text.

7 Draw a horizontal line across the first and second columns below the headline to separate it from the main text. The line should be between 1 and 3 pt weight. Ensure the line does not touch any text.

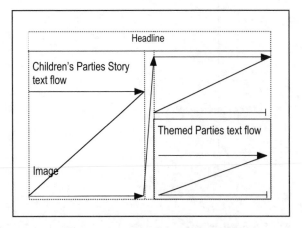

Figure C3.3 Layout for drawing line

8 Using the spell check facility, correct the spelling errors that appear in the text.

9 Copyfit your publication to ensure that:

- headings and related text are grouped together
- one line or less of text is grouped with the rest of related text (ie there are no widows or orphans)
- text/graphics are adjusted so that they are not superimposed on other text or images (except where specified)
- paragraph spacing is consistent.

10 Save the finished publication as **PARTY1** and print one copy.

Proof copy for Consolidation 3 Part 2

[Insert your name

PARTY TIME

Children's Parties

Children love parties, however, organising a party for a large number of small children can seem a very daunting task. We have some ideas that should take the stress out of the event and make it a memorable occasion for your child.

The secret of a good party is planning. First of all you need to decide the type of party you are going to hold and the number of guests. As a general rule, the younger the child, the smaller the number of guests, as very young children need to be supervised closely. Limit the number to as many as you feel you can supervise adequately and ensure you have some adult helpers on the day. The venue will also determine the number of people you can invite. Although it is obviously more expensive to hire a venue, such as a church or school hall, it does mean that the children will have somewhere to expend their energy without ruining your home.

The food and drink you are going to provide needs to be considered well in advance. Make sure that you provide plenty of variety as children can be very fussy about what they eat. Remember to include some vegetarian options. Sandwiches, dips, crisps, biscuits and ice-cream are always popular. If you can provide hot food, then pizza is a great favourite with almost all children.

The entertainment you provide is also very important. You should plan what is going to happen well in advance so that the children are kept occupied throughout the whole event. Traditional games such as pin the tail on the donkey and pass the parcel are still enjoyed by most children. If you can afford to hire a clown or magician, then this will keep the children occupied for an hour or so. Puppit shows are very popular with younger children and perhaps you could organise for a friend or older child to do this. Whatever you decide, remember that the party will not last for ever and before you realise it will be time for the children to go home.

Themed Parties

Most children enjoy a themed party and they do not have to be exppensive. Our ideas for the best parties include:

Teddy Bears' Picnic. Younger children will enjoy a teddy bears' picnic party. Ask the guests to bring a teddy and provide picnic food. You can purchase small food boxes that are just right for this occasion.

Pirate Party. For children aged around 5–7, a pirate party can be lots of fun. The guests should dress up as pirates and a prize can be given for the best costume. Treasure hunt games will keep the children occupied and a small bag of chocalate coins will provide the perfect going home present.

Disco Party. Older children will enjoy a disco party. If you do not want to hire a hall, then ensure the party area is clear of furnature to enable the children to jump around. Disco music, ( ) plenty of fizzy drinks and pizza will make children feel very grown up.

Consolidation 4

Part 1

1 Load Publisher 2000 and set up a two-page document. The paper size should be A4 and the orientation set to portrait. Specify three equal columns with a 4.5 mm (0.45 cm) gutter. Margins should be as follows:

Top   20 mm (2 cm)
Bottom   20 mm (2 cm)
Left   20 mm (2 cm)
Right   20 mm (2 cm)

2 Set up a style sheet with the following styles:

Style Name	Typeface	Point Size	Alignment
Body text	Serif	13	Left
Subheading	Serif, italic	16	Left
Headline	Sans serif, bold	18	Left

3 Set a header and footer as follows, using the body text typestyle:

Header   Article (Right aligned)
Footer   Your name (left aligned)   Page Number (centred)

Page numbering should start from page 8.

4 Save the file as a master page using the following filename: **WILDLIFE**.

5 Load the master page **WILDLIFE**. Import the text file called **ANIMALS**. The text should start in the left-hand column of your first page. It will fill the columns on your first page and flow onto a second page.

6 Select and apply the three different styles, prepared in Step 2, to the three appropriate areas of the text.

7 Import the supplied images called **OTTER** (Image 1) and **HARE** (Image 2) and display them as shown in C4.1. Place Image 1 at the bottom of the second column of the first page and Image 2 at the bottom of the first column on the second page.

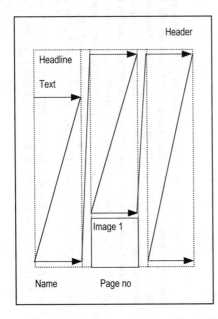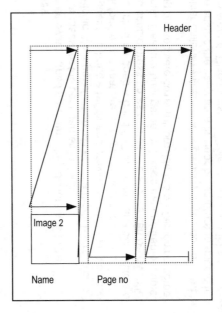

Figure C4.1 Layout for Consolidation 4 Part 1

8 Save your document as **WILDLIFE1** and print one copy.

9 Image 1 on the first page at the bottom of the second column should be resized to extend across the full width of columns 2 and 3. The image *must* be kept in proportion. Ensure that the finished publication takes no more than 2 pages. If necessary, Image 2 may also be resized to achieve this.

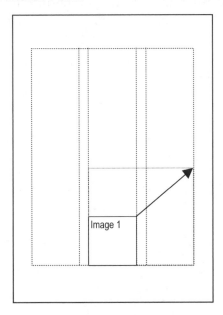

Figure C4.2 Resize Image 1

10 Copyfit your publication to ensure that:

- headings and related text are grouped together
- one line or less of text is grouped with the rest of the related text (ie there are no widows or orphans)
- text/graphics are adjusted so that they are not superimposed on other text or images
- paragraph spacing is consistent.

11 Save your document as **WILDLIFE2** and print one copy.

Part 2

1 Load the document **TOYS**.

2 Changes to the style sheet need to be made as follows:

Style Name	Typeface	Point Size	Alignment
Headline	Bold, italic	18	
Subheading	Serif, bold	16	Right
Bullet text	Italic	12	Left

3 Amendments to the publication need to be made. The instructions for the amendments are indicated on the proof copy on page 97.

4 In the **TOY MARKET** story, insert a bullet character at the beginning of the following three paragraphs:

Children are ...
Huge competition ...
Children prefer ....

Ensure that all bullet text is indented from the bullet point.

5 In the **TEDDY BEARS** story, overlay the text so that it is superimposed on the **TEDDY** image. Ensure that the text is at the front and that the image can be seen in the background.

6 Place a box with **square** corners around the headline text, ensuring that the edges of the box do not touch the text. Ensure that the headline remains centred

7 Draw a horizontal line across the second column below the **TOY MARKET** story to separate it from the **TEDDY BEARS** story. The line should be between 3 and 5 pt weight. Ensure the line does not touch any text.

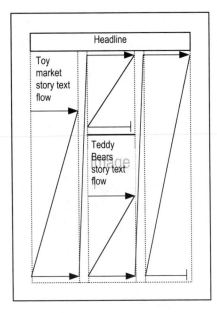

Figure C4.3 Layout for drawing line

8 Using the spell check facility, correct the spelling errors that appear in the text.

9 Copyfit your publication to ensure that:

- headings and related text are grouped together
- one line or less of text is grouped with the rest of the related text (ie there are no widows or orphans)
- text/graphics are adjusted so that they are not superimposed on other text or images (except where specified)
- paragraph spacing is consistent.

10 Save the finished publication as **TOYS1** and print one copy.

Proof copy for Consolidation 4 Part 2

CHILDREN'S TOYS

The Toy Market

The toy market has beeen declining over the past decade. Some of the reasons for this decline are given below:

Children are maturing earlier and therefore the age at which they stop playing with toys is decreasing.

Huge competition from the electronic and computerised game market.

Children prefer to watch telivision rather than play with toys.

Although the reasons are based in truth, children of today do still enjoy playing with toys. It should be remebered that toys and games provide an essential aid to learning. *Research has shown that children enjoy playing with traditionel type toys such as teddy bears, Yo-Yos, train sets, construction bricks and dolls. Although toys such as character merchandice can enjoy extreme popularity, this is very often short-lived. *A common complaint from parents is that there are hardly any toy shops left in this country. Many department stores have stopped selling toys. Where can parents find interesting toys at reasonable prices? There are a number of mail order businesses that offer a range of interesting products. The Internet is another good sorce with several large ~~companies~~ businesses

selling a variety of items. It is well worth finding a good toy supplier as your children will remember favourite toys for the rest of their lives.

Teddy Bears

We are all familiar with the teddy bear. They come in all shapes and sizes and appear on many household and children's items. When did teddy bears first become popular?

It is thought that the first teddy bear, as we know them today, appeared in 1903. They were made by a German company named Steiff. This company which still makes teddies today, had been making stuffed

bears since as far back as 1892. However, these were rigid models that were much more like real bears.

The teddy made in 1903 was called BAR55PB. He was a jointed model and as his name suggests, he was 55 cm high. The response to the new model was very slow with only one company placing an order. This American company ordred 3000 teddies and not one of these bears is known to be in existance today. If one could be found it would be worth a large amount of money.

The following year another model was designed, this time slightly smaller at 35cm. This model proved to be much more popular and around 12,000 were sold. Over the following few years the bears were constantly redesigned until Steiff felt that they had developed the best model in 1905.

Today Steiff are still delighting generations of children with their wide range of soft toys.

Insert your name

Exam Practice 3
OCR Stage II DTP

Element 1 – Set up and produce a publication

Before you start Task 1 make sure you have on disk the following text file and graphic images. These need to be imported into your desktop publishing publication.

Text file called: **SHOES**
Image 1 called: **COBBLER**
Image 2 called: **PLATFORMS**

Assessment Objectives

1.1a, 1.1b, 1.1c,
1.1d, 1.1e, 1f

1 Enter the desktop publishing system and create a new publication which meets the following specifications:

Number of pages	2
Page size	A4
Page orientation	Portrait/Tall
Number of columns	3
Gutter space	0.5 cm (5 mm) space between columns
Margins	Left 2.5 cm (25 mm)
	Right 2.5 cm (25 mm)
	Top 2.5 cm (25 mm)
	Bottom 2.5 cm (25 mm)

1.2a, 1.2b, 1.2c,
1.2d, 1.2e

2 Prepare three styles according to the following specifications:

Style Name	Typeface	Point Size	Alignment
Body text	Sans serif	11	Justified
Subhead	Sans serif, bold	16	Left
Headline	Serif, bold, italic	18	Justified

1.4a, 1.4b, 1.4c

3 Insert the following **header**:

ARTICLE (right aligned)

Insert the following footer:

XX (XX being replaced by your name) Page Number Stage II

(Left aligned)   (Centred)   (Right aligned)

Page numbering should start at 3.

1.5a

4 Save the file as a master page using the filename **SHOES1** and ask your tutor to verify this.

1.6a

5 Import the supplied text file called **SHOES**. The text should start in the left-hand column of your first page. It will fill the columns on your first page and flow onto a second page.

1.3a

6 Select and apply the three different styles prepared in step 2 to the three appropriate areas of the text.

1.7a

7   Import the supplied images called: **COBBLER** (Image 1) and **PLAT-FORMS** (Image 2) and display these as shown in Figure EP3.1. Place Image 1 in the middle of the second column on the first page and Image 2 at the top of the third column on the second page.

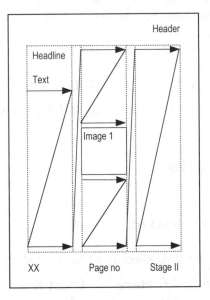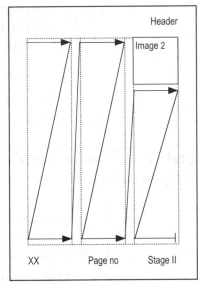

Figure EP3.1 Page layout for Element 1

1.9a

8   Save *two copies* of your work, using the names **SHOES2** and **SHOES3**. Ask your tutor to verify this.
Continue working in **SHOES3**. **SHOES2** can either be printed now or later as instructed by your tutor.

1.7c

9   Image 2 on the second page at the top of the third column should be resized to extend across the full width of columns 2 and 3. The image must be kept in proportion. Ensure that the finished publication takes no more than 2 pages. If necessary Image 1 may also be resized to achieve this.

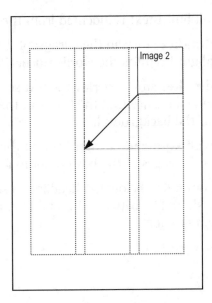

Figure EP3.2 Resize Image 2

1.8a, 1.8b, 1.8c, 1.8d	**10**	Copyfit your publication to ensure that:

- headings and related text are grouped together
- one line or less of text is grouped with the rest of the related text (ie there are no widows or orphans)
- text/graphics are adjusted so that they are not superimposed on other text or images
- paragraph spacing is consistent.

1.9a	**11**	Save the finished publication **SHOES3**. Ask your tutor to verify this.
1.10a	**12**	Print **SHOES3** and ensure that **SHOES2** is also printed as instructed by your tutor.

Element 2 – Edit a Publication

Assessment Objectives

2.1a	**1**	Load the file: **COOKERY**.

2.2a, 2.2b	**2**	Changes to the style sheet need to be made as follows:

Style Name	Typeface	Point Size	Alignment
Body text	Serif	14	
Bullet text	Serif		Justified
Subhead	Italic	16	
Headline	Bold		Right

2.3a	**3**	Amendments to the publication need to be made. The instructions for the amendments are indicated on the proof copy on page 102.
2.5a	**4**	In the **Breadmaker** story, insert a bullet character at the beginning of the following four paragraphs:

Cake making.
Jam and marmalade.
Pizzas.
Rolls and fancy breads.

2.5b		Ensure that all bullet text is indented from the bullet point.
2.4a	**5**	In the **Breadmaker** story, in the paragraph beginning **Who doesn't enjoy...** highlight in italics the words **no artificial preservatives.**
2.7a	**6**	In the **Breadmaker** story, overlay the text so that it is superimposed on the **Bread** image. Ensure that the text is at the front and that the image can be seen in the background.
2.9a, 2.9b	**7**	Place a box with **squared** corners around the story **Coffee Grinder**, ensuring that the edges of the box do not touch the text.
2.8a	**8**	Draw a horizontal line below the headline to separate it from the body text. The line should be between 4 and 8 pt rule weight. Ensure the line does not touch any text.

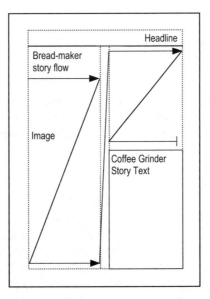

Figure EP3.3 Layout for drawing line

2.6a

9 Using the spell check facility of the desktop publishing system, correct the spelling errors that appear in the text.

2.10a, 2.10b, 2.10c, 2.10d

10 Copyfit your publication to ensure that:
   – Headings and related text are grouped together;
   – One line or less of text is grouped with the rest of the related text (ie there are no widows or orphans)
   – Text/graphics are adjusted so that they are not superimposed on other text or images unless specified
   – Paragraph spacing is consistent

2.11a

11 Save the finished publication, using the filename **COOKERY1** and ask your tutor to verify this.

2.12a

12 Print the finished publication.

Proof copy for Exam Practice 3 Element 2

What's new in the kitchen?

As home cooking rises in poplarity, there is an increasing number of sophisticated gadgits available to assist the busy cook. This week we will look at two of the new appliances that will help you save time in the kitchen.

Close up

Breadmaker

Who doesn't enjoy the taste of freshly-baked homemade bread? A breadmaker will produce a freshly-baked loaf without any of the time consuming processes that have to be proformed by hand. All you do is weigh the ingrediants, place them in the machine and switch it on.

A few hours later you will have a loaf of bread that tastes fantastic and has no artificial preservatives.

Many modern breadmakers have a timer facility that can be used so that you can wake to a just-baked loaf for breakfast. However, if you plan to do this you will need the loaf to finish approximately half an hour before you

want to eat it. This is because the loaf needs to rest for a while to allow it to cool sufficiently to be cut.

As well as plain white or wholemeal loaves, you can bake a variaty of different breads. Olive, sun-dried tomato and cheese and onion are all simple to make. Other uses for the breadmaker, depending on the model, can include:

Cake making. Some models will bake large cakes, but it is important to follow the given recipe carefully.

Jam and marmalade. These can be made in the appliance with reletive ease, however, they can be a little runny.

Pizzas. The breadmaker makes excellent pizza dough. All you need do is roll out, top and bake.

rolls and fancy breads. Depending on the model and recipe you can make any number of different breads and rolls. As with pizza dough, you must remove the dough from the machine, shape and then bake.

We have tried a number of ~~machines~~ *appliances* stet and have had excellent results from all. We highly reccomend these machines to our readers. ~~They cost from approximately £50.~~

Coffee Grinder

Although these are not new appliances we feel it is worth drawing atttention to these handy gadgets. One quick blast from the coffee grinder and you have freshly ground coffee that tastes wonderful. Just the thing to go with the freshly baked bread!

The majority of grinders have a control that will allow you to choose how finely the coffee will be ground. This means they are suitable for both percolators and cafetières.

Coffee beans are readily available in supermarkets. Many enthusiasts combine beans of different types until they have created their 'own blend'. The only drawback we encountered is that cleaning around the blades can be difficult. Care should be taken as the blades are sharp. *and delicatessens*

Insert your name
Cookery Special

Exam Practice 4
OCR Stage II DTP

Element 1 – Set up and produce a publication

Before you start Task 1 make sure you have on disk the following text file and graphic images. These need to be imported into your desktop publishing publication.

Text file called:	**AGA**
Image 1 called:	**COOK**
Image 2 called:	**FOOD**

Assessment Objectives

1.1a, 1.1b, 1.1c, 1.1d, 1.1e, 1.1f

1 Enter the desktop publishing system and create a new publication which meets the following specifications:

Number of pages	2	
Page size	A4	
Page orientation	Landscape/Wide	
Number of columns	3	
Gutter space	5 mm (0.5 cm) space between columns	
Margins	Left	25 mm (2.5 cm)
	Right	25 mm (2.5 cm)
	Top	25 mm (2.75 cm)
	Bottom	25 mm (2.75 cm)

1.2a, 1.2b, 1.2c, 1.2d, 1.2e

2 Prepare three styles according to the following specifications:

Style Name	Typeface	Point Size	Alignment
Body text	Serif	12	Left
Subhead	Sans serif, bold	16	Right
Headline	Serif, bold	18	Left

1.4a, 1.4b, 1.4c

3 Insert the following **header**:

XX (XX being replaced by your name)   Cookery Article
(left aligned)   (right aligned)

Insert the following **footer**:

Page Number   (left aligned)

Page numbering should start at 6.

1.5a

4 Save the file as a master page using the filename **AGA** and ask your tutor to verify this.

1.6a

5 Import the supplied text file called **AGA**. The text should start in the left-hand column of your first page. It will fill the columns on your first page and flow onto a second page.

1.3a

6 Select and apply the three different styles prepared in step 2 to the three appropriate areas of the text.

1.7a

7 Import the supplied images called: **COOK** (Image 1) and **FOOD** (Image 2) and display these as shown in Figure EP4.1. Place Image 1 at the top of the first column on the first page and Image 2 at the bottom of the first column on the second page.

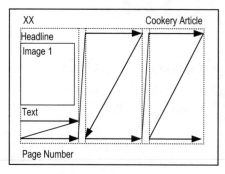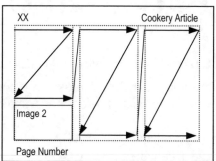

Figure EP4.1 Page layout for Element 1

1.9a

8 Save *two copies* of your work, using the names **AGA1** and **AGA2**. Ask your tutor to verify this.

Continue working in **AGA2**. **AGA1** can either be printed now or later as instructed by your tutor.

1.7c

9 Image 2 on the second page at the bottom of the first column should be resized to extend across the full width of columns 1 and 2. The image must be kept in proportion. Ensure that the finished publication takes no more than 2 pages. If necessary Image 1 may also be resized to achieve this.

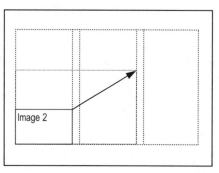

Figure EP4.2 Resize Image 2

1.8a, 1.8b, 1.8c, 1.8d

10 Copyfit your publication to ensure that:

– headings and related text are grouped together
– one line or less of text is grouped with the rest of the related text (ie there are no widows or orphans)
– text/graphics are adjusted so that they are not superimposed on other text or images
– paragraph spacing is consistent.

1.9a

11 Save the finished publication **AGA2**. Ask your tutor to verify this.

1.10a

12 Print **AGA2** and ensure that **AGA1** is also printed as instructed by your tutor.

Element 2 – Edit a Publication

Assessment Objectives

2.1a	**1**	Load the file: **HOME**.

2.2a, 2.2b   **2**   Changes to the style sheet need to be made as follows:

Style Name	Typeface	Point Size	Alignment
Body text			
Bullet text	Serif	10	Justified
Subhead	Bold	16	
Headline	Bold	20	Centred

2.3a   **3**   Amendments to the publication need to be made. The instructions for the amendments are indicated on the proof copy on page 107.

2.5a   **4**   In the **Choosing a Mortgage** story, insert a bullet character at the beginning of the following five paragraphs:

Variable rate loan.
Fixed rate loan.
Discount rate loan.
Capped rate loan.
Flexible loans.

2.5b   Ensure that all bullet text is indented from the bullet point.

2.4a   **5**   In the **Choosing A New Home** story, in the paragraph beginning **If you can...** highlight in bold and italics the words **Don't forget, properties are placed on the market every day**.

2.7a   **6**   In the **Choosing A New Home** story, overlay the text so that it is superimposed on the **HOUSE** image. Ensure that the text is at the front and that the image can be seen in the background.

2.9a, 2.9b   **7**   Place a box with **rounded** corners around the headline, ensuring that the edges of the box do not touch the text.

2.8a   **8**   Draw a horizontal line below the **Choosing a New Home** story to separate it from the **Choosing a mortgage** story. The line should be between 2 and 4 pt rule weight. Ensure the line does not touch any text.

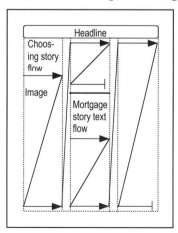

Figure EP4.3 Layout for drawing line

2.6a	**9**	Using the spell check facility of the desktop publishing system, correct the spelling errors that appear in the text.
2.10a, 2.10b, 2.10c, 2.10d	**10**	Copyfit your publication to ensure that: – headings and related text are grouped together – one line or less of text is grouped with the rest of the related text (ie there are no widows or orphans) – text/graphics are adjusted so that they are not superimposed on other text or images unless specified – paragraph spacing is consistent.
2.11a	**11**	Save the finished publication, using the filename **HOME1** and ask your tutor to verify this.
2.12a	**12**	Print the finished publication.

Proof copy for Exam Practice 4 Element 2

Guide to Property Buying

Choosing a New Home

Obviously one of the biggest restrictions on your choice of new home is your buget. The first thing you need to do is find out how much you will be able to borrow from a morgage lender. As a rough guide, most lenders will allow around three

times the joint salaries, although some will allow three and three quarters. Remember, you will probably have to find a deposit, around five to ten percent of the purchase price of the property.

Once you have worked out how much you can afford then you can start to look for your dream home. Before you start, think about the following points.
Do you have a particular type of property in mind, such as a Victorian home or a brand new property? Are you willing to compromise on this? Is a garage or off-road parking a must? What about the size of the garden? Are you willing to carry out repair or redecoration works? These decisions will help you in your search. Visit as many estate agents as possable. Discuss your requirements thoroughly with each so that they understand the type of property you are looking for. The more information you can give them, the more chance they have of finding something suitable.

View as many different houses as you can. Be prepared to look at some properties that may not seem immmediately suitable. You may be surprised to find that your tastes can change as you look at different properties.

If you can, be prepared to spend several weeks finding a property. Don't forget, properties are placed on the market every day. Do not feel as though you have to buy the first house that comes along. Your new home will probably be the bigggest single purchase you will ever make. You will want to get it right straightaway first time.

Choosing a Mortgage

The mortgage market can be a minfield to many of us. The range of products available is huge and it changes rapidly. However, this should not deter you from shopping around to ensure you obtain the best deal available at the time. Given below is a breif description of some of the types of mortgage you may encounter.
Variable rate loan. This is the most common type of loan and the interest rate moves up or down according to the Bank of England base rates. With this type of loan you must be prepared for the possibility of your mortgage payments increasing. In the late 1980s mortgage rates almost doubled in a matter of a year or so. Conversely, if the base rate falls then so will your mortgage repayments.
Fixed rate loan. This type of loan has a fixed interest rate for a specified period. It may be for

as little a time as one year or could be for as long as ten years. The advantage of this type of loan is that you know how much your monthly repayments will be for the fixed period. This can be very useful.
Discount rate loan. These loans offer a discount on the variable rate offered at the time. Some are garanteed to be at least a certain percentage lower than the base rate for a specified period of time. Your mortgage payments can rise or fall as with the variable rate, albeit at a lower rate.
Capped rate loan. With a capped rate, the interest rate will not rise above a certain specified amount during the period for which it is capped. This means that if interest rates rise sharply, your mortgage will be protected at a certain level, usually around one or two percent lower. However, if mortgage rates fall, then your monthly payments will decrease in line with the base rate.
Flexiable loans. These have become more popular in recent years with a large number of new products being developed by mortgage lenders. With this type of loan you have the flexibility of paying larger or smaller amounts than usual, depending on your circumstances. Some products will allow you to take a 'payment break' or even withdraw some of your payments.

Whichever type of mortgage loan you are interested in, it is advisable to seek advice from a financial advisor or mortgage expert.

Stage II Checklist

Did you remember to	Assessment Objective	Con 3	Con 4	Exam 3	Exam 4
...set up two pages, A4 with the orientation as specified?	1.1a 1.1b 1.1c				
...select the correct number of columns and set accurate margins and gutter space?	1.1d 1.1e 1.1f				
...set up the style sheet as specified, using the correct type size, font, alignment and enhancements?	1.2a 1.2b 1.2c 1.2d 1.2e				
...apply the text styles correctly?	1.3a				
...set up the header/footer correctly and page number accurately?	1.4a 1.4b 1.4c				
...save the blank template?	1.5a				
...import the text and images as specified in the design brief?	1.6a 1.7a 1.7b				
...resize the image correctly and in proportion?	1.7c 1.7d				
...copyfit the document in accordance with instructions?	1.8a 2.10a 1.8b 2.10b 1.8c 2.10c 1.8d 2.10d				
...save and print your document correctly?	1.9a 2.11a 1.10a 2.12a				
...make the specified amendments to the style sheet accurately?	2.2a 2.2b 2.2c 2.2d 2.2e				
...make amendments to the text as indicated in the design brief?	2.3a				
...enhance the specified text?	2.4a				
...use bullets as appropriate and indent the text correctly?	2.5a 2.5b				
...use the spellcheck accurately?	2.6a				
...layer the text and image correctly?	2.7a				
...draw a line in the specified place, using the correct line weight?	2.8a 2.8b				
...draw a box in the specified place using the correct corners?	2.9a 2.9b				

PART 3

STAGE III
Advanced Desktop Publishing

Before you start Part 3 make sure you can:

- load Publisher 2000
- set up templates and master pages
- create a new document
- open an existing file
- save and print documents
- set up page layouts
- set up column guides
- set up style sheets
- import text and images
- resize images in proportion
- copyfit your work
- multi-layer text and images.

In Part 3 of the book you will learn about:

- designing a page layout
- producing an alternative version of a publication
- using a non-standard page size.

Designing a page layout

In this chapter you will learn how to:
- set up a page layout following a design brief
- set up a table
- create dropped capitals
- use advanced copyfitting tools.

10.1 Set up a page layout following a design brief

In Part 2 you looked at creating documents using specified measurements for margins, gutters and style sheets. You are now going to try designing your own documents from a design brief.

In the workplace, as in examinations, you may be given a sketch of the page layout with various instructions dotted around the page to work from. Use this as a checklist and mark each instruction as you complete it.

It may be that you will be able to choose the margins and gutter space. If this is the case look at the amount of text and graphics you have to place and keep the margins and guides to a minimum size. A gutter space of 5 mm (0.5 cm) and margins of 15 mm (1.5 cm) would usually be acceptable.

You may have to key in some text, for example, the headline. If you are unsure as to how it should be displayed, the design brief should give you some guidance. For example, if the headline has been written on the design brief in capitals, then key it in in capitals. The alignment of the text can also be seen from the design brief. If it is clear that the heading stretches from margin to margin, then make sure you do the same. Once you have finished keying in the headline, or any text, check it carefully for typographical and spelling errors.

Exercise 19.1

1 Create an A4 size publication following the design brief on page 112. Gutter space can be as you wish. Use lines/rules where indicated in the design brief.

2 Set up a style sheet for the headline, subheading and body text as shown in the design brief. Choose point sizes to fill the publication. Import the text files: **Autumn**, **Loyalty**, **Warehouse** and **Online** and apply the appropriate styles. Save the document as **CLOTHES**.

3 In the **Autumn** article, insert the following new paragraph at the end of the article, after the paragraph ending **...to a high specification.**
Both the Classic and Casual ranges can be seen at any of our stores, in our mail-order catalogue and on our website.

Design brief for Exercise 19.1

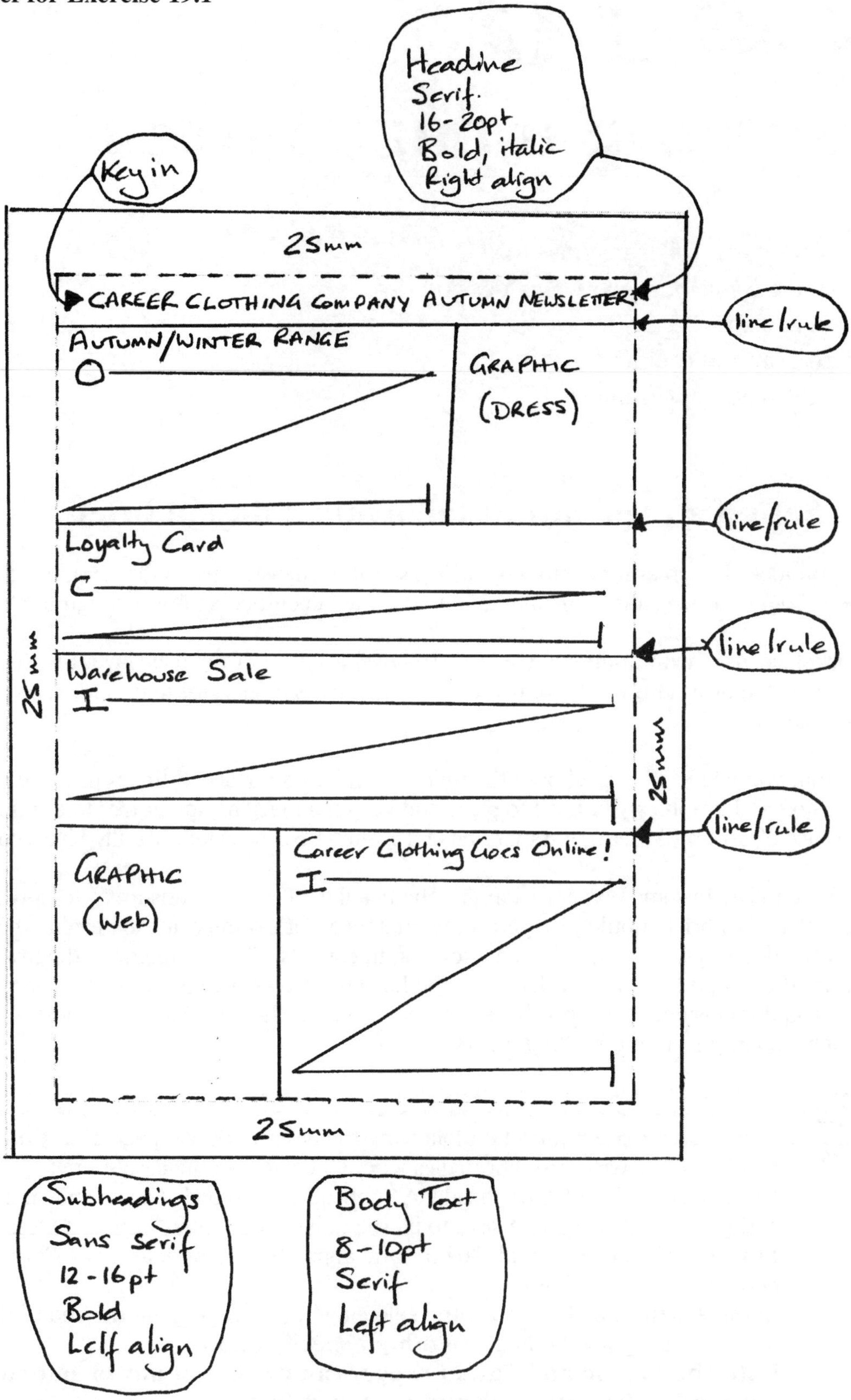

Key in

Headline
Serif.
16-20pt
Bold, italic
Right align

25mm

► CAREER CLOTHING COMPANY AUTUMN NEWSLETTER ◄

line/rule

AUTUMN/WINTER RANGE

O

GRAPHIC
(DRESS)

line/rule

Loyalty Card

C

line/rule

Warehouse Sale

I

25mm

25mm

line/rule

GRAPHIC
(Web)

Career Clothing Goes Online!

I

25mm

Subheadings
Sans serif
12-16pt
Bold
Left align

Body Text
8-10pt
Serif
Left align

METHOD

1 Load Publisher.
2 Make sure the orientation is portrait.
3 Check margins are 25 mm (2.5 cm).
4 Draw separate text frames for the heading and the four articles as per the design brief. (Don't forget to set the margins for the text frames to 0 cm.)

TIP

You may find it easier if you draw some guidelines. Although, in this instance, none of the text is actually set in columns, the design could benefit from being split vertically into three – i.e. the Autumn/Winter article approximately takes up a width of two columns, while the DRESS graphic next to it takes up the third column width. Likewise the WEB graphic takes up approximately one column width while the accompanying article (Career Clothing Goes On Line) takes up approximately the width of both the second and third columns.

An easy way to get column guides on your page is to set it up in the **Layout Guides** dialogue box:

1 From the **Arrange** menu, select: **Layout Guides**.
2 In the **Grid Guides** section, key in **3** in the **Columns** box.

Your document should now look something like this:

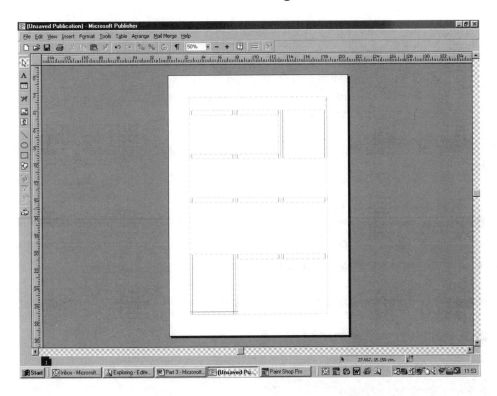

Figure 10.1 Text boxes drawn

5 Set up style sheets as per the design brief. Choose font sizes mid-way between the range provided for the moment (Headline 18 pt; Subheading 14 pt; Body Text 9 pt). You can alter these later if necessary so that the text fits and fills the page. Set a first line indent for the body text as is usual in desktop publishing.
6 Key in and import the text and apply the styles.

TIP

You may find that some of the text does not fit the text boxes you have drawn – or does not fill them. You can either change the font size (making sure you keep within the specified range) or change the sizes of the text boxes (again, making sure that you keep within the guidelines of the design brief). Of course, you could also do a combination of the two.

7 Add lines as specified on the design brief. As there is no point size given, you can choose this yourself – but make sure it is consistent for all the lines. As the body text is quite small it would probably look better if you used a small size – for example, I or 2 pts.

10.2 Set up a table

The text that you import may already contain a table, or you might have to key in a table yourself.

Exercise 19.4 You must format the table at the end of the **Warehouse** article. Set up two columns, left aligned with column headings:

Order Value   Postage and Packing

Formatting an existing table

You need to ensure that a tab or a comma has been inserted between each entry and a paragraph mark has been inserted at the end of each row. When you have ensured that this is the case – and inserted tabs (by pressing the **Tab** key) or commas (by pressing the **Comma** key) in between each entry if they were not already there – you are ready to create your table.

METHOD

I Highlight the text that is to be turned into a table (in this case, from **Order Value** to **Post free**).

2 Either:
- From the **Edit** menu, select: **Copy**, or
- Press: **CTRL +C**, or
- Click on: the 📋 **Copy** button.

3 From the **Edit** menu, select: **Paste Special**.

The **Paste Special** dialogue box will appear on screen:

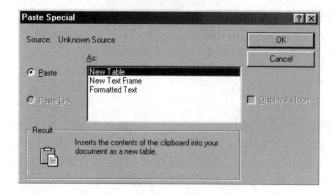

Figure 10.2 Paste Special dialogue box

4 In the **As** box, select **New Table**.
5 Click on: **OK**.

You will now have a table floating above your text. Notice also that the original table text is still in your document:

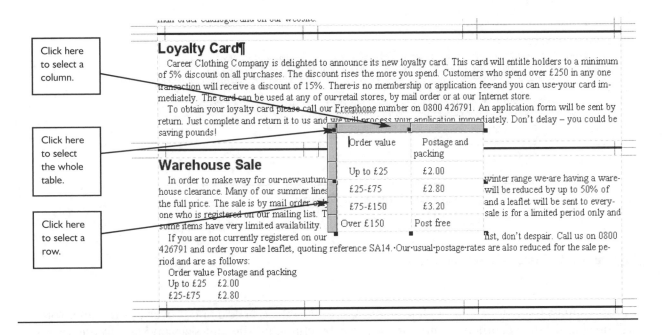

Figure 10.3 Table floating over text

You need to take the first line indent off the text in the table and ensure that the text is not inset within the table, otherwise it looks untidy.

> 6 Select the whole table by clicking on the top left-hand corner.
> 7 From the **Format** menu, select: **Indents and Lists**.
> 8 Key in **0cm** in the **First Line** box.
> 9 From the **Format** menu, select: **Table Cell Properties**.
> 10 Key in **0cm** in all the margin boxes.

You also need to increase the width of the columns so that the headings fit on one line and decrease the height of the rows so that the table does not take up so much room.

> 11 Ensure that the table is still selected.
> 12 Drag the middle right-hand handle to the right until the second heading is all on one line.
> 13 Drag the middle bottom handle up as much as you can without any of the text being obscured.

You now need to delete the original text and move the new table to where it is to go.

> 14 Delete the text in the normal way.
> 12 Hover the mouse over the table until the cursor changes to the **Move** cursor (the one with a little lorry).
> 13 Drag the table to its correct position.
> 14 Click anywhere in the page margin to deselect the table.

Your table should now look something like this:

Warehouse Sale

In order to make way for our new autumn/winter range we are having a warehouse clearance. Many of our summer lines will be reduced by up to 50% of the full price. The sale is by mail order only and a leaflet will be sent to everyone who is registered on our mailing list. The sale is for a limited period only and some items have very limited availability.

If you are not currently registered on our list, don't despair. Call us on 0800 426791 and order your sale leaflet, quoting reference SA14. Our usual postage rates are also reduced for the sale period and are as follows:

Order value	Postage and packing¤
Up to £25	£2.00
£25-£75	£2.80
£75-£150	£3.20
Over £150	Post-free

Career Clothing Goes Online!

If you like our garments, but don't enjoy shopping, visit our new website at careerclothes.co.uk for the latest ranges and sales information. The website

Figure 10.4 Table resized and moved

Unfortunately, the table is still too tall for the Warehouse Sale article and it overlaps the line. You will need to fix the document again (for example, by changing the font sizes and text frame sizes – within the specifications of the design brief). You might prefer to leave it for now, as there are further changes to be made to the document in the following sections which may also result in the need to fix the document again.

Keying in the table

If the text for the table is not already there and you need to key it in, you can use the ▦ **Table Frame Tool** button on the Object toolbar.

METHOD

1 Place the cursor where you want to insert the table.
2 Click on: the ▦ **Table Frame Tool**.
3 Draw a box where you wish the table to appear.

As soon as you have finished drawing the box, the **Create Table** dialogue box will appear asking you to key in the number of rows and columns you need.

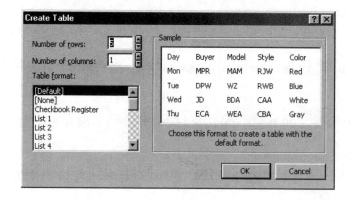

Figure 10.5 Create Table dialogue box

4 Key in the number of rows and columns you require
5 Click on: **OK**. A grid will appear on screen.
6 Key in the text, remembering to press the **Tab** key to move from column to column and the **Return** key to move from row to row.

Aligning your table
You should always try to ensure that your table alignment is consistent. This is to ensure your work looks as professional as possible. It does not matter whether you decide to centre, left, or right align each column as long as they are all the same.

10.3 Create dropped capitals

You may wish to set up dropped capital(s). Look at the example below.

T his is a dropped capital. You may have noticed these in newspapers and magazines. Note that the text is neatly aligned.

Exercise 19.5 Produce dropped capitals for the first letter of **each** article. Maintain consistent text flow of the body text around the dropped capitals.

   1 Click anywhere in the first paragraph of the text box.
   2 From the **Format** menu, select: **Drop Cap**.
   3 Choose **Drop Cap**

The **Drop Cap** dialogue box will appear on screen (see Figure 10.6).

   4 Click on: the **Custom Drop Cap** tab.

You will then be able to fill in the number of lines you would like the capital to drop and also the font style, type and size.

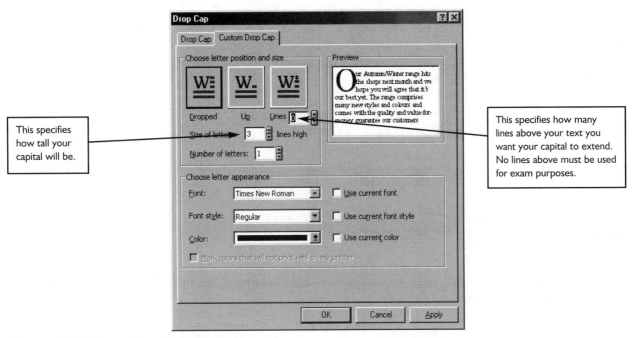

Figure 10.6 Drop Cap dialogue box

5 Key in **0** in the **Lines** box and **3** in the **Size of letters** box. Make sure that the **Number of letters** box says **I**.

6 Keep the same font and style as the body text by ensuring that **Use current font** and **Use current font style** are both ticked.

7 Repeat the process for all the articles as specified in the design brief.

TIP

Two things are important when setting dropped capitals:
- The space between the dropped capital and the rest of the text. In the example on p117, a space of 1 mm was set to make a neat margin.
- The number of lines the capital is dropped. In the example on p117, it was set at three lines.

Place the two image files: **Dress** and **Web** as indicated in the design brief, maintaining the original proportions.

10.4 Use advanced copyfitting tools

Copyfit your publication to ensure:
- all material is displayed on one page
- text/graphics/lines are not superimposed on each other
- headings and related text are grouped together
- one line or less of text is grouped with the rest of related text (ie there are no widows or orphans)
- paragraph spacing is consistent
- leading is consistent
- there are no more than 5 hyphenated line endings on the page
- there is no more than 10 mm (1 cm) of vertical white space at each end of each article.

You looked at some ways of copyfitting your material in Part 2. However, there are a few more advanced tools that you can use to ensure your work looks neat and tidy.

Displaying the material on one page
In the workplace, you may have to ensure that your work fits on one page. This is common sense, as a leaflet that extended just a few lines onto a second page would look unprofessional and untidy. In order to keep your work on one page, you can try one or more of the following:

■ Change your point sizes, so that the text fits on the page. Remember to keep the size within the specified range given on the design brief.
■ Change the size of the image(s). Remember to keep them in the area specified on the design brief.
■ Adjust the **tracking**. See below for more information on tracking.
■ Adjust the **leading**. See below for more information on leading.

Tracking
Tracking is the space between characters. The default setting for this is usually 'normal'. Look at Figure 10.7 to see how tracking works.

This is a sentence typed in a size 12, serif font. The tracking is on the default setting of normal.

This is a sentence typed in a size 12, serif font. The tracking has been set to very loose.

This is a sentence typed in a size 12, serif font. The tracking has been set to very tight.

Figure 10.7 Tracking

METHOD 1 Select the text you want to change
 2 From the **Format** menu, select: **Character Spacing**.

The **Character Spacing** dialogue box will appear on screen.

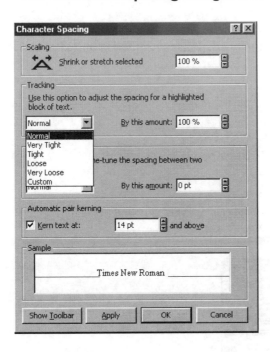

Figure 10.8 Character Spacing dialogue box

In the **Tracking** section, you can select a tracking option or you can set your own figure as a percentage. Alter the value to suit your document. It is easiest to use the preset values in the drop-down menu – **Normal**, **Very Tight**, **Tight**, **Loose** and **Very Loose** rather than changing the percentages in the **By this amount** box. However, if you want more control you can change the percentages manually.

TIP
> As you can see, adjusting the tracking can make a great deal of difference. However, if you choose to alter the tracking, remember the text must still be legible.

Adjust the leading
Leading is the technical term for the space between lines of text. It can be adjusted to give different affects. Look at Figure 10.9.

This is a sentence typed in a 12 point serif font. The leading is set on 14 points and the words are easy to read from line to line. Most desktop publishing software uses points to measure the space between lines. Publisher's default measurement, however, is linespaces. It is better to use points, though, as you have more control. To change to points, you can simply key in **pt** instead of **sp** in the relevant spaces (see below). It is usually best to use a leading that is one or two points more than your font size.

To condense the lines slightly alter the leading so that the space between the lines of text is smaller. This example has used a 12-point serif font and leading of 9 points.

To expand the lines, alter the leading so that the space between the lines of text is larger.

This example has used a 12-point serif font and leading of 20 points.

Figure 10.9 Leading

Note: the text set with 9-point leading has been clipped. This is not acceptable, it would have been better to use a 13-point leading.

To change the leading within the style sheet:

  1 From the **Format** menu, select: **Text Style**.
  2 Select the style you want to change.
  3 Click on: **Change this style**.
  4 Click on: **Line spacing**.

  The **Line Spacing** dialogue box appears on screen.

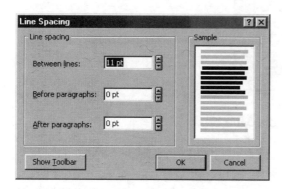

Figure 10.10 Line Spacing dialogue box

  5 In the **Between lines** box, key in the points you want to change to (ensuring that you key in **pt** instead of **sp**.
  6 Remember to change the leading for other relevant parts of the document (see tip below).

TIP

It is important that the leading is kept consistent throughout the publication. The best place to adjust the leading is within your style sheet. This will ensure that all the body text will have the same leading. Do not forget to include any tables or other text that has been keyed in as a separate story.

White Space
The areas around graphics/text and at the top and bottom of the page or columns are known as white space. Look at the example in Figure 10.11.

As you can see, the white space in this example is uneven at the top and bottom of the columns and around the graphic. The columns should be neatly aligned where possible with only the third column having white space at the bottom, although for the OCR Stage III Desktop Publishing exam, this should not be more than 10 mm. In order to ensure that this is the case you can do any of the following:

- Enlarge or reduce the size of the graphic (as long as you have not been given a specific size).
- Adjust the leading to ensure a neat fit (as long as you have not been given a specific leading value).
- Adjust the tracking to ensure a neat fit.
- Ensure the text flow is from the top to the bottom of each column – in Figure 10.11 the text box does not stretch from the top to the bottom in the second and third columns.

Exercise 19.8   Save the document and print one copy.

Exercise 20

1   Create an A4 size publication following the given design brief. Gutter space can be as you wish. Use line/rules where indicated in the design brief.

2   Set up a style sheet for the headline, subheading and body text as shown in the design brief. Choose point sizes to fill the publication. Import the text files: **About, Soon, Christmas** and **Trips** and apply the appropriate styles.

3   In the **Christmas** article, insert the following sentence at the end of the paragraph ending **half going to a local charity...**
The rest of the profits are put towards the cost of running the film club.

4   You must format the table at the end of the **Trips** article. Set up three columns, left aligned with column headings:
Date   Film   Location

5   Produce dropped capitals for the first letter of **each** article. Maintain consistent text flow of the body text around the dropped capitals.

6   Place the three image files: **Clip, Lights** and **Film** as indicated in the design brief, maintaining the original proportions.

7   Copyfit your publication to ensure:
   - all material is displayed on one page
   - text/graphics/lines are not superimposed on each other
   - headings and related text are grouped together
   - one line or less of text is grouped with the rest of related text (ie there are no widows or orphans)
   - paragraph spacing is consistent
   - leading is consistent
   - there are no more than 5 hyphenated line endings on the page
   - there is no more than 10 mm of vertical white space at each end of each article.

8   Save the document as **FILM** and print one copy.

Design brief for Exercise 20

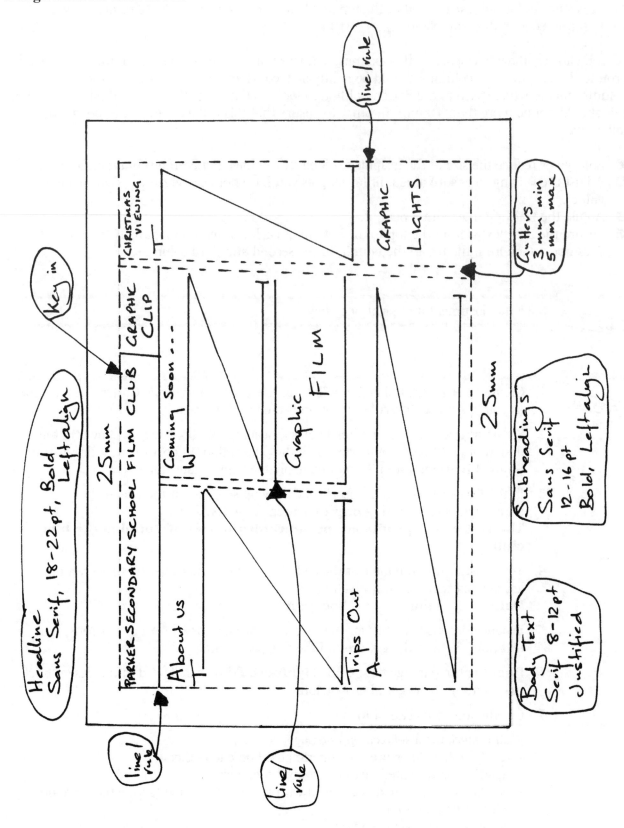

Figure 10.11 White space

Chapter 11

Producing an Alternative Version of a Publication

In this chapter you will learn how to:

■ crop graphics

■ create irregular text wrap

■ amend kerning.

You may decide that you would like to see an alternative version of a document you have created, or perhaps your boss would like to see several ideas on a page layout.

You may want to work on a copy of the document you have already created or start again. If you decide to work on your existing publication you must ensure that you work on a copy and that the original has been saved. If you decide to start again you must be very careful to ensure that the text styles are the same and that you only change what you are asked to change.

You should make sure that you work on a new version of your document (by saving it as a different filename). This way, the original will still be saved, so that if you make any large mistakes you have the original to refer to. Also, in the OCR Stage III Desktop Publishing exam, you need to print the original version as well as the alternative version, so it is best to have them both as different files, in case you can only print at the end of the exam.

You may be given a second design brief to work from for the alternative layout. Some of the new layout may be specified, for example, placing one of the stories in a specific place. You can then choose how to set out the rest of the publication. Remember, for examination work, you must *not* change the font or font sizes.

It may be that you will have to delete some of the text. If this is the case, then make sure you take out only the text specified – no more, no less.

Exercise 21.1

1 Open the file: **CLOTHES**. Save it as **CLOTHES1** and design a landscape layout based on the alternative page sketch on page 124.
2 Delete from the **Warehouse** article the sentence beginning **Our usual postage and packing rates... and the two-column table.**
3 Note that the first article must be **Autumn**.
   You must use the same fonts and the same point sizes that you chose in Exercise 19.

Alternative page sketch for Exercise 21.1

CAREER CLOTHING COMPANY AUTUMN NEWSLETTER

Autumn Winter Range

① You may select any number of columns

② Place the remaining articles and graphic files to suit your layout.

Dropped capitals should NOT appear in this task

Keep the graphic 'WEB' with the article 'on line'.

METHOD
1 From the **File** menu, choose **Page Setup**.
2 Click on: the **Landscape** orientation.
3 Click on: **OK**.

You will now have to move the various text boxes, lines and graphics manually to fit the new layout. In order to move the items:

METHOD
1 Click anywhere within the text box or image.
2 Drag the text box or image to the new position.

To change the size of the text box:

METHOD
1 Click anywhere within the text box so that the handles are selected.
2 Move the cursor over one of the handles and drag the box to the correct size.

Remember when you are resizing graphic images, if you use a corner handle, the box will change size proportionately. You do not need to do this as the boxes can be moved to any size.

You may also need to change the size of any lines you have drawn. However, unless specified, you do not have to keep lines in the alternative layout.

To change the size of a line:

METHOD
1 Click on the line and select one of the handles.
2 Drag the handle until the line is the required size.

The instructions have asked for text to be deleted.

To delete text from within an article:

METHOD
1 Highlight the text you wish to delete by dragging the mouse over the text.
2 Press **Delete**.

To delete a table:

If you have used the insert table method and you wish to delete the table:

METHOD
1 Click anywhere within the table to select it.
2 From the **Edit** menu choose **Delete Object**.

The table, and its contents, should now disappear.

The instructions also state that dropped capitals should not appear in the alternative layout. To remove dropped capitaals from your document:

METHOD
1 Highlight the dropped capital you wish to remove, note that each capital has to be removed individually.
2 From the **Format** menu select **Change Drop Cap**.
3 The **Drop Cap** options box will appear on screen. Click on: **Remove**.
4 Click on: **OK**.

Repeat these instructions for each dropped capital.

11.1 Crop graphics

Cropping graphics means that you cut some of the graphic out. Look at Figure 11.1.

This is the original graphic   This graphic has been cropped to remove the cake and fork at the top

Figure 11.1 Cropping graphics

Crop the **Dress** graphic to remove the shoes at the bottom of the image.

METHOD

1 Click on: the **Dress** graphic to select it – and to bring up the Picture Formatting toolbar.
2 Click on: the ⬚ **Crop Picture** button on the Picture Formatting toolbar.
3 Move the cursor down to the bottom middle handle of the picture frame – until the cursor turns to a pair of scissors.
4 Click and drag upwards to just below the bottom of the dress.
5 Release the mouse button.

This takes a little practice to get right. Make sure that you do not cut too much off the graphic or leave any little bits. If you are working in page view or 75% view, you may need to zoom in so that you can see if there are any dots left behind.

Although the graphic appears to be cut, the full graphic is in fact still there. If you make a mistake or want to see the full graphic again, then just place the cropping tool back over the relevant handle and click and drag out again. You will see that the graphic reappears in its full form.

11.2 Create irregular text wrap

It is possible to set irregular text wrap around the graphic so that the text is actually set around the shape of the graphic rather than in a square box. Look at Figure 11.2.

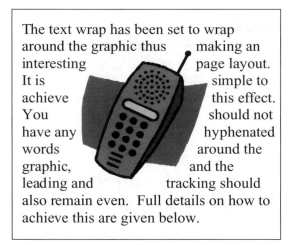

Figure 11.2 Irregular text wrap

As you can see the text is brought in to fit around the graphic rather than have a box effect.

Use irregular text wrap around the image **Web**. Do not include any hyphenation in text that wraps around the graphic.

METHOD
1 Select the **Web** graphic.
2 Click on: the 🖼 **Wrap Text to Picture** button on the Picture Formatting toolbar.

The graphic will now automatically change to irregular text wrap. You can now move it around to find the best place to put it. (Make sure it stays with the **On line** article as specified in the design brief.)

Turning off hyphenation around wrapped text
If you already turned the hyphenation off then there will be no hyphenation around the graphic. However, if you have not turned it off, it is important that you do so as it will look much better and also, in the OCR Stage III examination, you must make sure there is no hyphenation in wrapped text.

11.3 Amend kerning

The kerning is the space between individual characters. There are pairs of letters that, when put together, have a small amount of space between them. For example, if you type the letters **AW** you can see that there is a space between them. If these letters are magnified to a size that might be used in a newsletter, logo or heading, you can see that this can look untidy. Look at Figure 11.3.

You can see the difference between the space separating the A and the W and that separating	# AW
the T and the R.	# TR

Figure 11.3 Kerning

Kerning can be used to tidy up the gap between the two letters, or it can be used to expand the letters as in the examples below:

Aw t r

Exercise 21.6 In the headline text, in the word **CLOTHING**, amend the kerning of the two letters, **L** and **O** so that they touch each other.

METHOD
1 Highlight the text you want to kern – ie the **L** and the **O** of **CLOTHING**.
2 From the **Format** menu, select: **Character Spacing**.

The **Character Spacing** dialogue will appear on screen:

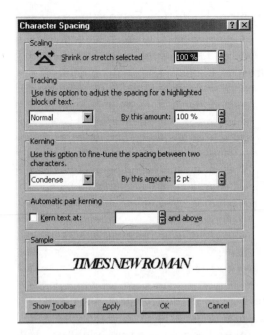

Figure 11.4 Character Spacing dialogue box

3 In the **Automatic pair kerning** section, click on **Kern text at** to turn the automatic kerning off.

4 In the **Kerning** section, select **Condense** from the drop-down menu to reduce the space between the letters.

5 In the **By this amount** box, key in: **2 pt**. The text in the **Sample** box will change and you will have a preview of how the text will look (change the amount until you are satisfied).

6 When you are satisfied with the text, click on: **Apply**.

7 Click on: **OK** to return to your work.

Exercise 21.7

7 Ensure that the publication fills the page by changing the leading of the body text. This must be visible when printed.

8 Copyfit your publication to ensure:
- all material is displayed on one page
- text/graphics are not superimposed on each other
- headings and related text are grouped together
- one line or less of text is grouped with the rest of the related text
- paragraph spacing is consistent
- leading is consistent
- no more than 5 hyphenated line endings on page
- no more than 10mm (vertical) white space unless specified in the design brief.

9 Save and print the publication.

Exercise 22

1 Open the file: **FILM** and save it as **FILM1**. Design a portrait layout based on the alternative page sketch below.

2 Delete from the **Christmas** article the paragraph beginning **It is customary ....** And ending with **by 8 December.**

3 Note that the first article must be **About**.
You must use the same fonts and the same point sizes that you chose in Exercise 20.

4 Crop the **Chair** graphic to remove both lights on either side of the chair.

5 Use irregular text wrap around the image **Film**. Do not include any hyphenation in text that wraps around the graphic.

6 In the headline text, in the word **School**, amend the kerning of the two letters **o** so that they overlap each other.

7 Ensure that the publication fills the page by changing the leading of the body text. This must be visible when printed.

8 Copyfit your publication to ensure:
   - all material is displayed on one page
   - text/graphics are not superimposed on each other
   - headings and related text are grouped together
   - one line or less of text is grouped with the rest of the related text
   - paragraph spacing is consistent
   - leading is consistent
   - no more than 5 hyphenated line endings on page
   - no more than 10mm (vertical) white space unless specified in the design brief.

9 Save and print the publication.

Alternative page sketch for Exercise 22

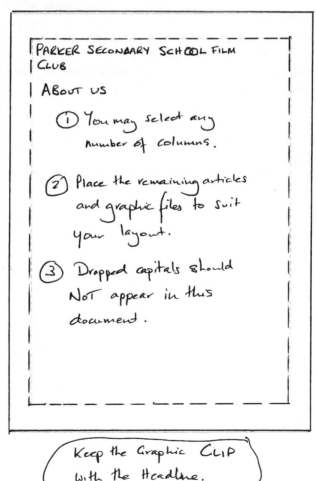

Chapter 12

Using a Non-standard Page Size

In this chapter you will learn how to:

■ set up non-standard page sizes
■ design your document
■ print colour separations
■ print crop marks.

12.1 Set up non-standard page sizes

Non-standard page sizes may be used in the workplace to produce posters, business cards, leaflets, etc. For the purposes of this book, you will be defining the page measurements for a page smaller than A4.

Exercise 23.1

1 Produce the publication from the page layout sketches on page 131. Follow the orientation and measurements given.
2 The text files for this exercise are **Address**, **Details**, **Loyal and Web**.
  The image files for this exercise are **Suit** and **Card**.
3 You will need to key in the text which appears on the page layout sketches, as this text is not included in your text files.
4 Ensure that you follow all the instructions on the page layout sketches.
5 Save as **FORM**.

Page 1 layout for Exercise 23

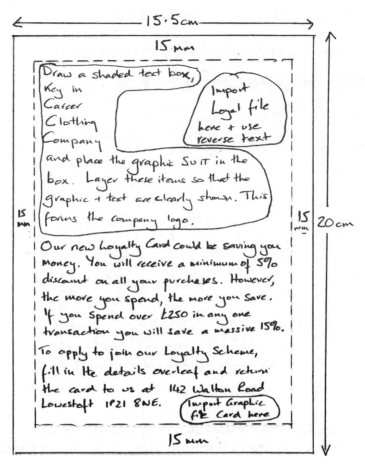

Page 2 layout for Exercise 23

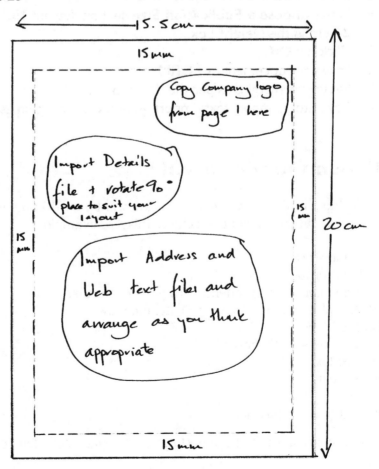

METHOD

1 Load Publisher.
2 From the **File** menu, select: **Page Setup**.

The **Page Setup** dialogue box appears on screen.

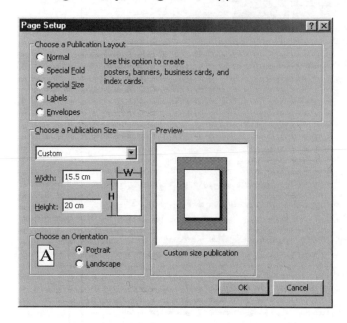

Figure 12.1 Page Setup dialogue box

3 In the **Choose a Publication Layout** section, click on: **Special Size**.
4 In the **Choose a Publication Size** section, select **Custom** from the drop-down list.
5 In the **Choose an Orientation** section, ensure that **Portrait** is selected.
6 In the **Choose a Publication Size** section, key in: **15.5 cm** in the **Width** box and **20 cm** in the **Height** box.
7 Click on: **OK**.
8 Save your document as **FORM**.
9 Set up the margins as per the design brief.
10 Key in text; import text; import graphics and position as per the design brief.

12.2 Design your document

If you are producing a leaflet or newsletter, you will want your document to be eye-catching. There are a number of ways in which you can achieve this. For example:

- Use of fonts and sizes
- Use of bold and/or italic
- Using boxes and lines to draw attention to parts of the text
- Placing the graphics and text in an eye-catching way
- Using shading for boxes
- Multi-layering boxes/text/images
- Using reversed text
- Using rotated text
- Using bullets
- Repeating text and/or images

You have already looked at most of these. However there are still a few to learn.

Shading
The page layout brief on page 131 specifies a shaded box for the logo which appears on both pages.

 METHOD

1 Select the text frame with the text **Career Clothing Company** in.

2 Click on: the Fill Color button.

3 Select: **More Colors** from the drop-down menu.

The **Colors** dialogue box appears on screen.

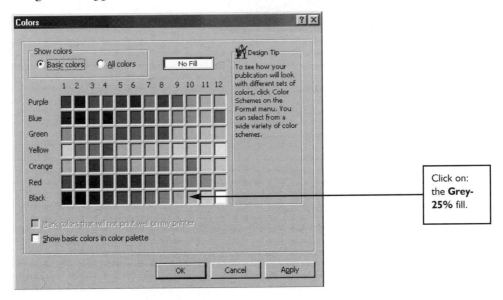

Figure 12.2 Colors dialogue box

You now need to select which shading to use. You should ensure that it is still possible to read the text through shading. Beware of making your shade colour too dark. Look at Figure 12.3 below.

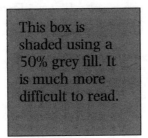

This box is shaded using a 25% grey fill. Note that you can still read the text.

This box is shaded using a 50% grey fill. It is much more difficult to read.

Figure 12.3 Shading

A shading of 25% is a good one to choose as the text is still easy to read, but the shading is dark enough for it to be clearly visible when printed.

4 Click on: the **Grey-25%** fill.

The graphic will probably have disappeared behind the text frame so you need to send the text frame to the back so that the graphic is visible in front of the text frame.

5 Click on: the **Send to Back** button on the Standard toolbar.

The graphic should now be in front of the text frame.

Reversed text
The page layout brief on page 131 specifies reversed text for the Loyalty Card text in the top right-hand corner of the first page.

Reversed text is different to shaded text. Look at Figure 12.4 below.

> Reversed text means white text on a black or coloured background. This can be very effective when used as a design feature in a publication.

Figure 12.4 Reversed text

METHOD

1 Highlight the text in the box.

2 Click on: the **A Text Color** button on the Text Formatting toolbar.

3 Select the white box from the drop-down menu (see Figure 12.5).

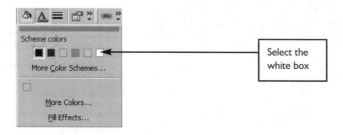

Figure 12.5 Font Color drop-down menu

The text will have disappeared from the screen – but don't worry, it's still there.

4 Click on: the text frame to select it.

5 Click on: the **Fill Color** button on the Picture Formatting toolbar.

6 Select the black box from the drop-down menu.

You should now have a black box with white writing in it.

Repeating text and/or images
Quite often a leaflet will repeat the company logo on each page or repeat the same information in a bid to get us to remember it.

The page layout brief on page 131 specifies that the logo on page 1 should be copied to page 2.

If you need to repeat items then copying them is quicker than importing them separately. This is particularly true if you have set up a multi-layered item and need to repeat it.

METHOD

First you need to group the text frame and the graphic so that they are treated as one item.

1 Click on the text frame and then, holding down the **Shift** key, click on the graphic.

A jigsaw icon appears indicating the items are not grouped.

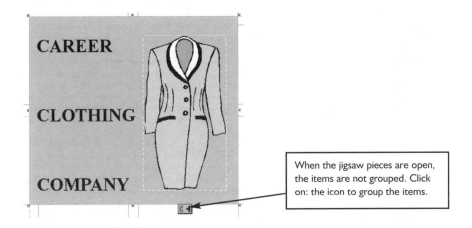

When the jigsaw pieces are open, the items are not grouped. Click on: the icon to group the items.

Figure 12.6 Grouping items

2 Click on: the [icon] **Group Objects** icon to group them.

You can now copy the items and paste them on to the next page.

3 **Either:**
  • Press: **Ctrl + C**
  Or:
  • Click on: the [icon] **Copy** button
  Or:
  • From the **Edit** menu, select: **Copy**.
4 Move to page 2.
5 **Either:**
  • Press: **Ctrl + V**
  Or:
  • Click on: the [icon] **Paste** button
  Or:
  • From the **Edit** menu, select **Paste**.

> *TIP*
>
> If you need to ungroup the items at a later point – for example, if you want to move one of them to a different position but not the other(s) – then just click on: the [icon] closed jigsaw button. The items will then ungroup.
>
> Remember, if you accidentally press delete while you have all your items selected, then you can get them back by clicking on: the [icon] **Undo** button.

The logo will now be on page 2 – you can move it around as necessary.

If you were just copying a single item, then you would only need to select the item and follow steps 3 to 4.

Rotated text
Rotated text can give an interesting effect. Look at Figure 12.7.

This text has beem
rotated 90°

This text has beem
rotated 90°

Figure 12.7 Rotated text

The page layout brief on page 131 specifies that the **Details** text on page 2 should be rotated 90°.

METHOD

1 Select the **Details** text frame.
2 **Either:**
   • From the **Arrange** menu, select: **Rotate or Flip** and then: **Custom Rotate**.
   Or:
   • Click on: the 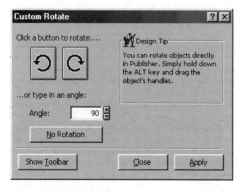 **Custom Rotate** button.

The **Custom Rotate** dialogue box will appear on the screen.

Figure 12.8 Custom Rotate dialogue box

3 In the **Angle** box, key in **90**.
4 Click on: **Apply**.
5 Click on: **Close**.

The text will now be rotated.

12.3 Print colour separations

Exercise 23.6

You must produce two printouts of each page, one of each colour. You may choose which images/parts of text are to be blue and which black. Be careful to ensure that each item of the publication appears on either the blue or the black printout. Please note that the worked examples show the final composite pages and not the colour separations. Composite pages are not acceptable in OCR examinations.

Printing your publication using colour-separation techniques is not nearly as difficult as it sounds. However, before you print the separations you need to decide which items to have as black and which to have as the specified colour (in this case blue).

You must make sure that you have assigned a colour to each item on the page as if you do not then either the items will not be printed at all, or will be printed on both separations. In order to assign a

colour to each item, including text, just highlight or select the text or item and either use the

Text Color button or the 🪣 **Fill Color** button.

You will also need to make sure there is nothing that is in a colour other than the two specified – ie nothing other black and blue. When you change the options of colour printing to spot colours, the graphic images in your document should change colour automatically to shades of grey. If this is not the case then you will have to recolour the graphic manually:

METHOD

1 Select the picture.
2 From the **Format** menu, select: **Recolor Picture**.

The **Recolor Picture** dialogue will appear on screen.

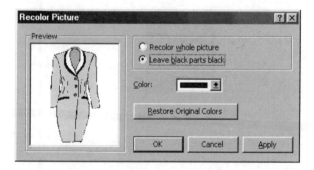

Figure 12.9 Recolor Picture dialogue box

3 Select the colour you require from the **Color** drop-down menu (click on: **More Colors** if you cannot find the one you want) – in this case, choose blue.
4 You can choose to colour the whole picture blue or to leave those parts that are already black, black. Choose the latter now.
5 Click on: **Apply**.
6 Click on: **OK**.
7 Repeat this process for the other pictures in the document. (Don't forget that you will need to ungroup any pictures that have been grouped with other items before you can select them.) You need to change any pictures to either blue or black.

In the printing process, colours are printed separately and so in order to print a two-page publication you will end up with four separate pages – two for each page of the two-page spread. Look at Figure 12.10 which shows the process for a two-colour separation, blue and black.

Page 1 of the publication – colour separated print outs

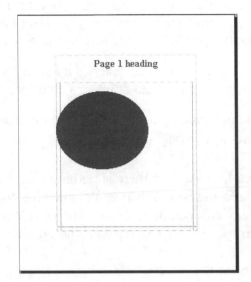

Black print out

Blue print out

Page 2 of the publication – colour separated print outs

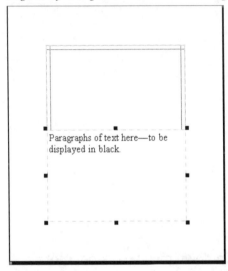

Black print out

Blue print out

Pages 1 and 2 of the publication – non separated print outs

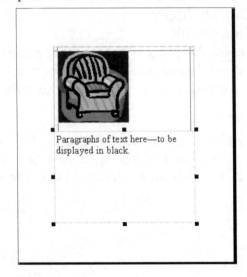

Page 1 composite

Page 2 composite

Figure 12.10 Two-colour separation – blue and black

You do not need a colour printer to do this as both separations can be printed in black.

You need to print the document as colour separations:

METHOD
1 From the **Tools** menu, select: **Commercial Printing Tools**, then select: **Choose Color printing**.

The **Color Printing** dialogue box will appear on screen.

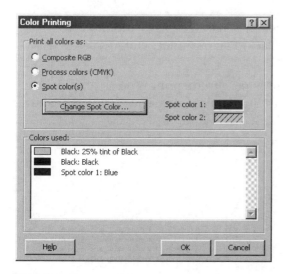

Figure 12.11 Color Printing

2 In the **Print all colors as** section, select: **Spot color(s)**.
3 Check that **Spot color 1** is blue. (If it's not you have probably not assigned your colours correctly. Click on: **Cancel** and go back to your document and check that everything is either blue or black. Then repeat steps 1 to 4.)
4 Click on: **OK**.
5 From the **File** menu, select: **Print**.

The **Print** dialogue box will appear on screen.

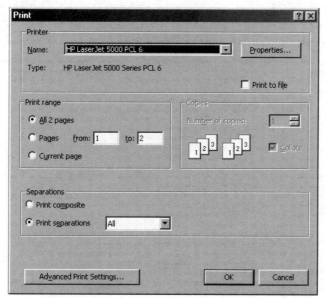

Figure 12.12 Print dialogue box

6 In the **Separations** section, click on: **Print separations**.
7 Click on: **OK**.

Your pages should now print as colour separations. You will notice that Publisher has automatically printed details outside the margins of which colour each separation is (as well as the file name, the page number and the date).

12.4 Using crop marks

Exercise 23.7 Ensure that crop marks are included on the colour-separated pages and indicate which page and colour is which (ie Page 1 – Black, Page 2 – Blue, etc).

Crop marks are used to show the printing area of a sheet of paper. In the print process printing is carried out on standard-size sheets of paper and then cut to the required size. The crop marks show exactly where the cuts need to be made. Look at Figure 12.13.

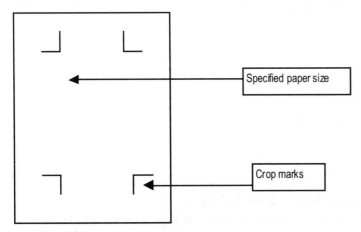

Figure 12.13 Crop marks

Many printers will automatically print the crop marks when you print colour separations. However, not all of them do. You will need to check whether your printer does this or not, and if not you will need to find out how to set it up to do so.

TIP
Unfortunately, Publisher does not show crop marks on screen. Ensure that, when you print your document, the crop marks can be seen clearly.

1 Produce the publication from the following page layout sketches. Follow the orientation and measurements given.

2 The text files for this exercise are **Raffle, Help** and **Films**. The image files for this exercise are **Clip, Tree, Party** and **Eats**.

3 You will need to key in the text which appears on the page layout sketches, as this text is not included in your text files.

4 Ensure that you follow all the instructions on the page layout sketches.

5 Save as **TICKET.**

6 You must produce two printouts of each page, one of each colour. You may choose which images/parts of text are to be green and which black. Be careful to ensure that each item of the publication appears on either the green or the black printout. Please note that the worked examples show the final composite pages and not the colour separations. Composite pages are not acceptable in OCR examinations.

7 Ensure that crop marks are included on the colour-separated pages and indicate which page and colour is which (ie Page 1 – Black, Page 2 – Green, etc).

Page 1 layout for Exercise 24

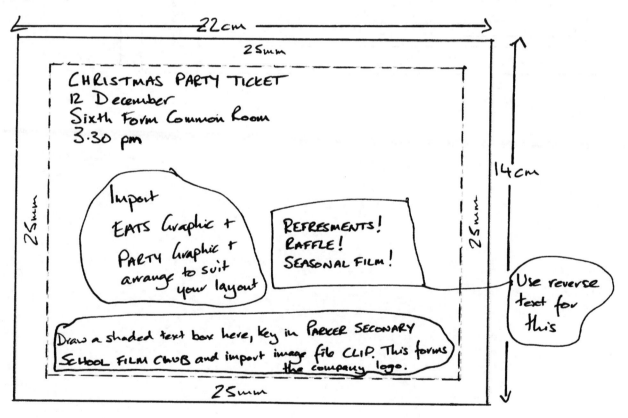

Page 2 layout for Exercise 24

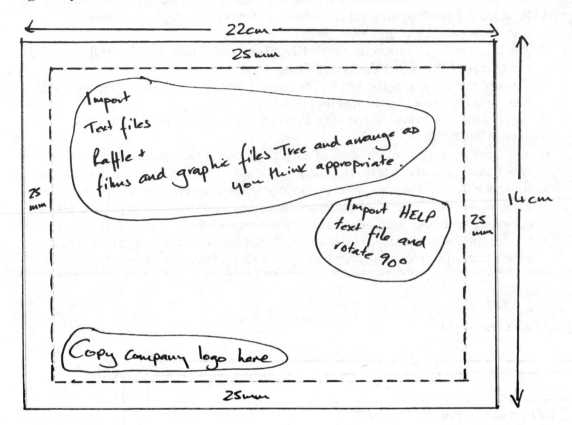

Consolidation 5

Part 1

Before you start Task 1, ensure you have on disk the following text and image files. These must be imported into your DTP publication.

Text files: **Auction**, **Clothing**, **PTA**, **Diary**

Image files: **People**, **Diary**

1   Create an A4 size publication following the design brief on page 144. Use lines/rules where indicated in the design brief.

2   Set up a style sheet for Headline, Subhead and Body text as shown in the design brief. Choose point sizes to fill the publication. Import the text files and apply the appropriate styles.

3   In the '**The PTA**' story, insert the following paragraph at the end of the article.

During the coming year we will need to replace 3 committee members as their children will be leaving the school. If you are interesting in joining please contact Marge Lovell, the committee secretary.

4   You must format the table within the **School Clothing** article. Set up two columns, left aligned with column headings: 'Item' and 'Price'.

5   Produce dropped capitals for the first letter of **each** article. Maintain consistent text flow of the body text around the dropped capitals.

6   Place the two image files as indicated in the design brief, maintaining the original proportions.

7   Copyfit your publication to ensure:

    -   All material is displayed on one page

    -   Text/graphics/lines are not superimposed on each other

    -   Headings and related text are grouped together

    -   One line or less of text is grouped with the rest of the related text

    -   Paragraph spacing is consistent

    -   Leading is consistent

    -   No more than 5 hyphenated line endings on a page

    -   No more than 1cm (10 mm) vertical white space unless specified in the design brief

8   Save as **NEWTOWN** and print the publication.

Design brief for Consolidation 5 Part 1

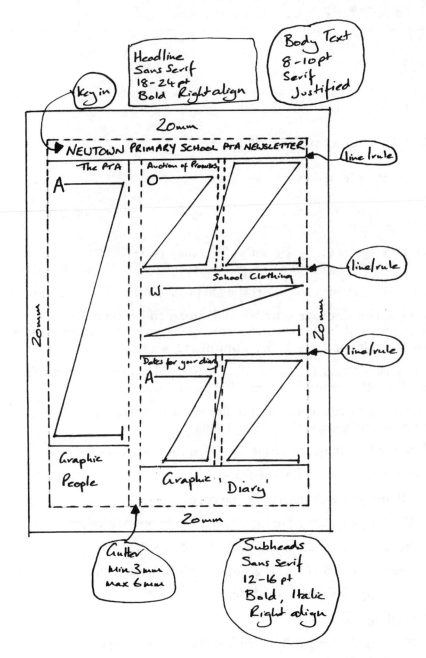

Part 2

You are required to produce an alternative version of the publication from Part 1 (**NEWTOWN**).

1   Design a landscape layout based on the alternative page layout sketch on page 145.

    Delete, from the 'The PTA' article, the paragraph beginning **If you would like to be involved in the PTA ...**

    Note that the first article must remain **The PTA**.

    You must use the same fonts and the same point sizes that you chose in Part 1.

2   Crop the **PEOPLE** graphic to remove the bottom row of figures.

3   Use irregular text wrap around the **DIARY** image. Do not include any hyphenation in text that wraps around the graphic.

4   In the Headline text, in the word 'SCHOOL' amend the kerning of the two letters 'O' so that they overlap each other.

5   Ensure the publication fills the page by changing the leading of the body text.

6   Copyfit your publication to ensure:

All material is displayed on one page

Text/graphics/lines are not superimposed on each other

Headings and related text are grouped together

One line or less of text is grouped with the rest of the related text

Paragraph spacing is consistent

Leading is consistent

No more than 5 hyphenated line endings on a page

No more than 1cm (10 mm) vertical white space unless specified in the design brief

7   Save as **NEWTOWN1** and print the publication.

Alternative page sketch for Consolidation 5 Part 2

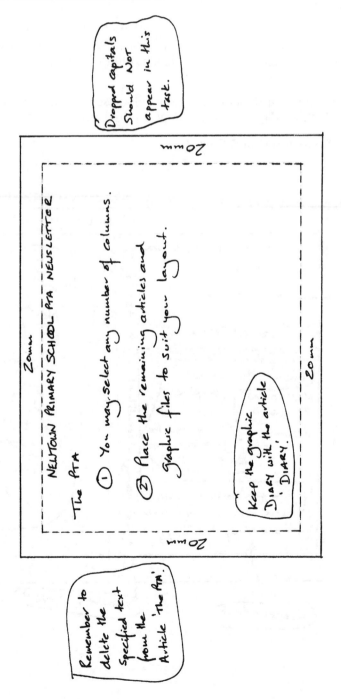

Part 3

For this task you are required to produce a document consisting of 2 pages. The publication should be designed and set up to produce a two-colour document in black and red. However, you do not need a colour printer.

Text files: **EVENING, LOTS, NEWTOWN**

Image files: **SCHOOL, DRINK, AUCTIONEER**

1   Produce the publication from the page layout sketches on pages 146 and 147. Follow the orientation and measurements given.

2   Design the layout of the pages from the page layout sketches.

3   You will need to key in the text which appears on the page layout sketches, as this text is not included in your text files.

4   Ensure that you follow all the instructions on the page layout sketches.

5   Save the document as **NEWTOWN2**.

6   You must produce two printouts of each page, one for each colour. You may choose which images/parts of text are to be red and which black. Be careful to ensure that each item of the publication appears on either the red or black printout. *Please note that the worked examples in this book only show the composite pages.*

Ensure that crop marks are included on the colour separated pages and indicate which page and colour is which (ie Page 1 – Black, Page 1 – Red, etc).

Page 1 layout for Consolidation 5 Part 3

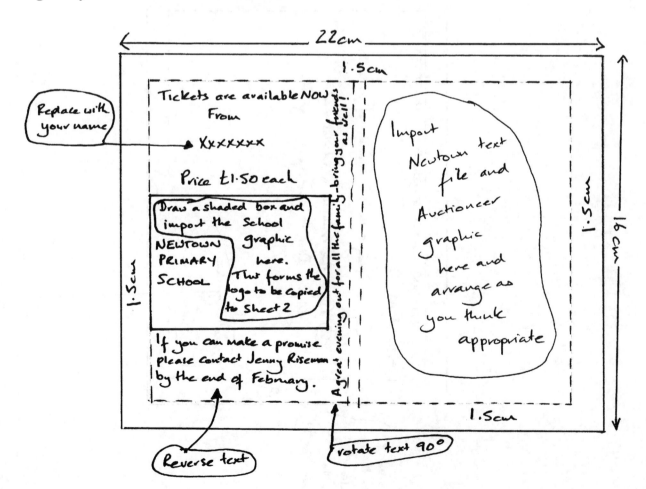

Page 2 layout for Consolidation 5 Part 3

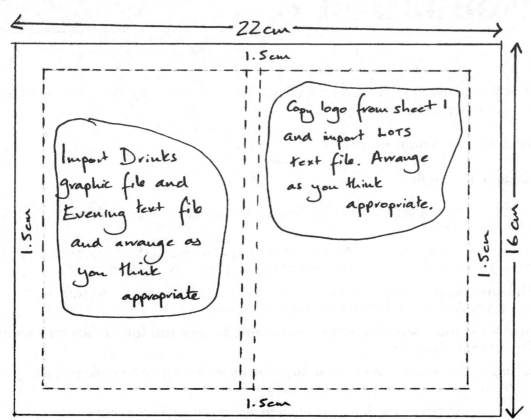

Consolidation 6

Part 1

Before you start Task 1, ensure you have on disk the following text and image files. These must be imported into your DTP publication.

Text files: **Belles**, **Gowns**, **Venue**, **Events**

Image files: **Logo**, **Veil**, **Couple**

1   Create an A4 size publication following the design brief on page 149. Use lines/rules where indicated in the design brief.

2   Set up a style sheet for Headline, Subhead and Body text as shown in the design brief. Choose point sizes to fill the publication. Import the text files and apply the appropriate styles.

3   In the '**Did you Know** ... story, insert the following sentence at the end of the paragraph beginning 'If you do decide to hold your wedding ceremony'.

   Your local Superintendent Registrar will be able to give you full details on how to apply for a special licence.

4   You must format the table within the **Wedding Gowns** article. Set up two columns, left aligned with column headings: 'Dress' and 'Price'.

5   Produce dropped capitals for the first letter of **each** article. Maintain consistent text flow of the body text around the dropped capitals.

6   Place the three image files as indicated in the design brief, maintaining the original proportions.

7   Copyfit your publication to ensure:

   All material is displayed on one page

   Text/graphics/lines are not superimposed on each other

   Headings and related text are grouped together

   One line or less of text is grouped with the rest of the related text

   Paragraph spacing is consistent

   Leading is consistent

   No more than 5 hyphenated line endings on a page

   No more than 1cm (10 mm) vertical white space unless specified in the design brief

8   Save as **WEDDING1** and print the publication.

Design brief for Consolidation 6 Part 1

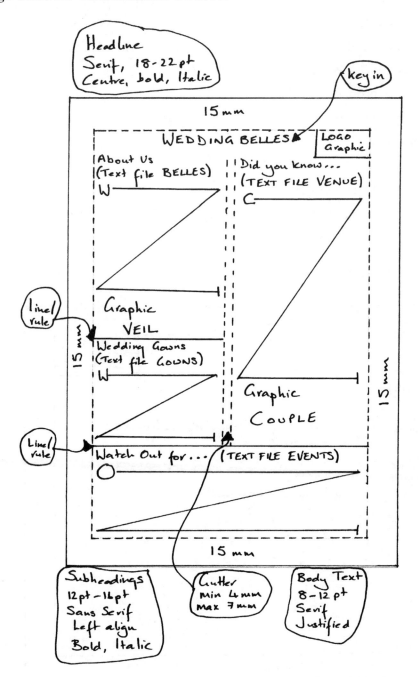

Part 2

You are required to produce an alternative version of the publication from Part 1 (**WEDDING1**).

1   Design a landscape layout based on the alternative page layout sketch on page 150.

Delete, from the '**Wedding Gowns**' article, the paragraph beginning **Given below are a few .... AND the table.**

Note that the first article must remain **About us**.

You must use the same fonts and the same point sizes that you chose in Part 1.

2   Crop the **VEIL** graphic to remove the veil, leaving only the bouquet image.

3   Use irregular text wrap around the **COUPLE** image. Do not include any hyphenation in text that wraps around the graphic.

4   In the Headline text, in the word 'WEDDING amend the kerning of the two letters 'D' so that they overlap each other.

5 Ensure the publication fills the page by changing the leading of the body text.

6 Copyfit your publication to ensure:

All material is displayed on one page

Text/graphics/lines are not superimposed on each other

Headings and related text are grouped together

One line or less of text is grouped with the rest of the related text

Paragraph spacing is consistent

Leading is consistent

No more than 5 hyphenated line endings on a page

No more than 1cm (10 mm) vertical white space unless specified in the design brief

7 Save as **WEDDING2** and print the publication.

Alternative page sketch for Consolidation 6 Part 2

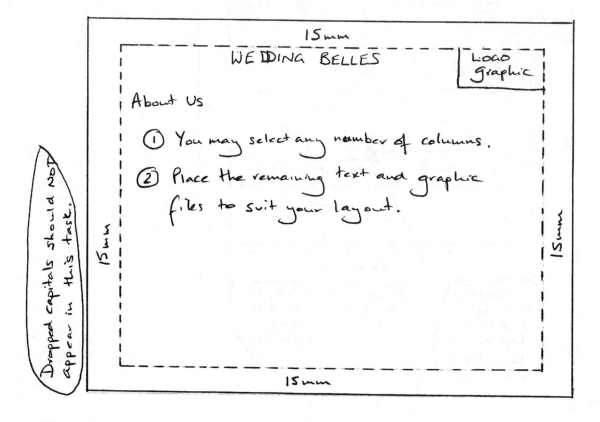

Part 3

For this task you are required to produce a document consisting of 2 pages. The publication should be designed and set up to produce a two-colour document in black and pink. However, you do not need a colour printer.

Text files: **ADMITTANCE, BRISTOL, PRIZES, STANDS**

Image files: **BELLS, CAKE, HEART, RINGS, HONEYMOON**

1 Produce the publication from the page layout sketches on page 151. Follow the orientation and measurements given.

2 Design the layout of the pages from the page layout sketches.

3 You will need to key in the text which appears on the page layout sketches, as this text is not included in your text files.

4 Ensure that you follow all the instructions on the page layout sketches.

5 Save the document as **WEDDING3**.

6 You must produce two printouts of each page, one for each colour. You may choose which images/parts of text are to be pink and which black. Be careful to ensure that each item of the publication appears on either the pink or black printout. *Please note that the worked examples in this book only show the composite pages.*

Ensure that crop marks are included on the colour separated pages and indicate which page and colour is which (ie Page 1 – Black, Page 1 – pink, etc).

Page 1 layout for Consolidation 6 Part 3   **Page 2 layout for Consolidation 6 Part 3**

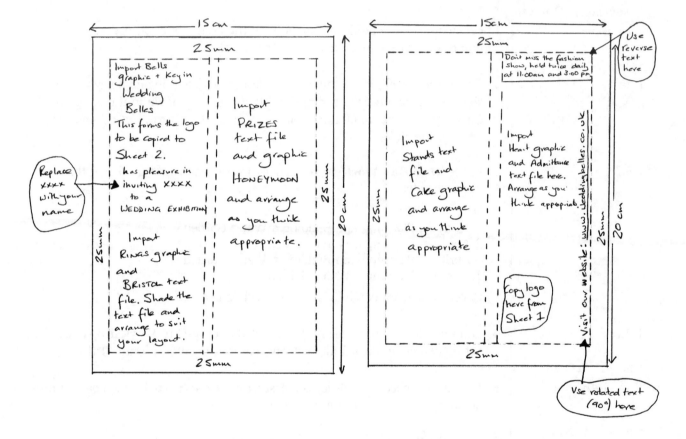

Exam Practice 5
OCR Stage III DTP

Element 1 – Create a pre-press publication from a design brief

Before you start Task 1, ensure you have on disk the following text files and image files. These must be imported into your DTP publication.

Text files: **MONTH, FURNITURE, WORKSHOPS, SUMMER**

Image files: **ORCHARD, CHAIR, GARDEN**

Assessment Objectives

1.1a	**1** Create an A4 size publication following the design brief on page 153. Use line/s rules where indicated in the design brief.
1.2a	**2** Key in the Headline as shown in the design brief. Set up and apply a style sheet for Headline, Subheadings and Body Text as shown in the design brief. Choose point sizes to fill the publication. Import the text files and apply the appropriate styles.
1.5a	**3** In the '**One-Day Workshops**' article, insert the following table at the end of the article:

Date   Title
31 May   Planning and Building a Water Garden
2 April   Planting a Water Garden
5 April   Planning and Building a Water Garden
11 April   Planting a Water Garden

Check your work carefully, as errors will be penalised.

1.3a	**4** You must format the table at the end of the '**One-Day Workshops**' article. Set up two columns, left aligned with column headings: 'Date' 'Title'.
1.4a, 1.4b	**5** Produce dropped capitals for the first letter of **each** article. Each capital must be dropped the same number of lines.
1.1a	**6** Place the three image files as indicated in the design brief.
	7 Copyfit your publication to ensure:
1.6a	- all material is displayed on one page
1.6b	- text/graphics/lines are not superimposed on each other
1.6c	- headings and related text are grouped together
1.6d	- one line or less of text is grouped with the rest of related text (ie there are no widows or orphans)
1.6e	- paragraph spacing is consistent
1.6f	- leading is consistent
1.6g	- there are no more than 5 hyphenated line endings on the page
1.6h	- there is no more than 10 mm of vertical white space at the end of each article.
1.7a	**8** Save as **GARDEN1** and print the publication A4 portrait.

Design brief for Exam Practice 5 Element 1

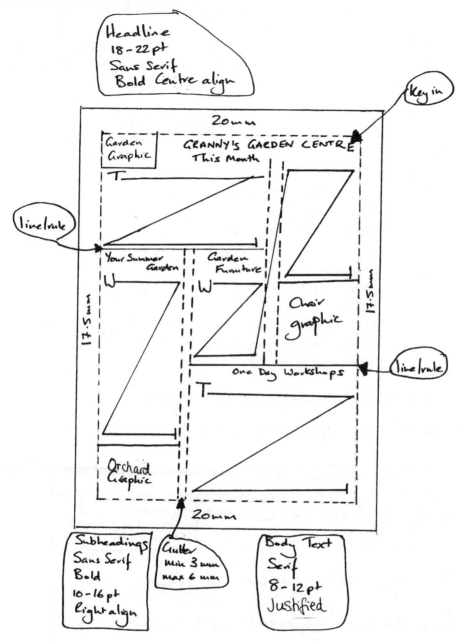

Element 2 – Produce alternative version of a publication

You are required to produce an alternative version of the publication from Element One. You may either work on a copy of the original or create a new publication.

Assessment Objectives

2.1a	**1** Design a landscape layout based on the alternative page layout sketch on page 154.
	(a) Delete, from the '**Your Summer Garden**' article, the two paragraphs beginning 'If you would like help ...' and '**Plant suggestions, colour schemes** ...'
	(b) Note that the first article must remain '**This Month**'.
	(c) You **must** use the same fonts and the **same** point sizes that you used in Task 1. Alterations will be penalised.
	(d) Dropped capitals should not appear in this task.
2.2a	**2** Crop the graphic **ORCHARD** to remove the clouds at the top of the graphic.

2.3a, 2.3b

3 Use irregular text wrap around the **CHAIR** graphic. Do not include any hyphenation in text that wraps around the **CHAIR** graphic.

2.4a

4 In the Headline text decrease the kerning (space between the letters) of the fourth and fifth letters of the word **GRANNY'S** so that the two Ns are overlapping.

2.5a

5 Increase the leading of the body text. There must be a visible difference from that used in Task 1. Ensure that the publication fills the page.

6 Copyfit your publication to ensure:

2.6a
- all material is displayed on one page

2.6b
- text/graphics/lines are not superimposed on each other

2.6c
- headings and related text are grouped together

2.6d
- one line or less of text is grouped with the rest of related text (ie there are no widows or orphans)

2.6e
- paragraph spacing is consistent

2.6f
- leading is consistent

2.6g
- there are no more than 5 hyphenated line endings on the page

2.6h
- there is no more than 10 mm of vertical white space at the end of each article.

2.7a

7 Save as **GARDEN2** and print the publication.

Alternative page sketch for Exam Practice 5 Element 2

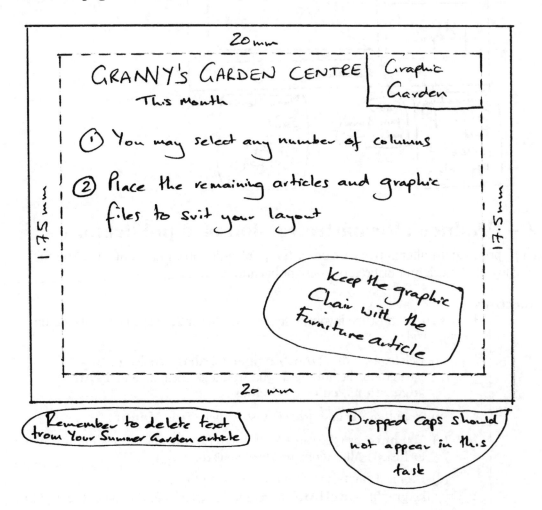

Element 3 – Prepare a publication for colour production

Before you start Task 3 make sure you have on disk the following text files and graphic images. There must be imported into your DTP publication.

Text Files: **SPRING, DATES, PROGRAMME, STOCKISTS**

Image Files: **FISH, SEEDS, GARDEN**

For this task you are required to produce a leaflet consisting of 2 pages.

The publication should be designed and set up to produce a two-colour leaflet, in blue and black. However, you do not need a colour printer.

Assessment Objectives

3.1a, 3.1b	**1** Produce the publication from the page layout sketches on page 156. You must use **portrait** orientation and the measurements given.
3.2a	**2** Design the layout of the pages from the page layout sketches. Use margins of at least 20 mm (2 cm).
3.6a	**3** You will need to key in the text which appears on the page layout sketches, as this text is not included in your text files. Check your work for accuracy as errors will be penalised.
3.3a, 3.3b, 3.3c, 3.4a, 3.5a	**4** Ensure that you follow all the instructions on the page layout sketches.
3.7a	**5** Save the document as **GARDEN3**.

You must produce colour separations of the publication, consisting of 2 printouts of each page, one for each colour. Composite printouts will not be accepted for assessment. You may choose which images/parts of text are to be blue and which black. Be careful to ensure that each item of the publication appears on **either** the blue printout **or** the black printout. *Please note that the worked examples in this book only show the composite pages.*

Indicate which pages contain the blue separations and which contain the black separations. (ie page 1 – black, page 1 – blue, page 2 – black, page 2 – blue).

Ensure that crop marks are printed on each page.

Page 1 layout for Exam Practice 5 Element 3   **Page 2 layout for Exam Practice 5 Element 3**

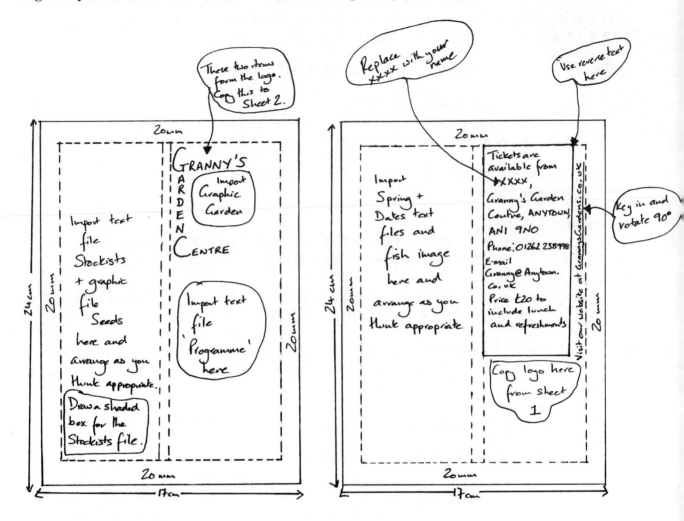

Exam Practice 6
OCR Stage III DTP

Element 1 – Create a pre-press publication from a design brief

Before you start Task 1, ensure you have on disk the following text files and image files. These must be imported into your DTP publication.

Text files: **FENCING, SPORT, FEES**

Image files: **SWORD, BALL**

Assessment Objectives

1.1a	**1**	Create an A4 size publication following the design brief on page 158. Use line/s rules where indicated in the design brief.
1.2a	**2**	Key in the Headline as shown in the design brief. Set up and apply a style sheet for Headline, Subheadings and Body Text as shown in the design brief. Choose point sizes to fill the publication. Import the text files and apply the appropriate styles.
1.5a	**3**	In the '**Focus on Fencing**' article, insert the following new paragraph between the paragraphs beginning 'The Sabre' and 'If you are new to this sport':

As with the foil, there are three scoring lights, a green, a red and a white, on the machine.

Check your work carefully, as errors will be penalised.

1.3a	**4**	You must format the table at the end of the '**Fee Information**' article. Set up two columns, left aligned with column headings: 'Activity' 'Cost'.
1.4a, 1.4b	**5**	Produce dropped capitals for the first letter of **each** article. Each capital must be dropped the same number of lines.
1.1a	**6**	Place the two image files as indicated in the design brief.
	7	Copyfit your publication to ensure:
1.6a		- all material is displayed on one page
1.6b		- text/graphics/lines are not superimposed on each other
1.6c		- headings and related text are grouped together
1.6d		- one line or less of text is grouped with the rest of related text (ie there are no widows or orphans)
1.6e		- paragraph spacing is consistent
1.6f		- leading is consistent
1.6g		- there are no more than 5 hyphenated line endings on the page
1.6h		- there is no more than 10 mm (1 cm) of vertical white space at the end of each article.
1.7a	**8**	Save as **SPORT1** and print the publication A4 landscape.

Design brief for Exam Practice 6 Element 1

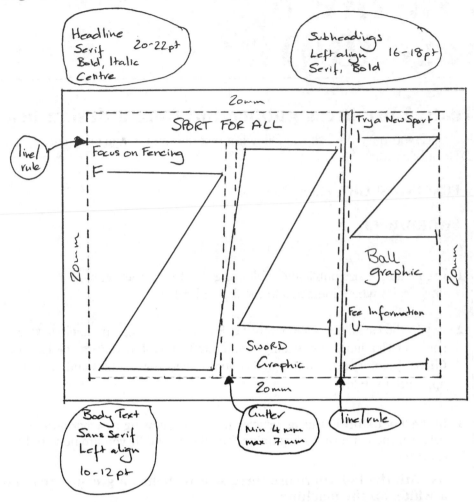

Headline
Serif 20-22pt
Bold, Italic
Centre

Subheadings
Left align 16-18pt
Serif, Bold

20mm

SPORT FOR ALL

Try a New Sport

line/rule

Focus on Fencing

20mm

Ball graphic

20mm

Fee Information

SWORD Graphic

20mm

Body Text
Sans Serif
Left align
10-12pt

Gutter
Min 4 mm
max 7 mm

line/rule

Element 2 – Produce alternative version of a publication

You are required to produce an alternative version of the publication from Element One. You may either work on a copy of the original or create a new publication.

Assessment Objectives

2.1a

1 Design a portrait layout based on the alternative page layout sketch on page 159.

(a) Delete, from the 'Fee Information' article, the paragraph beginning **The new structure will be as follows ... AND the table**.

(b) Note that the first article must be **Try a New Sport**.

(c) You **must** use the same fonts and the **same** point sizes that you used in Task 1. Alterations will be penalised.

(d) Dropped capitals should not appear in this task.

2.2a

2 Crop the graphic **BALL** to remove the small bounce marks on the left of the graphic.

2.3a, 2.3b

3 Use irregular text wrap around the **SWORD** graphic. Do not include any hyphenation in text that wraps around the **SWORD** graphic.

2.4a

4 In the Headline text decrease the kerning (space between the letters) of the second and third letters of the word **SPORT** so that the letter P and the letter O are overlapping.

2.5a

5 Increase the leading of the body text. There must be a visible difference from that used in Task 1. Ensure that the publication fills the page.

6 Copyfit your publication to ensure:

2.6a - all material is displayed on one page

2.6b - text/graphics/lines are not superimposed on each other

2.6c - headings and related text are grouped together

2.6d - one line or less of text is grouped with the rest of related text (ie there are no widows or orphans)

2.6e - paragraph spacing is consistent

2.6f - leading is consistent

2.6g - there are no more than 5 hyphenated line endings on the page

2.6h - there is no more than 10 mm (1 cm) of vertical white space at the end of each article.

2.7h

7 Save as **SPORT2** and print the publication.

Alternative page sketch for Exam Practice 6 Element 2

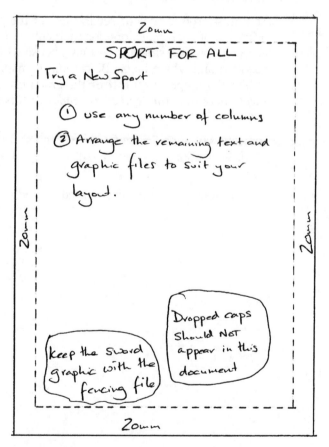

Element 3 – Prepare a publication for colour production

Before you start Task 3 make sure you have on disk the following text files and graphic images. There must be imported into your DTP publication.

Text Files: **WESTON, EXERCISE, CLUBS, OPENING, CAFE**

Image Files: **BALL, DIVER, CAFE, SWIMMER, PLAYER**

For this task you are required to produce a leaflet consisting of 2 pages.

The publication should be designed and set up to produce a two-colour leaflet, in green and black. However, you do not need a colour printer.

Assessment Objectives

3.1a, 3.1b	**1** Produce the publication from the page layout sketches on page 161. You must use **landscape** orientation and the measurements given.
3.2a	**2** Design the layout of the pages from the page layout sketches. Use margins of at least 15 mm (1.5 cm).
3.6a	**3** You will need to key in the text which appears on the page layout sketches, as this text is not included in your text files. Check your work for accuracy as errors will be penalised.
3.3a, 3.3b, 3.3c, 3.4a, 3.5a	**4** Ensure that you follow all the instructions on the page layout sketches.
3.7a	**5** Save as **SPORT3**.

You must produce colour separations of the publication, consisting of 2 printouts of each page, one for each colour. Composite printouts will not be accepted for assessment. You may choose which images/parts of text are to be green and which black. Be careful to ensure that each item of the publication appears on **either** the green printout **or** the black printout. *Please note that the worked examples in this book only show the composite pages.*

Indicate which pages contain the green separations and which contain the black separations. (ie page 1 – black, page 1 – green, page 2 – black, page 2 – green).

Ensure that crop marks are printed on each page.

Page 1 layout for Exam Practice 6 Element 3

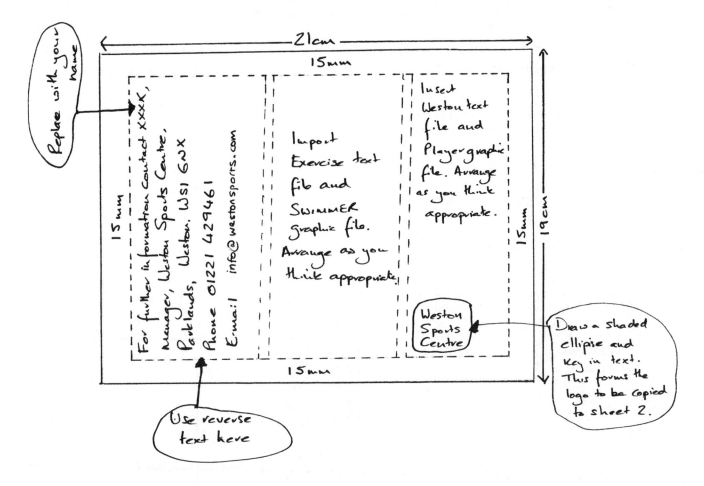

Page 2 layout for Exam Practice 6 Element 3

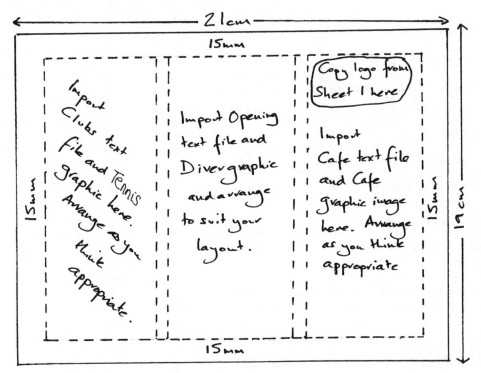

Stage III Checklist

Did you remember to	Assessment Objective	Con 5	Con 6	Exam 5	Exam 6
...design a page layout displaying the text, graphics and lines as specified?	1.1a				
...create a style sheet and apply the text styles correctly?	1.2a				
...set up a table, aligning the columns consistently?	1.3a				
...create dropped capitals for the first letter of each article, ensuring that the text flow around the capitals remained consistent?	1.4a				
...key in all the required text without error?	1.5a 3.6a				
...copyfit the document in accordance with instructions?	1.6a 2.6a 1.6b 2.6b 1.6c 2.6c 1.6d 2.6d 1.6e 2.6e 1.6f 2.6f 1.6g 2.6g 1.6h 2.6h				
...save and print your document correctly?	1.7a 2.7a 3.7a				
...design an alternative layout as specified?	2.1a				
...crop the graphic as specified?	2.2a				
...create irregular text wrap around the graphic without hyphenation?	2.3a 2.3b				
...amend the kerning as specified?	2.4a				
...amend the leading as specified?	2.5a				
...create a non-standard page size, with orientation and page measurements as specified and showing crop marks?	3.1a 3.1b 3.7a				
...design a page layout within the given specifications?	3.2a				
...produce multi-layer items and use shading and reverse text as specified?	3.3a 3.3b 3.3c				
...copy the text and images as specified?	3.4a				
...rotate text as specified?	3.5a				

Worked Examples

AFFORDABLE ANTIQUES

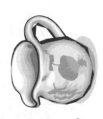

Modern Collectables

We have all heard about those lucky people who have found valuable antiques in their attics or at a car boot sale. However, most of us feel that our possessions are worthless or at best, have sentimental value.

Before you throw away household items that you consider to be worthless, check again. Items from the 1940s to 1970s have become collectable in recent years. Items of particular interest include pottery, tableware, jewellery and kitchenware. Your granny's pottery milk jug and sugar bowl may be worth much much more than she paid for them.

A paste brooch, which although pretty has no real value, may well be of interest to a collector. They may be prepared to pay a sum not far off the price of a real piece of jewellery today.

The national press have recently featured articles on the popularity of pop memorabilia. If you are fortunate enough to own old pop memorabilia such as signed records or pictures from a group such as the Beatles, these may be worth a considerable sum of money.

How can you find out whether your possessions have any monetary value? Your local auction house may be able to help. They will often give you an estimated value of an item free of charge. Another way is to look at any of the large number of books that have been published on this subject. Many recent books concentrate on collectable items rather than traditional antiques. These can also be found in the reference section of your local library. Why not look through your cupboards and see if you are in fact worth a small fortune?

Restoration

What do you do when one of your precious antiques breaks or becomes damaged? Most experts agree that the one thing you should not do is attempt to repair the item yourself. A badly repaired item will lose much of its value, whereas a repair carried out by an expert could minimise the loss.

If the worst happens and your Clarice Cliff plate has a chipped rim or your antique walnut bureau becomes scratched, who should you call? The answer is an antique restoration company. You may be able to find details of these in your local telephone directory.

Before you leave your valuable antiques with them, check the quality of their work. It may be possible for them to supply you with one or two names of customers who will be pleased to vouch for the quality of their work. Alternatively, get in touch with your local antiques dealer or auction house. They may be willing to recommend companies who have worked for them in the past. Another good source of recommendation is by word of mouth. Ask your friends and family if they know of anyone who could do the work for you.

KEEPING SMALL ANIMALS

If you would like to own a pet but do not have the time or commitment to keep a dog or cat then you should consider keeping a small animal. Animals such as rabbits, guinea pigs, hamsters, mice and rats make good pets. They do not require too much attention and do not mind if you are out at work all day. This article will look at keeping rabbits.

Rabbits

These make excellent pets and they enjoy being handled. In fact the more you handle your pet the more tame it will become. Rabbits enjoy company and it is possible to keep two rabbits of the same type housed together.

However, you should not allow a young rabbit to be housed with a mature buck or doe. Rabbits should be handled correctly. When you pick up your rabbit, put one hand under its chest and use your other hand to support its hindquarters. Never pick a rabbit up by its ears.

To feed your rabbit buy a good quality rabbit mix made from maize, wheat, oats, bran and grass pellets. Greens should be fed sparingly or not at all. A well scraped carrot will provide a treat for your pet. Alternatively, you can purchase a range of specially prepared treats from your local pet shop. Fresh water must be available at all times. A water bottle that is attached to the cage is the most convenient. You should clean and refill the bottle each day.

The hutch should be of good quality and should have a sheltered area for sleeping. Fresh bedding must be provided and should be changed regularly, at least twice a week. Hay, straw or wood chippings are suitable for this purpose. These can be obtained easily from your local pet supply shop. The hutch should be positioned so that it does attract some sunlight, but do not place it in direct sunlight as it may become too hot for your pet.

If you have a garden, then a run will provide your pet with regular exercise. You should not put your rabbit in the run on a cold or wet day as they are susceptible to chills.

Guinea Pigs

Rabbits and guinea pigs will live together happily. We will look at keeping guinea pigs in our next article.

Exercise 6 – ANTIQUE2

AFFORDABLE ANTIQUES

Modern Collectables may be worth a considerable sum of money.

We have all heard about those lucky people who have found valuable antiques in their attics or at a car boot sale. However, most of us feel that our possessions are worthless or at best, have sentimental value.

Before you throw away household items that you consider to be worthless, check again. Items from the 1940s to 1970s have become collectable in recent years. Items of particular interest include pottery, tableware, jewellery and kitchenware. Your granny's pottery milk jug and sugar bowl may be worth much much more than she paid for them.

A paste brooch, which although pretty has no real value, may well be of interest to a collector. They may be prepared to pay a sum not far off the price of a real piece of jewellery today.

The national press have recently featured articles on the popularity of pop memorabilia. If you are fortunate enough to own old pop memorabilia such as signed records or pictures from a group such as the Beatles, these

or your antique walnut bureau becomes scratched, who should you call? The answer is an antique restoration company. You may be able to find details of these in your local telephone directory.

Before you leave your valuable antiques with them, check the quality of their work. It may be possible for them to supply you with one or two names of customers who will be pleased to vouch for the quality of their work. Alternatively, get in touch with your local antiques dealer or auction house. They may be willing to recommend companies who have worked for them in the past.

Another good source of recommendation is by word of mouth. Ask your friends and family if they know of anyone who could do the work for you.

How can you find out whether your possessions have any monetary value? Your local auction house may be able to help. They will often give you an estimated value of an item free of charge. Another way is to look at any of the large number of books that have been published on this subject. Many recent books concentrate on collectable items rather than traditional antiques. These can also be found in the reference section of your local library. Why not look through your cupboards and see if you are in fact worth a small fortune?

Restoration

What do you do when one of your precious antiques breaks or becomes damaged? Most experts agree that the one thing you should not do is attempt to repair the item yourself. A badly repaired item will lose much of its value, whereas a repair carried out by an expert could minimise the loss.

If the worst happens and your Clarice Cliff plate has a chipped rim

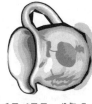

Exercise 5.13 – ANIMAL2

KEEPING SMALL ANIMALS

If you would like to own a pet but do not have the time or commitment to keep a dog or cat then you should consider keeping a small animal. Animals such as rabbits, guinea pigs, hamsters, mice and rats make good pets. They do not require too much attention and do not mind if you are out at work all day. This article will look at keeping rabbits.

Rabbits

These make excellent pets and they enjoy being handled. In fact the more you handle your pet the more tame it will become. Rabbits enjoy company and it is possible to keep two rabbits of the same type housed together. However, you should not allow a young rabbit to be housed with a mature buck or doe.

Rabbits should be handled correctly. When you pick up your rabbit, put one hand under its chest and use your other hand to support its hindquarters. Never pick a rabbit up by its ears.

To feed your rabbit buy a good quality rabbit mix made from maize, wheat, oats, bran and grass pellets.

Greens should be fed sparingly or not at all. A well scraped carrot will provide a treat for your pet. Alternatively, you can purchase a range of specially prepared treats from your local pet shop. Fresh water must be available at all times. A water bottle that is attached to the cage is the most convenient. You should clean and refill the bottle each day.

The hutch should be of good quality and should have a sheltered area for sleeping. Fresh bedding must be provided and should be changed regularly, at least twice a week. Hay, straw or wood chippings are suitable for this purpose. These can be obtained easily from your local pet supply shop. The hutch should be positioned so that it does attract some sunlight, but do not place it in direct sunlight as it may become too hot for your pet.

If you have a garden, then a run will provide your pet with regular exercise. You should not put your rabbit in the run on a cold or wet day as they are susceptible to chills.

Guinea Pigs

Rabbits and guinea pigs will live together happily. We will look at keeping guinea pigs in our next article.

Exercise 8.7 – ANTIQUE3

AFFORDABLE ANTIQUES

Modern Collectables

We have all heard about those lucky people who have found valuable antiques in their attics or at a car boot sale. However, most of us feel that our possessions are worthless or at best, have sentimental value.

Before you throw away household items that you consider to be worthless, check again. Items from the 1940s to 1970s have become collectable in recent years. Items of particular interest include pottery, tableware, jewellery and kitchenware. Your granny's pottery milk jug and sugar bowl may be worth much much more than she paid for them.

A paste brooch, which although pretty has no real value, may well be of interest to a collector. They may be prepared to pay a sum not far off the price of a real piece of jewellery today.

The national press have recently featured articles on the popularity of pop memorabilia. If you are fortunate enough to own old pop memorabilia such as signed records or pictures from a group such as the Beatles, these experts agree that the

may be worth a considerable sum of money.

How can you find out whether your possessions have any monetary value? Your local auction house may be able to help. They will often give you an estimated value of an item free of charge. Another way is to look at any of the large number of books that have been published on this subject. Many recent books concentrate on collectable items rather than traditional antiques. These can also be found in the reference section of your local library. Why not look through your cupboards and see if you are in fact worth a small fortune?

one thing you should not do is attempt to repair the item yourself. A badly repaired item will lose much of its value, whereas a repair carried out by an expert could minimise the loss.

If the worst happens and your Clarice Cliff plate has a chipped rim or your antique walnut bureau becomes scratched, who should you call? The answer is an antique restoration company. You may be able to find details of these in your local telephone directory.

Before you leave your valuable antiques with them, check the quality of their work. It may be possible for them to supply you with one or two names of customers who will be pleased to vouch for the quality of their work. Alternatively, get in touch with your local antiques dealer or auction house. They may be willing to recommend companies who have worked for them in the past.

Another good source of recommendation is by word of mouth. Ask your friends and family if they know of anyone who could do the work for the you.

Restoration

What do you do when one of your precious antiques breaks or becomes damaged? Most

---

Exercise 7.8 – ANIMAL3

KEEPING SMALL ANIMALS

If you would like to own a pet but do not have the time or commitment to keep a dog or cat then you should consider keeping a small animal. Animals such as rabbits, guinea pigs, hamsters, mice and rats make good pets. They do not require too much attention and do not mind if you are out at work all day. This article will look at keeping rabbits.

Rabbits

These make excellent pets and they enjoy being handled. In fact the more you handle your pet the more tame it will become. Rabbits enjoy company and it is possible to keep two rabbits of the same type housed together. However, you should not allow a young rabbit to be housed with a mature buck or doe.

Rabbits should be handled correctly. When you pick up your rabbit, put one hand under its chest and use your other hand to support its hindquarters. Never pick a rabbit up by its ears.

To feed your rabbit buy a good quality rabbit mix made from maize, wheat, oats, bran and grass pellets. Greens should be fed sparingly or not at all. A well scraped carrot will provide a treat for your pet. Alternatively, you can purchase a range of specially prepared treats from your local pet

shop. Fresh water must be available at all times. A water bottle that is attached to the cage is the most convenient. You should clean and refill the bottle each day.

The hutch should be of good quality and should have a sheltered area for sleeping. Fresh bedding must be provided and should be changed regularly, at least twice a week. Hay, straw or wood chippings are suitable for this purpose. These can be obtained easily from your local pet supply shop. The hutch should be positioned so that it does attract some sunlight, but do not place it in direct sunlight as it may become too hot for your pet.

If you have a garden, then a run will provide your pet with regular exercise. You should not put your rabbit in the run on a cold or wet day as they are susceptible to chills.

Guinea Pigs

Rabbits and guinea pigs will live together happily. We will look at keeping guinea pigs in our next article.

Consolidation 1 – SOLAR1

THE SOLAR SYSTEM

The solar system is made up of the sun and everything in orbit around it. This includes 9 major planets and asteroids. Our own planet, the Earth, is part of the solar system.

The planets are kept in order by the sun's gravity. Under this influence the orbits followed by the planets are ellipses. As the planets move constantly they do not fall towards the sun. The speed at which they travel helps balance the pull of gravity from the sun. The planets farthest from the sun move more slowly. Pluto, which is the furthest, is on average 10 times slower than the nearest which is Mercury.

In the first of an occasional series, we will be looking at 2 of the 9 major planets – Pluto and Mercury.

PLUTO

As stated above, Pluto is one of the slowest planets, the journey around the sun made by this planet is the biggest and it takes a thousand times longer than Mercury to complete an orbit. It is however, the smallest of the nine major planets.

It is thought that Pluto consists of a core of ice and rock which is covered with water-based ice, around 150 miles thick. The atmosphere of the planet changes according to the distance from the sun. The nearer the sun the thicker the atmos-phere. This is because the increase in warmth releases gases from the frost on the planet's surface.

It takes Pluto 63,872 days to spin once and the tilt of its axis is 57 degrees. Although it is the smallest planet, its diameter is 1,466 miles.

MERCURY

This is the second smallest planet after Pluto and is the closest to the sun. Although Mercury spins slowly it orbits the sun faster than any other planet. It takes approximately 59 Earth days to spin once and spins only 3 times for every 2 journeys around the sun.

It is thought that Mercury is one of the most cratered planets in the solar system with a surface shaped by volcanic eruptions and impacts. Its crust is wrinkled in places and this is because Mercury shrank a little when its surface cooled. As the planet is so close to the sun it is extremely hot. It does not have any atmosphere and gravity is very weak. The temperature during the day can reach 400 degrees Celsius (750 degrees Fahrenheit. This is hot enough to melt tin and lead. At night, the temperature drops dramatically with temperatures of below -180 degrees Celsius (-290 degrees Fahrenheit).

Consolidation 1 – SOLAR

THE SOLAR SYSTEM

The solar system is made up of the sun and everything in orbit around it. This includes 9 major planets and asteroids. Our own planet, the Earth, is part of the solar system.

The planets are kept in order by the sun's gravity. Under this influence the orbits followed by the planets are ellipses. As the planets move constantly they do not fall towards the sun. The speed at which they travel helps balance the pull of gravity from the sun. The planets farthest from the sun move more slowly. Pluto, which is the furthest, is on average 10 times slower than the nearest which is Mercury.

In the first of an occasional series, we will be looking at 2 of the 9 major planets – Pluto and Mercury.

PLUTO

As stated above, Pluto is one of the slowest planets, the journey around the sun made by this planet is the biggest and it takes a thousand times longer than Mercury to complete an orbit. It is however, the smallest of the nine major planets.

It is thought that Pluto consists of a core of ice and rock which is covered with water-based ice, around 150 miles thick. The atmosphere of the planet changes according to the distance from the sun. The nearer the sun the thicker the atmosphere. This is because the increase in warmth releases gases from the frost on the planet's surface.

It takes Pluto 63,872 days to spin once and the tilt of its axis is 57 degrees. Although it is the smallest planet, its diameter is 1,466 miles.

MERCURY

This is the second smallest planet after Pluto and is the closest to the sun. Although Mercury spins slowly it orbits the sun faster than any other planet. It takes approximately 59 Earth days to spin once and spins only 3 times for every 2 journeys around the sun.

It is thought that Mercury is one of the most cratered planets in the solar system with a surface shaped by volcanic eruptions and impacts. Its crust is wrinkled in places and this is because Mercury shrank a little when its surface cooled.

As the planet is so close to the sun it is extremely hot. It does not have any atmosphere and gravity is very weak. The temperature during the day can reach 400 degrees Celsius (750 degrees Fahrenheit). This is hot enough to melt tin and lead. At night, the temperature drops dramatically with temperatures of below -180 degrees Celsius (-290 degrees Fahrenheit).

SHORT BREAK HOLIDAYS

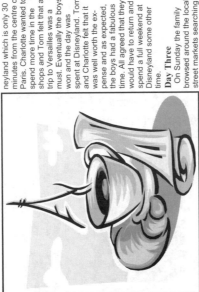

We sent Charlotte Marsh (38) and her husband Tom (41) and children Caleb (9) and Jules (7) to Paris on a 3-day break. They travelled from their home in Wiltshire by train and then, after a short trip across London boarded the Eurostar service from Waterloo. They were in the centre of Paris 3 hours later.

Day One

The two-star hotel is situated in the centre of the city, ideal for sightseeing and surrounded by cafes and restaurants with plenty of shops nearby. The Marshes decided to have a family room as this provided the best value with the children staying for free in the room. The hotel provided breakfast, but all other meals were to be taken locally.

The first stop for the Marshes was the Eiffel Tower. Although Charlotte confessed to being scared of heights she said the views from the top of the tower were 'amazing'. Caleb and Jules thought it was 'fantastic .... you could see for miles'. After a short break the family spent the rest of the day shopping and sightseeing around Paris.

Day Two

Day two and there is a family disagreement! The boys wanted to go to Disneyland which is only 30 minutes from the centre of Paris. Charlotte wanted to spend more time in the shops and Tom felt that a trip to Versailles was a must. Eventually the boys won and the day was spent at Disneyland. Tom and Charlotte felt that it was well worth the expense and as expected, the boys had a fabulous time. All agreed that they would have to return and spend a full weekend at Disneyland some other time.

Day Three

On Sunday the family browsed around the local street markets searching for bargains. After some energetic haggling, a leisurely lunch at a family-owned restaurant was needed. This was followed by a boat trip along the Seine which was enjoyed by all. At 4 pm it was time to make their way back to the train for the long journey home.

Final verdict? 'It was fantastic – we had a marvellous time and can't believe that we could pack so much into a 3-day break. We will definitely take more weekend breaks' The cost for the 3-day break including train travel and accommodation was £175 per person.

Consolidation 2 – BREAKS

SHORT BREAK HOLIDAYS

We sent Charlotte Marsh (38) and her husband Tom (41) and children Caleb (9) and Jules (7) to Paris on a 3-day break. They travelled from their home in Wiltshire by train and then, after a short trip across London boarded the Eurostar service from Waterloo. They were in the centre of Paris 3 hours later.

Day One

The two-star hotel is situated in the centre of the city, ideal for sightseeing and surrounded by cafes and restaurants with plenty of shops nearby. The Marshes decided to have a family room as this provided the best value with the children staying for free in the room. The hotel provided breakfast, but all other meals were to be taken locally.

The first stop for the Marshes was the Eiffel Tower. Although Charlotte confessed to being scared of heights she said the views from the top of the tower were 'amazing'. Caleb and Jules thought it was 'fantastic .... you could see for miles'. After a short break the family spent the rest of the day shopping and sightseeing around Paris.

Day Two

Day two and there is a family disagreement! The boys wanted to go to Disneyland which is only 30 minutes from the centre of Paris. Charlotte wanted to spend more time in the shops and Tom felt that a trip to Versailles was a must. Eventually the boys won and the day was spent at Disneyland. Tom and Charlotte felt that it was well worth the expense and as expected, the boys had a fabulous time. All agreed that they would have to return and spend a full weekend at Disneyland some other time.

Day Three

On Sunday the family browsed around the local street markets searching for bargains. After some energetic haggling, a leisurely lunch at a family-owned restaurant was needed. This was followed by a boat trip along the Seine which was enjoyed by all. At 4 pm it was time to make their way back to the train for the long journey home.

Final verdict? 'It was fantastic – we had a marvellous time and can't believe that we could pack so much into a 3-day break. We will definitely take more weekend breaks' The cost for the 3-day break including train travel and accommodation was £175 per person.

Exam Practice 1 – HOME1

LEAVING HOME

Renting a Flat

Once you have decided to leave the family home and become independent you have to find somewhere to live. Not many young people are able to buy their own home straight away. Renting a flat or bedsitter is the first stage to living on your own.

If you are looking for somewhere to live there are a few points to bear in mind.

Cost of Independence

First of all you must make sure you will be able to afford the rent. At first glance the weekly sum may not seem

too much. However, there are many hidden costs. You must not forget to include bills in your calculations. These include water rates, gas, electricity and telephone. You should of course add insurance for your belongings. Buildings insurance is usually the responsibility of the landlord. If you own a television set, you will need to pay for a licence.

You will also need to pay your community charge. This is a sum that has to be paid to your local council. You may be able to pay this charge in monthly instalments. The cost varies from house to house and depends on how much the property is worth. You can ask your local authority how much this will be before you commit yourself to renting a flat. You may find this charge is included in the rent.

Once you have added together all these costs you will be able to work out how much money you have left each week. From this amount you will have to deduct money for food and travel to work if necessary. Whatever is left after these deductions is yours to spend. If you are now showing a minus figure you will need to think again!

You may decide that a cheaper alternative is to share a flat with one or two others. You will have some ready-made friends and the costs will be shared. It can be great fun if everyone gets on well together. If this is your choice you will need to have some house rules. These should be agreed by everyone. You will need to agree on such important issues as who cleans up, cooks and buys food and on whether it is OK to have friends to stay.

If you still feel that an independent life is for you then take your time and find somewhere you feel you could enjoy living. Happy house hunting!

Exam Practice 1 – HOME

LEAVING HOME

Renting a Flat

Once you have decided to leave the family home and become independent you have to find somewhere to live. Not many young people are able to buy their own home straight away. Renting a flat or bedsitter is the first stage to living on your own.

If you are looking for somewhere to live there are a few points to bear in mind.

Cost of Independence

First of all you must make sure you will be able to afford the rent. At first glance the weekly sum may not seem too much. However, there are many hidden costs. You must not forget to include bills in your calculations. These include water rates, gas, electricity and telephone. You should of course add insurance for your belongings. Buildings insurance is usually the responsibility of the landlord. If you own a television set, you will need to pay for a licence.

You will also need to pay your community charge. This is a sum that has to be paid to your local council. You may be able to pay this charge in monthly instalments. The cost varies from house to house and depends on how much the property is worth. You can ask your local authority how much this will be before you commit yourself to renting a flat. You may find this charge is included in the rent.

Once you have added together all these costs you will be able to work out how much money you have left each week. From this amount you will have to deduct money for food and travel to work if necessary. Whatever is left after these deductions is yours to spend. If you are now showing a minus figure you will need to think again!

You may decide that a cheaper alternative is to share a flat with one or two others. You will have some ready-made friends and the costs will be shared. It can be great fun if everyone gets on well together. If this is your choice you will need to have some house rules. These should be agreed by everyone.

You will need to agree on such important issues as who cleans up, cooks and buys food and on whether it is OK to have friends to stay.

If you still feel that an independent life is for you then take your time and find somewhere you feel you could enjoy living. Happy house hunting!

Exam Practice 2 – STONE1

Romancing the Stone

Diamonds

'Diamonds are a girl's best friend' is a well known saying placing the stones higher than boyfriends or husbands and on an equal basis with man's best friend – the dog. Why are diamonds so popular with women?

The beauty of diamond jewellery must be one of the reasons. Diamonds sparkle and glitter. They look fabulous set in gold, silver or platinum. They can be dressed up and, with care, look suitable during the day. They can raise the spirits if you are feeling low. If bought by a romantic partner, even one that is now an ex, they can make a woman feel glamorous and desirable.

Secondly, they are, of course, valuable. Women used to feel that their diamond jewellery gave them a sense of security. In the days when traditionally women did not work or own their own home, diamonds could always be sold to raise money in troubled times. Zsa Zsa Gabor tells us that you should never hate a man enough to return his diamonds!

In the middle ages diamonds were deemed to be symbols of strength and invincibility, only worthy to be worn by kings. However, in 1477 Archduke Maximilian of Austria gave a diamond ring to his beloved Mary of Burgundy. He placed the ring on the third finger of her left hand and is responsible for the fashion in diamond engagement rings that has lasted since then. The reason for choosing the third finger of the left hand is that Ancient Egyptians believed that the vein of love runs from the heart to the top of the third finger of the left hand.

Famous Diamonds

There have been many famous diamonds with interesting stories attached. Some are said to bring bad luck to whoever wear them. Some are famous for their size, weight or clarity.

The late Wallis Simpson, wife of Edward, Prince of Wales was famous for her collection of jewels. She built up a collection that was auctioned for £31.4 million in 1987.

Richard Burton bought his then wife Elizabeth Taylor a diamond costing $305,000 in 1968. This was a huge sum of money at the time. He bought her the legendary Krupp diamond which is one of the most famous of recent times.

More and more money is being spent on diamond jewellery. In 1998 an estimated £800 million was spent on diamond jewellery, compared to £600 million in 1983.

Exam Practice 2 – STONE

Romancing the Stone

Diamonds

'Diamonds are a girl's best friend' is a well known saying placing the stones higher than boyfriends or husbands and on an equal basis with man's best friend – the dog. Why are diamonds so popular with women?

The beauty of diamond jewellery must be one of the reasons. Diamonds sparkle and glitter. They look fabulous set in gold, silver or platinum. They can be dressed up and, with care, look suitable during the day. They can raise the spirits if you are feeling low. If bought by a romantic partner, even one that is now an ex, they can make a woman feel glamorous and desirable.

Secondly, they are, of course, valuable. Women used to feel that their diamond jewellery gave them a sense of security. In the days when traditionally women did not work or own their own home, diamonds could always be sold to raise money in troubled times. Zsa Zsa Gabor tells us that you should never hate a man enough to return his diamonds!

In the middle ages diamonds were deemed to be symbols of strength and invincibility, only worthy to be worn by kings. However, in 1477 Archduke Maximilian of Austria gave a diamond ring to his beloved Mary of Burgundy. He placed the ring on the third finger of her left hand and is responsible for the fashion in diamond engagement rings that has lasted since then. The reason for choosing the third finger of the left hand is that Ancient Egyptians believed that the vein of love runs from the heart to the top of the third finger of the left hand.

Famous Diamonds

There have been many famous diamonds with interesting stories attached. Some are said to bring bad luck to whoever wear them. Some are famous for their size, weight or clarity.

The late Wallis Simpson, wife of Edward, Prince of Wales was famous for her collection of jewels. She built up a collection that was auctioned for £31.4 million in 1987.

Richard Burton bought his then wife Elizabeth Taylor a diamond costing $305,000 in 1968. This was a huge sum of money at the time. He bought her the legendary Krupp diamond which is one of the most famous of recent times.

More and more money is being spent on diamond jewellery. In 1998 an estimated £800 million was spent on diamond jewellery, compared to £600 million in 1983.

Exercise 11.5 – HOLIDAYS1 – Page 1

Article

Holidays in the UK

Many people are becoming tired of long delays, cancelled flights and the inconvenience sometimes incurred at airports. They are choosing to spend their holidays in the UK. A number have found that the United Kingdom has plenty to offer both young and old alike.

Although the weather is generally uncertain, you can be sure of finding beautiful countryside, historic sites and plenty to entertain the whole family wherever you go. From canal boat holidays to activity breaks there will be something to suit you. We tested a number of UK holidays and this is what we found.

Self-Catering in Pembrokeshire

The Pembrokeshire coastline is spectacular. Endless stretches of the most beautiful beaches and fabulous rolling countryside await you in this unspoiled part of Wales. We rented a cottage in the small village of Broad Haven. Broad Haven is approximately seven miles from Haverfordwest, a ma-jor Welsh town. Wherever you stay in Broad Haven you are never more than a ten-minute stroll from the beach.

The beach is fabulous – a long stretch of sand with rock pools full of sea life. Magnificent cliffs surround the beach and the cliff walks are part of the Pembrokeshire Coastal Path.

At low tide you can walk the half mile or so across the beach to Little Haven, a tiny village with quaint fishermen's cottages and a minute quayside. Although there is little to do in Broad Haven apart from the beach, there are plenty of things to do in and around the area.

St David's, the smallest city in the United Kingdom has a magnificent cathedral which is situated next to the fascinating ruins of a bishop's palace. The city centre, although small, is pretty with some interesting gift shops selling the best of Welsh crafts. A visit to the sea life centre in St David's will provide fun for the children.

A little further afield is Oakwood Theme Park. This is a great attraction for all the family. The theme park has plenty to amuse children of all ages with a well thought out area for younger children. The facilities at Oakwood include a large indoor play area so bad weather will not interrupt the fun. There are plenty of cafés and fast food stalls to keep those hunger pangs at bay and you will find there is something to suit all tastes. Oakwood also offers kennel facilities so you can leave your pet safe in the knowledge that it will be well looked after.

If you are interested in castles and historic sites you will find plenty to visit. We found a most interesting ruined castle at the end of a country lane. To visit the castle you must collect the key from the local post office.

Going back further in time is an Iron Age hill fort at Castell Henlys. This is well worth a visit to see the reconstructed village at the top of a hill. Remember to wear suitable footwear though.

We spent a fantastic week in Pembrokeshire and will definitely make a return visit.

Weekend Break in Cambridge

For a relaxing weekend Cambridge has a lot to offer. Wonderful walks, a town rich in history, excellent shopping facilities and fabulous restaurants – who could ask for more.

One of the things you must do in Cambridge is to take a walk along the Backs. This riverside walk takes you past the backs of some of the most famous colleges. The beautiful, solemn architecture combined with the leafy

Holiday Feature   Sharon Spencer   3

Exercise 11.5 – HOLIDAYS1 – Page 2

Article

tree-lined riverside walk is very special. You will feel as though you have been transported back in time to a more elegant age where life passed by much more slowly and peacefully than in these hectic times. You will not believe that a bustling town centre is only a few minutes away. If you prefer to travel in style take a trip in a punt. There are many different companies vying for business and each punt has its own guide who does all the hard work. Sit back, relax and enjoy the marvellous views. At around £5 per person, this is a very reasonable cost for such a romantic expedition.

The colleges themselves are well worth visiting if possible. Not all are open to the public and others have guided tours just once or twice a week. However, if it is possible for you to visit during your stay, do take advantage.

The shopping facilities in Cambridge are excellent with a wide variety of boutiques, chain stores and high street names. The shopping centre is spread throughout the town, so remember to wear comfortable shoes. At the heart of the town centre is a busy market place. A large market selling everything under the sun operates twice a week.

There are plenty of restaurants in the town centre offering cuisine from every corner of the world, most at reasonable prices.

We stayed in a pretty guest house that was wonderfully clean and comfortable.

Canal Boat Trip

For a holiday with something different, try a canal boat. We hired a barge for one week, received some basic training and off we went. Our journey along the Kennet and Avon canal was fantastic. Beautiful countryside, small villages and some larger towns and cities, such as Bath, were all encountered on our journey. The handling of the canal boat took some getting used to, but we managed quite well. The children really enjoyed sitting on deck watching the world go by, and found the rather cramped living quarters great fun. The living quarters for the boat we hired were small for two large teenagers and two adults, however, it was well equipped and extremely clean.

As an activity holiday this is hard to beat, plenty of exercise and fresh air combined with a leisurely pace of life. The only setback to a holiday such as this could be the weather. In pouring rain and stormy weather the holiday may not be so much fun.

There are many companies offering canal boat hire and for the more adventurous, there are agencies in Eire, France, Holland and even the USA.

Holiday Feature   Sharon Spencer   4

Feature

ers. However, this proved to be impossible to enforce. Taxes on tea remained high until 1784 when it was reduced in order to prevent smuggling.

Tea drinking was a very social act and became part of any entertainment. By 1732, an evening spent dancing or watching fireworks would be rounded off by serving tea. Tea gardens opened all over the country at weekends with tea being served as the high point of the afternoon. This in turn lead to tea dances appearing. These remained fashionable in Britain until World War II.

In 1864 the first tea shop was started. This was immensely popular as for the first time women could enjoy meeting their friends and partaking of refreshments without having to be chaperoned. Tea shops quickly caught on all over the country and still enjoy popularity today.

Two World Wars

In World War I the German U-boat blockade drastically reduced the amount of tea imported into Britain. The ensuing black market led to rationing for civilians and prices were fixed by the Government to overcome this problem.

The rationing of tea was far less drastic during World War II. Tea drinking was believed to be a national morale booster and tea stocks were dispersed in over 500 different locations around the country to minimise the chances of destruction by air raid. Tea was drunk in vast quantities by civilians and the armed forces alike. By D-Day for example, the Royal Navy alone was drinking nearly 4000 tonnes of tea each year.

Tea Today

Tea drinking has lost some popularity in the last three decades with more and more people preferring to drink coffee. However, the demand for tea continues to be great and it is still considered to be our national beverage. There is nothing better when you are feeling low than 'a nice cup of tea'. It is offered as a panacea for all troubles with a common phrase in times of crisis being: 'I'll make us some tea'.

Sharon Spencer

7

Feature

TEA TIME

Discovery

According to Chinese mythology, the Chinese Emperor Shen Nung was sitting beneath a tree while his servant boiled drinking water. A leaf from the tree fell into the water and Shen Nung decided to drink the brew. This happened in 2737 BC and tea has been a popular drink ever since.

From its early days, tea has been renowned for its properties as a healthy and refreshing drink. By the 3rd century AD, stories were being told about the benefits of tea drinking. At the time of the Tang Dynasty, AD 618–906, tea became the national drink of China.

The first book on tea 'Ch'a Ching', was written around AD 780 by Lu Yu. It comprises three volumes and includes historical summary, early tea plantations through to making and drinking the beverage. There are many illustrations of tea-making utensils and it is thought that the book inspired the Buddhist priests to create the Japanese tea ceremony.

The Tea Plant

The plant *Camellia sinensis* is an evergreen plant of the Camellia family. It has smooth, shiny, pointed leaves which look similar to the privet hedge leaf found in this country. The *Camellia sinensis* is indigenous to China and parts of India. The wild tea plant can develop into a tree 30 metres high. Monkeys were trained to pick the leaves and throw them for collection below. Today, however, under cultivation the *Ca-*

mellia sinensis is kept to a height of approximately 1 metre to allow for easy picking. There are more than 1500 teas from over 25 countries around the world. The main producers are India, Sri Lanka, Kenya, Malawi, Indonesia and China. Tea is cultivated as a plantation crop. It likes acidic soil, a warm climate and at least 50 inches of rain per annum.

Tea in Europe

The first mention of tea outside of China and Japan is said to be by the Arabs in AD 850. It is reputed that the Arabs were responsible for bringing tea to Europe via the Venetians in around 1550. However it is the Portuguese and Dutch who claim the credit for this. It is thought that the Portuguese opened up the sea routes to China in around 1515. Jesuit priests travelling on the ships are reputed to have brought the tea-drinking habit back to Portugal. However, Dutch sailors manning the ships were said to have encouraged the Dutch merchants to enter the trade and had set up a regular shipment of tea to ports in France, Holland and the Baltic coast by 1610. England did not enter the trade until the mid to late 17th century.

Tea in Britain

The East India Company, under their charter granted by Elizabeth I to the Directors, had the monopoly of importing goods from outside Europe. However, there are no records of tea trading with Chinese merchants until 1644.

The merchant Thomas Garway was among the first to trade tea in Britain. He offered it in dry

and liquid form at his coffee house in Exchange Alley in London, holding its first public sale in 1657.

In 1660 Garway issued the first press release for tea stating it was 'wholesome, preserving perfect health until extreme old age, good for clearing the sight' among other benefits. Tea was sold for around £6 to £10 per pound – a tremendous amount of money in those days.

However, not everyone was pleased to see that tea was fast becoming popular. Innkeepers and in turn the Government were unhappy that the sales of hard liquor were declining in favour of tea drinking. The revenues that came from taxes levied on spirits also declined.

In order to control this situation Charles II forbade the sale of tea, coffee, chocolate and sherbet from private houses. However this act was so unpopular it never became statute law. The Act XII of 1676 imposed a duty on the sale of such beverages and required licences for coffee house keep-

Sharon Spencer

6

Exercise 13.6 – HOLIDAYS2 – Page 1

Article

Holidays in the UK

Many people are becoming tired of long delays, cancelled flights and the inconvenience sometimes incurred at airports. They are choosing to spend their holidays in the UK. A number have found that the United Kingdom has plenty to offer both young and old alike.

Although the weather is generally uncertain, you can be sure of finding beautiful countryside, historic sites and plenty to entertain the whole family wherever you go. From canal boat holidays to activity breaks there will be something to suit you. We tested a number of UK holidays and this is what we found.

Self-Catering in Pembrokeshire

The Pembrokeshire coastline is spectacular. Endless stretches of the most beautiful beaches and fabulous rolling countryside await you in this unspoiled part of Wales. We rented a cottage in the small village of Broad Haven. Broad Haven is approximately seven miles from

Haverfordwest, a major Welsh town. Wherever you stay in Broad Haven you are never more than a ten-minute stroll from the beach.

The beach is fabulous – a long stretch of sand with rock pools full of sea life. Magnificent cliffs surround the beach and the cliff walks are part of the Pembrokeshire Coastal Path.

At low tide you can walk the half mile or so across the beach to Little Haven, a tiny village with quaint fishermen's cottages and a minute quayside.

Although there is little to do in Broad Haven apart from the beach, there are plenty of things to do in and around the area. St David's, the smallest city in the United Kingdom has a magnificent cathedral which is situated next to the fascinating ruins of a bishop's palace. The city centre, although small, is pretty with some interesting gift shops selling the best of Welsh crafts. A visit to the sea life centre in St David's will provide fun for the children.

A little further afield is Oakwood Theme Park. This is a great attraction for all the family. The theme park has plenty to amuse children of all ages with a well thought out area for younger children. The facilities at Oakwood include a large indoor play area so bad weather will

not interrupt the fun. There are plenty of cafés and fast food stalls to keep those hunger pangs at bay and you will find there is something to suit all tastes. Oakwood also offers kennel facilities so you can leave your pet safe in the knowledge that it will be well looked after.

If you are interested in castles and historic sites you will find plenty to visit. We found a most interesting ruined castle at the end of a country lane. To visit the castle you must collect the key from the local post office.

Going back further in time is an Iron Age hill fort at Castell Henlys. This is well worth a visit to see the reconstructed village at the top of a hill. Remember to wear suitable footwear though.

We spent a fantastic week in Pembrokeshire and will definitely make a return visit.

Weekend Break in Cambridge

For a relaxing weekend Cambridge has a lot to offer. Wonderful walks, a town rich in history, excellent shopping facilities and fabulous restaurants – who could ask for more.

One of the things you must do in Cambridge is to take a walk along the Backs. This riverside walk takes you past the backs of some of the most famous colleges. The beautiful, solemn

Holiday Feature   Sharon Spencer   3

Exercise 13.6 – HOLIDAYS2 – Page 2

Article

architecture combined with the leafy tree-lined riverside walk is very special. You will feel as though you have been transported back in time to a more elegant age where life passed by much more slowly and peacefully than in these hectic times. You will not believe that a bustling town centre is only a few minutes away. If you prefer to travel in style take a trip in a punt. There are many different companies vying for business and each punt has its own guide who does all the hard work. Sit back, relax and enjoy the marvellous views. At around £5 per person, this is a very reasonable cost for such a romantic expedition.

The colleges themselves are well worth visiting if possible. Not all are open

to the public and others have guided tours just once or twice a week. However, if it is possible for you to visit during your stay, do take advantage. The shopping facilities in Cambridge are excellent with a wide variety of boutiques, chain stores and high street names. The shopping centre is spread throughout the town, so remember to wear comfortable shoes. At the heart of the town centre is a busy market place. A large market selling everything under the sun operates twice a week.

There are plenty of restaurants in the town centre offering cuisine from every corner of the world, most at reasonable prices.

We stayed in a pretty guest house that was

wonderfully clean and comfortable.

Canal Boat Trip

For a holiday with something different, try a canal boat. We hired a barge for one week, received some basic training and off we went. Our journey along the Kennet and Avon canal was fantastic. Beautiful countryside, small villages and some larger towns and cities, such as Bath, were all encountered on our journey. The handling of the canal boat took some getting used to, but we managed quite well. The children really enjoyed sitting on deck watching the world go by, and found the rather cramped living quarters great fun. The living quarters for the boat we hired were small for two large teenagers and two adults, however, it was well equipped and extremely clean.

As an activity holiday this is hard to beat, plenty of exercise and fresh air combined with a leisurely pace of life. The only setback to a holiday such as this could be the weather. In pouring rain and stormy weather the holiday may not be so much fun.

There are many companies offering canal boat hire and for the more adventurous, there are agencies in Eire, France, Holland and even the USA.

Holiday Feature   Sharon Spencer   4

Exercise 16 – DOGS1

DOGS

OWNING A DOG

Dogs make great pets and can soon become a much-loved member of the family. They provide companionship, are fun to be with and give you a good excuse to take regular exercise. However, they do require time, money and commitment from their owners.

Dogs are very social animals and do not enjoy being left on their own for long periods of time. If you work full time and are thinking of getting a dog you may consider taking on an older rescue dog that does not need constant attention.

Think carefully before choosing a dog. There are many aspects of dog ownership that need to be taken into consideration before you make a final choice.

Firstly, you should consider your home environment. For example, if you live in a flat or house with no garden, then a small dog would probably be the most suitable. If you must have a larger dog then you need to consider where you will be able to exercise it.

Most dogs need regular, outdoor exercise. Some breeds require much more exercise than others. Be realistic about how much time you can spare to walk your pet.

Cost is another important consideration. Large dogs can eat a great deal of food and this can cost a considerable sum over a few weeks. If you add to the cost of food, vet bills, kennel fees, bedding, leads, toys and other accessories you can see the bills mount up.

If you do decide to have a pet dog you will soon find the advantages far outweigh the disadvantages.

CHOOSING A BREED

As mentioned, there are some general considerations that have to be taken into account before you decide to own a dog. However, once the decision has been made, you need to choose which breed to own.

Some breeds make much better family pets than others. You may wish to own a particular type of dog such as a gundog or toy dog. You also need to consider whether you are interested in showing your animal.

Some of the most popular breeds are given below.

- Labrador Retriever. These make excellent family pets. They are usually even-tempered, intelligent animals and are good with children. They can also make good guard dogs.
- Cairn Terrier. These are very friendly small dogs. They make excellent companions as they are intelligent and loyal. Cairn terriers do however require regular grooming.
- Cocker Spaniel. These medium-sized dogs make excellent companions. They require regular grooming and lots of exercise. This is very important as they do have a tendency to put on weight.
- Mongrels. Usually very hardy dogs, they make excellent family pets. Depending on the type, they may not require much grooming but do enjoy regular exercise.

Exercise 15.4 – BEAUTY1

LOOKING GOOD

Cleansing

In order to look good you need to spend some time on your cleansing and moisturising regime. Clean, fresh skin will automatically make you feel and look years younger. Here are a few of our top tips.

If you wear make-up it is essential that all traces are removed before you go to bed. Leaving make-up on overnight will block the pores, preventing skin from breathing. Spots and blackheads may also appear.

Your first step to wonderful looking skin is to remove your make-up. There are many different make-up removers available and you should choose one that will suit your skin type. Using cotton wool and a good quality cleanser, ensure that all traces of make-up and grime have been removed.

The second step is to clean your face. There are many types of cleanser on the market, ranging from face scrubs, which contain tiny particles that exfoliate the skin, to cleansing milks which are heavier and creamier in consistency. Some well-known brands sell special types of soap that are designed especially for use on the face. A sales advisor will be able to help you determine the best cleanser for your skin type.

The last step is to apply a good quality moisturiser. Again, you should find one that suits your skin type. Gently apply to your face and neck every night. Within a few months you should be able to see the difference this 5-minute routine makes. Hopefully others will notice as well.

Hair

People probably spend more time and money on their hair than on any other part of their body. The many different colours and styles that can be achieved are used as fashion statements or as a form of self-expression. Strange, considering that hair has no obvious biological function. It is an appendage of skin consisting of threads of cells filled with keratin, a protein which is also found in finger and toenails.

Each hair is anchored in a tiny pit called a follicle underneath the skin. It is the shape of the follicle which determines the appearance of the hair. A round follicle will produce a straight hair, an oval follicle produces wavy hair and a spiral follicle will give you curly hair.

The pigments that give hair its colour are found in the middle of the three layers that make up a strand of hair. This layer is known as the cortex. Black, brown and fair hair all contain varying concentrations of the pigment melanin. Red hair, however, contains the pigment trichosiderin, which contains iron.

Some interesting hair facts are given below.

- *There is no such thing as a grey hair. It is a mixture of natural colour hair and strands that no longer contain the coloured pigment. These are actually white hairs.*
- *Hair grows at a rate of around 0.015 inches each day. It grows faster at night and in warm weather. Black hair grows faster than blonde.*
- *The number of hairs on the head varies with the natural colour. Blondes have around 14,000 hairs, dark-haired people have around 108,000 while redheads have only 90,000 strands of hair.*

Sharon Spencer Health and Beauty

DOGS

OWNING A DOG

Dogs make great pets and can soon become a much-loved member of the family. They provide companionship, are fun to be with and give you a good excuse to take regular exercise. However, they do require time, money and commitment from their owners.

Dogs are very social animals and do not enjoy being left on their own for long periods of time. If you work full time and are thinking of getting a dog you may consider taking on an older rescue dog that does not need constant attention.

Think carefully before choosing a dog. There are many aspects of dog ownership that need to be taken into consideration before you make a final choice.

Firstly, you should consider your home environment. For example, if you live in a flat or house with no garden, then a small dog would probably be the most suitable. If you must have a larger dog then you need to consider where you will be able to exercise it.

Most dogs need regular, outdoor exercise. Some breeds require much more exercise than others. Be realistic about how much time you can spare to walk your pet.

Sharon Spencer

Cost is another important consideration. Large dogs can eat a great deal of food and this can cost a considerable sum over a few weeks. If you add to the cost of food, vet bills, kennel fees, bedding, leads, toys and other accessories you can see the bills mount up.

If you do decide to have a pet dog you will soon find the advantages far outweigh the disadvantages.

CHOOSING A BREED

As mentioned, there are some general considerations that have to be taken into account before you decide to own a dog. However, once the decision has been made, you need to choose which breed to own.

Some breeds make much better family pets than others. You may wish to own a particular type of dog such as a gundog or toy dog. You also need to consider whether you are interested in showing your animal.

Some of the most popular breeds are given below.

- Labrador Retriever. These make excellent family pets. They are usually even-tempered, intelligent animals and are good with children. They can also make good guard dogs.
- Cairn Terrier. These are very friendly small dogs. They make excellent companions as they are intelligent and loyal. Cairn terriers do however require regular grooming.
- Cocker Spaniel. These medium-sized dogs make excellent companions. They require regular grooming and lots of exercise. This is very important as they do have a tendency to put on weight.
- Mongrels. Usually very hardy dogs, they make excellent family pets. Depending on the type, they may not require much grooming but do enjoy regular exercise.

LOOKING GOOD

Cleansing

In order to look good you need to spend some time on your cleansing and moisturising regime. Clean, fresh skin will automatically make you feel and look years younger. Here are a few of our top tips.

If you wear make-up it is essential that all traces are removed before you go to bed. Leaving make-up on overnight will block the pores, preventing skin from breathing. Spots and blackheads may also appear.

Your first step to wonderful looking skin is to remove your make-up. There are many different make-up removers available and you should choose one that will suit your skin type. Using cotton wool and a good quality cleanser, ensure that all traces of make-up and grime have been removed.

The second step is to clean your face. There are many types of cleanser on the market, ranging from face scrubs, which contain tiny particles that exfoliate the skin, to cleansing milks which are heavier and creamier in consistency. Some well-known brands sell special types of soap that are designed especially for use on the face. A sales advisor will be able to help you determine the best cleanser for your skin type.

The last step is to apply a good quality moisturiser. Again, you should find one that suits your skin type. Gently apply to your face and neck every night. Within a few months you should be able to see the difference this 5-minute routine makes. Hopefully others will notice as well.

Hair

People probably spend more time and money on their hair than on any other part of their body. The many different colours and styles that can be achieved are used as fashion statements or as a form of self-expression. Strange, considering that hair has no obvious biological function. It is an appendage of skin consisting of threads of cells filled with keratin, a protein which is also found in finger and toenails.

Each hair is anchored in a tiny pit called a follicle underneath the skin. It is the shape of the follicle which determines the appearance of the hair. A round follicle will produce a straight hair, an oval follicle produces wavy hair and a spiral follicle will give you curly hair.

The pigments that give hair its colour are found in the middle of the three layers that make up a strand of hair. This layer is known as the cortex. Black, brown and fair hair all contain varying concentrations of the pigment melanin. Red hair, however, contains the pigment trichosiderin, which contains iron.

Some interesting hair facts are given below:

- There is no such thing as a grey hair. It is a mixture of natural colour hair and strands that no longer contain the coloured pigment. These are actually white hairs.
- Hair grows at a rate of around 0.015 inches each day. It grows faster at night and in warm weather. Black hair grows faster than blonde.
- The number of hairs on the head varies with the natural colour. Blondes have around 14,000 hairs, dark-haired people have around 108,000 while redheads have only 90,000 strands of hair.

Sharon Spencer Health and Beauty

INTERNET FEATURE

means that you will be able to exchange ideas and discuss issues with fellow collectors or hobbyists.

The many auction sites that have been set up will also be of interest to you. You may find that people are trying to sell just what you have been looking for. It is an easy way to find goods without have to spend a great deal of time trying to track them down by phone, fax or letter.

Because the web is worldwide, you will be able to purchase goods from overseas without delay. A real boon for collectors.

International Shopping

One of the benefits of web shopping is that you can easily purchase goods from overseas. Many companies are unwilling to send heavy paper catalogues overseas as the expense in relation to orders received in this way is too great. However, once their catalogue is posted on the net then customers can order without any extra expense to the company.

This will allow dedicated consumers plenty of opportunity to shop around for the best prices on items they wish to purchase, without even leaving their home. Good examples of items that are regularly purchased in this way include CDs, books, and DVDs.

There are of course some setbacks to this method. Not all companies are willing to ship items abroad. It can be very frustrating to have chosen your goods, spent some time going through the checkout to find that at the last possible moment your order is refused.

Postage costs can also be very high. Before you commit yourself to having items shipped over because they appear to be very inexpensive, count in the cost of postage. The other major setback of shopping abroad occurs, of course, if the goods are incorrect or broken. It is obviously costly to send the goods back to, for example, the USA.

However, if you shop carefully or

would like to have items that are not available in this country, then this is a good method of shopping.

Overall, shopping via the Internet may play a large part of shopping in the future. However, nothing will replace the enjoyment many people find in browsing around the shops, examining the goods they wish to purchase before they buy.

Sharon Spencer　　　5

INTERNET FEATURE

SHOPPING WORLDWIDE
Background

According to many, shopping on the Internet is going to be a boom industry for many years to come. Experts have predicted that as our lives become even busier and the roads more congested, more and more people will switch to shopping over the Internet.

Although there are certainly signs that the number of people purchasing by this method is increasing, a degree of caution should be employed. This article sets out to discuss some of the implications of shopping over the Internet.

Using the worldwide web to source and purchase goods is not as new as you might think. It has been possible to purchase goods in this way for more than five years. However, during the last two years many new Internet stores have been created and many of our best-known retailers have invested heavily in websites. Is this really because large numbers of people are changing the way they shop, or is it because these retailers are frightened they may miss out?

Large sums of money have been invested in setting up brand new e-tailers, (the jargon used for

retailers who sell through a website). These companies exist purely to sell via the net. Although it is early days for these businesses it should be noted that few of them are reporting profits at present.

Many small specialist companies use the web to promote their goods which may be hard to find and highly sought after. It is, of course, possible to purchase from overseas which opens up many new choices for consumers.

Just how easy is it to locate goods and order through the Internet? Is it really time saving and convenient? Only time will tell in the long term, but we can look at how successful Internet shopping is today.

Supermarkets

Most of the leading supermarkets in this country are now offering an Internet service. You click onto the site, browse around a 'virtual store', choose the goods you require and then venture to the checkout. Here you check the goods you have ordered are correct, enter your credit card details and within minutes you should have received an order confirmation.

Many supermarkets offer same or next-day delivery but recent reports suggest that delivery is not always as reliable as one would wish. One tester stated that she was told there were no delivery slots free until the

following week! Not very useful if you need something for tea the same evening.

Other reports have claimed that orders have arrived incomplete or incorrect. On one occasion, the supermarket in question had to purchase some of the customer's goods from a nearby rival supermarket as they were out of stock!

Once the goods have been delivered to your door, they need to be checked against the order to ensure that the order is correct. If you have ordered a large number of items, this could take quite some time.

However, many users say that this service is 'the best thing since sliced bread'. They state that they save a

great deal of time and effort by using this service. It should be pointed out however, that most of the reports regarding Internet supermarket shopping have had testers ordering only a small number of items, say eight to ten. An average family's weekly shopping would include around fifty to sixty items. This in turn means that there is a much wider margin for error when receiving your order.

All in all, Internet supermarket shopping is obviously useful to many people, particularly those who make small, regular purchases. However, for those who enjoy picking out special offers and trying out new foods then the virtual supermarket will probably not be the most suitable way of shopping at present.

Specialist Items

If you have a hobby or interest such as collecting model cars or old records, then the Internet can be of great interest to you. You may find that companies who advertise in specialist magazines now boast a website, so you can immediately browse through their catalogue without delay. You will be able to e-mail these businesses with a question and receive a reply without too much delay.

You may also find that your hobby or interest has a chatroom. This

Sharon Spencer　　　4

means that you will be able to exchange ideas and discuss issues with fellow collectors or hobbyists.

The many auction sites that have been set up will also be of interest to you. You may find that people are trying to sell just what you have been looking for. It is an easy way to find goods without have to spend a great deal of time trying to track them down by phone, fax or letter.

Because the web is worldwide, you will be able to purchase goods from overseas without delay. A real boon for collectors.

International Shopping

One of the benefits of web shopping is that you can easily purchase goods from overseas. Many companies are unwilling to send heavy paper catalogues overseas as the expense in relation to orders received in this way is too great. However, once their catalogue is posted on the net then customers can order without any extra expense to the company.

This will allow dedicated consumers plenty of opportunity to shop around for the best prices on items they wish to purchase, without even leaving their home. Good examples of items that are regularly purchased in this way include CDs, books, and DVDs.

There are of course some setbacks to this method. Not all companies are willing to ship items abroad. It can be very frustrating to have chosen your goods, spent some time

going through the checkout to find that at the last possible moment your order is refused.

Postage costs can also be very high. Before you commit yourself to

having items shipped over because they appear to be very inexpensive, count in the cost of postage. The other major setback of shopping abroad occurs, of course, if the goods are incorrect or broken. It is obviously costly to send the goods back to, for example, the USA.

However, if you shop carefully or would like to have items that are not available in this country, then this is a good method of shopping.

Overall, shopping via the Internet may play a large part of shopping in the future. However, nothing will replace the enjoyment many people find in browsing around the shops, examining the goods they wish to purchase before they buy.

Sharon Spencer   5

SHOPPING WORLDWIDE
Background

According to many, shopping on the Internet is going to be a boom industry for many years to come. Experts have predicted that as our lives become even busier and the roads more congested, more and more people will switch to shopping over the Internet.

Although there are certainly signs that the number of people purchasing by this method is increasing, a degree of caution should be employed. This article sets out to discuss some of the implications of shopping over the Internet.

Using the worldwide web to source and purchase goods is not as new as you might think. It has been possible to purchase goods in this way for more than five years. However, during the last two years many new Internet stores have been created and many of our best-known retailers have invested heavily in websites. Is this really because large numbers of people are changing the way they shop, or is it because these retailers are frightened they may miss out?

Large sums of money have been invested in setting up brand new e-tailers, (the jargon used for

retailers who sell through a website). These companies exist purely to sell via the net. Although it is early days for these businesses it should be noted that few of them are reporting profits at present.

Many small specialist companies use the web to promote their goods which may be hard to find and highly sought after. It is, of course, possible to purchase from overseas which opens up many new choices for consumers.

Just how easy is it to locate goods and order through the Internet? Is it really time saving and convenient? Only time will tell in the long term, but we can look at how successful Internet shopping is today.

Supermarkets

Most of the leading supermarkets in this country are now offering an Internet service. You click onto the site, browse around a 'virtual store', choose the goods you require and then venture to the checkout. Here you check the goods you have ordered are correct, enter your credit card details and within minutes you should have received an order confirmation.

Many supermarkets offer same or next-day delivery but recent reports suggest that delivery is not always as reliable as one would wish. One tester stated that she was told there were no delivery slots free until the

following week! Not very useful if you need something for tea the same evening.

Other reports have claimed that orders have arrived incomplete or incorrect. On one occasion, the supermarket in question had to purchase some of the customer's goods from a nearby rival supermarket as they were out of stock!

Once the goods have been delivered to your door, they need to be checked against the order to ensure that the order is correct. If you have ordered a large number of items, this could take quite some time.

However, many users say that this service is 'the best thing since sliced bread'. They state that they save a

great deal of time and effort by using this service. It should be pointed out however, that most of the reports regarding Internet supermarket shopping have had testers ordering only a small number of items, say eight to ten. An average family's weekly shopping would include around fifty to sixty items. This in turn means that there is a much wider margin for error when receiving your order.

All in all, Internet supermarket shopping is obviously useful to many people, particularly those who make small, regular purchases. However, for those who enjoy picking out special offers and trying out new foods then the virtual supermarket will probably not be the most suitable way of shopping at present.

Specialist Items

If you have a hobby or interest such as collecting model cars or old records, then the Internet can be of great interest to you. You may find that companies who advertise in specialist magazines now boast a website, so you can immediately browse through their catalogue without delay. You will be able to e-mail these businesses with a question and receive a reply without too much delay.

You may also find that your hobby or interest has a chatroom. This

Sharon Spencer   4

Article

WILDLIFE TODAY

The Dormouse

Sadly, the common dormouse is now extinct in seven British counties. The main reason for this is the loss of woodlands and hedgerows, the natural habitat of the dormouse. It is thought that the dormouse is also vulnerable to changes in the climate which may interrupt its winter hibernation.

The dormouse is a small creature around 6–9cm in length, excluding its tail. It feeds on pollen and blossom in the spring and insects and fruit in the summer. During autumn it builds up its body weight in preparation for hibernation by eating hazelnuts. In fact, trying to find a dormouse is a very difficult task, but if you find a small pile of discarded hazelnuts, then a dormouse may not be too far away.

The hibernation period lasts from the first frosts of late October to March or April. The dormouse makes its bed in leaf litter or by burying a few inches below the soil. This means it is at risk of discovery by predators such as badgers and foxes. Unfortunately, many dormice perish during the hibernation period, not just through being discovered by predators, but also because humidity levels can affect them adversely.

Since 1995, English Nature has funded a dormouse captive breeding programme. This programme aims to raise animals for release into the wild, specifically in areas where

dormice no longer breed naturally. This programme has been relatively successful and it is hoped that eventually dormice will again populate the woodlands and hedgerows of the UK.

The Otter

The Eurasian river otter is the only otter native to this country. It can also be found throughout Europe, as far north as the Artic Circle, across most of Asia and in northern Africa. The average length of an otter is from 55–90cm. It has a long, slim body and powerful jaws. The otter is well adapted to aquatic life and has webbed toes and a powerful rudder-like tail which is used for propulsion under water. An otter is capable of closing its eyes and nostrils while underwater and has two types of fur – a water-proof coat and a fine underfur which provides insulation.

In Britain, otters are fresh and saltwater animals, although in Scotland and the Shetlands, they must have access to freshwater pools in order to clean their insulating fur.

The otter is quite a solitary creature and is active at dusk and during the night. Seldom seen during the day, it rests in holts which are burrows in the river bank. Its diet consists of fish, crustaceans, water birds, voles and frogs.

This species is considered an endangered species and has become extinct in many of its

natural habitats. Unfortunately, its numbers are still decreasing at present. Otters are protected by the Wildlife and Countryside Act (1981) and cannot be kept, sold or killed without a licence.

Hedgehog

The hedgehog is the only mammal in Britain to have spines. The upper parts of the head and body are covered in short yellow-tipped spines with adults having up to 5,000 spines. The rest of the body is covered with brown fur. Hedgehogs have short tails.

The natural habitat of hedgehogs is forest, scrub and cultivated land and they often live in gardens. Their diet consists of snails, slugs, beetles and earthworms and so hedgehogs are a welcome guest in any garden. Less welcome is the fact that hedgehogs also eat eggs and chicks of ground nesting birds.

Solitary animals by nature, the hedgehog is at its most active during the night, particularly after a heavy rainfall. The hedgehog's home in summer is a temporary nest of leaves, grass and moss. Hedgehogs hibernate from October to March or April, typically under hedgerows. Unfortunately most hedgehog deaths occur during the hibernation period. The dense covering of spines offers the hedgehog protection from predators such as foxes, stoats and badgers. When disturbed it rolls into a tight ball to protect its head and soft underside. Although its eyesight is poor, its sense of smell and hearing is very good. Hedgehogs can swim and climb well.

Sharon Spencer

8

PARTY TIME

Children's Parties

Children love parties, however, organising a party for a large number of small children can seem a very daunting task. We have some ideas that should take the stress out of the event and make it a memorable occasion for your child.

The secret of a good party is planning. First of all you need to decide the type of party you are going to hold and the number of guests. As a general rule, the younger the child, the smaller the number of guests, as very young children need to be supervised closely. Limit the number to as many as you feel you can supervise adequately and ensure you have some adult helpers on the day. The venue will also determine the number of people you can invite. Although it is obviously more expensive to hire a venue, such as a church or school hall, it does mean that the children will have somewhere to expend their energy without ruining your home.

The food and drink you are going to provide needs to be considered well in advance. Make sure that you provide plenty of variety as children can be very fussy about what they eat. Remember to include some vegetarian options. Sandwiches, crisps, dips, biscuits and ice-cream are always popular. If you can provide hot food, then pizza is a great favourite with almost all children.

The entertainment you provide is also very important. You should plan what is going to happen well in advance so that the children are kept occupied throughout the whole event. Traditional games such as pin the tail on the donkey and pass the parcel are still enjoyed by most children. If you can afford to hire a clown or magician, then this will keep the children occupied for an hour or so. Puppet shows are very popular with younger children and perhaps you could organise for a friend or older child to do this.

Themed Parties

Most children enjoy a themed party and they do not have to be expensive. Our ideas for the best parties include:

- Teddy Bears' Picnic. Younger children will enjoy a teddy bears' picnic party. Ask the guests to bring a teddy and provide picnic food. You can purchase small food boxes that are just right for this occasion.
- Pirate Party. For children aged around 5–7, a pirate party can be lots of fun. The guests should dress up as pirates and a prize can be given for the best costume. Treasure hunt games will keep the children occupied and a small bag of chocolate coins will provide the perfect going home present.
- Disco Party. Older children will enjoy a disco party. If you do not want to hire a hall, then ensure the party area is clear of furniture to enable the children to jump around. Disco music, plenty of fizzy drinks and pizza will make children feel very grown up.

Sharon Spencer

Consolidation 4, Part 1, Step 11 – WILDLIFE2 – Page 1

Article

WILDLIFE TODAY

The Dormouse

Sadly, the common dormouse is now extinct in seven British counties. The main reason for this is the loss of woodlands and hedgerows, the natural habitat of the dormouse. It is thought that the dormouse is also vulnerable to changes in the climate which may interrupt its winter hibernation.

The dormouse is a small creature around 6–9cm in length, excluding its tail. It feeds on pollen and blossom in the spring and insects and fruit in the summer. During autumn it builds up its body weight in preparation for hibernation by eating hazelnuts. In fact, trying to find a dormouse is a very difficult task, but if you find a small pile of discarded hazelnuts, then a dormouse may not be too far away.

The hibernation period lasts from the first frosts of late October to March or April. The dormouse makes its bed in leaf litter or by burying a few inches below the soil. This means that it is at risk of discovery by predators such as badgers and foxes. Unfortunately, many dormice perish during the hibernation period, not just through being discovered by predators, but also because humidity levels can affect them adversely.

Since 1995, English Nature has funded a dormouse captive breeding programme. This programme aims to raise animals for release into the wild, specifically in areas where dormice no longer breed naturally. This programme has been relatively successful and it is hoped that eventually dormice will again populate the woodlands and hedgerows of the UK.

The Otter

The Eurasian river otter is the only otter native to this country. It can also be found throughout Europe, as far north as the Artic Circle, across most of Asia and in northern Africa. The average length of an otter is from 55–90cm. It has a long, slim body and powerful jaws. The otter is well adapted to aquatic life and has webbed toes and a powerful rudder-like tail which is used for propulsion under water. An otter is capable of closing its eyes and nostrils while underwater and has two types of fur – a waterproof coat and a fine underfur which provides insulation.

In Britain, otters are fresh and saltwater animals, although in Scotland and the Shetlands, they must have access to freshwater pools in order to clean their insulating fur.

The otter is quite a solitary creature and is active at dusk and during the night. Seldom seen during the day, it rests in holts which are burrows in the river bank. Its diet consists of fish, crustaceans, water birds, voles and frogs.

This species is considered an endangered species and has become extinct in many of its natural habitats. Unfortunately, its numbers are still decreasing at present. Otters are protected by the Wildlife and Countryside Act (1981) and cannot be kept, sold or killed without a licence.

Hedgehog

The hedgehog is the only mammal in Britain to have spines. The upper parts of the head and body are covered in short yellow-tipped spines with adults having up to 5,000 spines. The rest of the body is covered with brown fur. Hedgehogs have short tails.

The natural habitat of hedgehogs is forest, scrub and cultivated land and they often live in gardens. Their diet consists of snails, slugs, beetles and earthworms and so hedgehogs are a welcome guest in any garden. Less welcome is the fact that hedgehogs also eat eggs and chicks of ground nesting birds.

Solitary animals by nature, the hedgehog is at its most active during the night, particularly after a heavy rainfall. The hedgehog's home in summer is a temporary nest of leaves, grass and moss. Hedgehogs hibernate from

Sharon Spencer

8

Consolidation 4, Part 1, Step 8 – WILDLIFE1 – Page 2

Article

Hedgehogs are also protected under the Wildlife and Countryside Act (1981) and may not be trapped without a licence. At present they are not considered to be endangered, although their numbers are declining, probably due to the loss of their natural habitat.

Brown Hare

The brown hare has a body length of approximately 48–70cm. This means it is larger than a rabbit and has longer limbs. Its black-tipped ears are equal in length to the head. When running, its tail is held down showing the black dorsal surface. The hare's fur moults during spring and autumn, the summer coat is lighter than the reddish winter coat.

Brown hares are widespread in central and western Europe, including England and Wales, however they are absent from Ireland and Scotland. Brown hares prefer temperate open habitats, using hedgerows and woodland as resting places during the day. These resting places are known as 'forms' and only the head and back of the hare is visible. They are mostly found in flat country among open grassland and arable farms, however, they can live at up to 1500m in the Pyrenees.

The brown hare is a more social animal than the otter and hedgehog as it will share its territory with other hares. It escapes its predators by outrunning them. The brown hare feeds mainly on herbs in the summer and grasses in the winter. It will also eat cereal and root crops.

The number of brown hares has declined in Britain and most of Europe since the 1960s. This is thought to be partly due to modern farming methods. At present they are shot for sport in Europe and sometimes hunted with dogs in the UK.

Badgers

Badgers range in size from approximately 55–85cm. They are easily recognisable by the black and white stripes which run from the nose to the shoulders. They are stocky animals with short black legs and silvery grey backs.

Badgers can be found in Europe, Japan and South China. In this country they are most common in southwest England, Wales and small areas of northeast England.

Their preferred habitat is forest and grassland. They live in underground burrows called setts. These are complex homes with chambers, passages and entrances and will be used by successive generations. Clean creatures, badgers will often bring the nesting material out to air in the sunshine during the day.

Badgers are social creatures and live in family groups of up to 12. They enjoy playing together and this in turn helps to strengthen their social bond. Their diet consists of earthworms, frogs, birds, eggs, lizards, insects, bulbs, seeds, berries and rodents.

The badger is not considered endangered but its numbers have declined in recent years. It is estimated that up to 50,000 badgers are killed each year in Britain on the roads. Badgers are often hunted for sport.

Sharon Spencer

9

Consolidation 4, Part 2, Step 10 – TOYS1

CHILDREN'S TOYS

The Toy Market

The toy market has been declining over the past decade. Some of the reasons for this decline are given below:

- Children are maturing earlier and therefore the age at which they stop playing with toys is decreasing.
- Huge competition from the electronic and computerised game market.
- Children prefer to watch television rather than play with toys.

Although the reasons are based in truth, children of today do still enjoy playing with toys. It should be remembered that toys provide an essential aid to learning. Research has shown that children enjoy playing with traditional type toys such as teddy bears, Yo-Yos, train sets, construction bricks and dolls. Although toys such as character merchandise can enjoy extreme popularity, this is very often short-lived.

A common complaint from parents is that there are hardly any toy shops left in this country. Many department stores have stopped selling toys. Where can parents find interesting toys at reasonable prices? There are a number of mail order companies that offer a range of interesting products. The Internet is another good source with several large companies selling a variety of items. It is well worth finding a good toy supplier as your children will remember favourite toys for the rest of their lives.

Teddy Bears

We are all familiar with the teddy bear. They come in all shapes and sizes and appear on many household and children's items. When did teddy bears first become popular?

It is thought that the first teddy bear, as we know them today, appeared in 1903. They were made by a German company named Steiff. This company which still makes teddies today, had been making stuffed bears since as far back as 1892. However, these were rigid models that were much more like real bears.

The teddy made in 1903 was called BAR55PB. He was a jointed model and as his name suggests, he was 55 cm high. The response to the new model was very slow with only one company placing an order. This American company ordered 3000 teddies and not one of these bears is known to be in existence today. If one could be found it would be worth a large amount of money.

The following year another model was designed, this time slightly smaller at 35 cm. This model proved to be much more popular and around 12,000 were sold. Over the following few years the bears were constantly redesigned until Steiff felt that they had developed the best model in 1905.

Today Steiff are still delighting generations of children with their wide range of soft toys.

Sharon Spencer

Consolidation 4, Part 1, Step 11 – WILDLIFE2 – Page 2

Article

October to March or April, typically under hedgerows. Unfortunately most hedgehog deaths occur during the hibernation period. The dense covering of spines offers the hedgehog protection from predators such as foxes, stoats and badgers. When disturbed it rolls into a tight ball to protect its head and soft underside. Although its eyesight is poor, its sense of smell and hearing is very good. Hedgehogs can swim and climb well.

Hedgehogs are also protected under the Wildlife and Countryside Act (1981) and may not be trapped without a licence. At present they are not considered to be endangered, although their numbers are declining, probably due to the loss of their natural habitat.

Brown Hare

The brown hare has a body length of approximately 48–70cm. This means it is larger than a rabbit and has longer limbs. Its black-tipped ears are equal in length to the head. When running, its tail is held down showing the black dorsal surface. The hare's fur moults during spring and autumn, the summer coat is lighter than the reddish winter coat.

Brown hares are widespread in central and western Europe, including England and Wales,

however they are absent from Ireland and Scotland. Brown hares prefer temperate open habitats, using hedgerows and woodland as resting places during the day. These resting places are known as 'forms' and only the head and back of the hare is visible. They are mostly found in flat country among open grassland and arable farms, however, they can live at up to 1500m in the Pyrenees.

The brown hare is a more social animal than the otter and hedgehog as it will share its territory with other hares. It escapes its predators by outrunning them. The brown hare feeds mainly on herbs in the summer and grasses in the winter. It will also eat cereal and root crops.

The number of brown hares has declined in Britain and most of Europe since the 1960s. This is thought to be partly due to modern farming methods. At present they are shot for sport in Europe and sometimes hunted with dogs in the UK.

Badgers

Badgers range in size from approximately 55–85cm. They are easily recognisable by the black and white stripes which run from the nose to the shoulders. They are stocky animals with short black legs and silvery grey backs.

Badgers can be found in Europe, Japan and South China. In this country they are most common in southwest England, Wales and small areas of northeast England.

Their preferred habitat is forest and grassland. They live in underground burrows called setts. These are complex homes with chambers, passages and

entrances and will be used by successive generations. Clean creatures, badgers will often bring the nesting material out to air in the sunshine during the day.

Badgers are social creatures and live in family groups of up to 12. They enjoy playing together and this in turn helps to strengthen their social bond. Their diet consists of earthworms, frogs, birds, eggs, lizards, insects, bulbs, seeds, berries and rodents.

The badger is not considered endangered but its numbers have declined in recent years. It is estimated that up to 50,000 badgers are killed each year in Britain on the roads. Badgers are often hunted for sport.

Sharon Spencer

9

ARTICLE

HISTORY OF FOOTWEAR

Pre 1900

The history of footwear is fascinating with the earliest recording of shoes being found in Missouri. Evidence has been found of shoes worn by Native Americans in 8000 BC. Shoes worn by 'Ice Man' from 3000 BC have been found in the French Alps. These primitive shoes were found stuffed with grass. Also from this period is evidence of murals of shoes and shoemakers found on the temple walls of the Egyptians.

Moving on to AD 600, Greek slaves were not allowed to wear shoes in order to distinguish them from free citizens. One hundred years later and the Roman emperor Aurelius proclaimed that only he and his successors could wear red sandals. A strange ruling perhaps, but not the only law relating to footwear. In the 1400s sumptuary law dictated the length of toes of shoes worn by knights. This was probably necessary as these shoes, called crackows, had toes of up to 24 inches in length.

The early 1500s brought high heels to shoe fashion. It is thought that Leonardo da Vinci may have invented them. This fashion caught on and by the mid 1500s platform shoes could be found rising to 30 inches. Various fashions in footwear continued and in the early 1600s the latest craze was shoelaces. As always, fashion goes in circles and by the mid 1600s platform shoes were back in fashion.

This time they were approximately 5 inches high and often highly decorated. Louis XIV, who, it is reported, was a short man, started this fad.

Around 100 years later, the first shoe production lines could be found. This meant that workers could concentrate on specific tasks rather than making a complete shoe.

By the late 1700s, shoe factories appeared. However, it was another 100 years before custom-made shoes became largely replaced. At about the same time, the first retail shoe shop was opened in Boston.

The early 1800s saw the return to popularity of flat shoes. Grecian type sandals were also fashionable. During the mid 1800s plimsolls were invented. These, of course, were the precursors of trainers, as we know them today. This century finished with a fashion for high buttoned shoes.

The 1900s

The 1900s saw great changes in the fashion, manufacture and materials used in footwear. The 19th century ended with a fashion for high buttoned leather shoes. Fashion dictated that narrow feet were stylish and people often wore shoes a full size too small in order to achieve this look. At its most extreme, some women even had their little toes removed in order to make their feet look smaller.

Most people wore boots during the day. However, elegance was the keyword for evening wear. Court shoes with a small Louis heel were the most popular. These were often decorated with metallic or embroidery thread. Another form of embellishment was glass or jet beading on the toes of the shoes. Common materials included soft kid or satin.

The manufacture of shoes shifted from cobblers to factories. These were popular because prices were much lower. This in turn meant that people could afford to look at shoes as accessories and own several pairs. This was a huge change, as until then people, men in particular, often owned just one pair of shoes that lasted several years.

As the Great War began, people were urged to be less frivolous and clothes and shoes were collected as part of the war effort. As clothing became more utilitarian, with men and women's shoes looking similar, it was decided that the materials used for shoe manufacture became much more varied. Often leather was mixed with coloured canvas or gabardine. Leathers were reversed to form suede shoes and often had a kid or patent finish. Removable buckles in cut steel, silver filigree, diamante or

ARTICLE

marcasite were used for both day and evening footwear.

In 1917 the first rubbered sole shoe was introduced to the American market. They were called 'sneakers' because they did not make a noise. All other shoes, with the exception of moccasins made a sound when you walked.

With the innovations in manufacturing in the 1920s, shoes became a focal point of fashion. Styles were influenced by crazes such as the Charleston dance. A securely fitting shoe that would not fly off was needed and so shoes with a closed toe, buttoned strap and low heels became the fashion. The materials used included dyed leather in bright colours and metallic finishes could be found. Luxury materials such as satin, brocade and velvet were also popular. The heel of the shoe was also decorated, often in lace or rhinestones.

Unfortunately, the 1930s brought a depression and this meant that clothes and shoes had to last longer. Sensible, low-heeled footwear became the order of the day. However, strappy evening sandals were popular with those who could afford luxury items. Platform shoes were again introduced, this time made of cork or wood.

The war years meant that yet again people needed to cut back. Because of a leather shortage, other materials needed to be found. Reptile skins and mesh proved to be the most suitable. Decorations were rare, although many women made their own.

In the United States, rules were introduced limiting the height of shoe heels to one inch and shoes were restricted to six colour choices.

Eventually the war ended and rationing gradually finished. In the fashion world extravagance became a keyword and shoes were available in every shape, size and colour. Designers urged people to have a different pair of shoes to match every outfit. The stiletto heel was introduced during the 1950s.

In the 1960s teenagers took over fashion and experimented with every style, textile, shape and colour imaginable. Footwear reflected this trend and anything and everything was possible. Knee length boots in vinyl or plastic were immensely popular and became something of a symbol for the 1960s.

Although the 1970s saw a return of economic depression, the pop culture of this decade saw people tottering around on shoes and boots with huge platform soles. These could be as high as 7–8 inches and were often lavishly embellished. By the end of the 70s, however, a more conservative approach was taken, with simple footwear. Some designers looked back in time for inspiration with Roman and Edwardian influences showing through. Running shoes became a popular item during this decade, but as a functional item.

The early 1980s brought a strange mixture of glamour and business. Power dressed women were very serious about their careers and in order to be taken seriously adopted a flat or low-heeled mode of footwear. The styles were classic and the colours muted – anything in fact to ensure they were not seen as frivolous women. However, the style of casual footwear compensated for this. Bright and colourful sandals, moccasins and espadrilles were popular with all.

At the beginning of the 21st century it appears that almost anything goes. People are no longer slavishly devoted to fashion. Comfort, it appears, has won the day.

Exam Practice 3, Element 1, Step 12 – SHOES3 – Page 1

ARTICLE

HISTORY OF FOOTWEAR

Pre 1900

The history of footwear is fascinating with the earliest recording of shoes being found in Missouri. Evidence has been found of shoes worn by Native Americans in 8000 BC. Shoes worn by 'Ice Man' from 3000 BC have been found in the French Alps. These primitive shoes were found stuffed with grass. Also from this period is evidence of murals of shoes and shoemakers found on the temple walls of the Egyptians.

Moving on to AD 600, Greek slaves were not allowed to wear shoes in order to distinguish them from free citizens. One hundred years later and the Roman emperor Aurelius proclaimed that only he and his successors could wear red sandals. A strange ruling perhaps, but not the only law relating to footwear. In the 1400s sumptuary law dictated the length of the toes of shoes worn by knights. This was probably necessary as these shoes, called crackows, had toes of up to 24 inches in length.

The early 1500s brought high heels to shoe fashion. It is thought that Leonardo da Vinci may have invented them. This fashion caught on and by the mid 1500s platform shoes could be found rising to 30 inches. Various fashions in footwear continued and in the early 1600s the latest craze was shoelaces. As always, fashion goes in circles and by the mid 1600s platform shoes were back in fashion.

This time they were approximately 5 inches high and often highly decorated. Louis XIV, who, it is reported, was a short man, started this fad.

Around 100 years later, the first shoe production lines could be found. This meant that workers could concentrate on specific tasks rather than making a complete shoe.

By the late 1700s, shoe factories appeared. However, it was another 100 years before custom-made shoes became largely replaced. At about the same time, the first retail shoe

shop was opened in Boston. The early 1800s saw the return to popularity of flat shoes. Grecian type sandals were also fashionable. During the mid 1800s plimsolls were invented. These, of course, were the precursors of trainers, as we know them today. This century finished with a fashion for high buttoned shoes.

The 1900s

The 1900s saw great changes in the fashion, manufacture and materials used in footwear. The 19th century ended with a fashion for high buttoned leather shoes. Fashion dictated that narrow feet were stylish and people often wore shoes a

full size too small in order to achieve this look. At its most extreme, some women even had their little toes removed in order to make their feet look smaller.

Most people wore boots during the day. However, elegance was the keyword for evening wear. Court shoes with a small Louis heel were the most popular. These were often decorated with metallic or embroidery thread. Another form of embellishment was glass or jet beading on the toes of the shoes. Common materials included soft kid or satin.

The manufacture of shoes shifted from cobblers to factories. These were popular because prices were much lower. This in turn meant that people could afford to look at shoes as accessories and own several pairs. This was a huge change, as until then people, men in particular, often owned just one pair of shoes that lasted several years.

As the Great War began, people were urged to be less frivolous and clothes and shoes were collected as part of the war effort. As clothing became more utilitarian in style so did the footwear, with men and women's shoes looking similar. It was at this time that the materials used for shoe manufacture became much more varied. Often leather was mixed with coloured canvas or gabardine. Leathers were reversed to form suede shoes and often had a kid or patent finish. Removable buckles in cut steel, silver filigree, diamante or

---

Exam Practice 3, Element 1, Step 12 – SHOES3 – Page 2

ARTICLE

marcasite were used for both day and evening footwear.

In 1917 the first rubbered sole shoe was introduced to the American market. They were called 'sneakers' because they did not make a noise. All other shoes, with the exception of moccasins made a sound when you walked.

With the innovations in manufacturing in the 1920s, shoes became a focal point of fashion. Styles were influenced by crazes such as the Charleston dance. A securely fitting shoe that would not fly off was needed and so shoes with a closed toe, buttoned strap and low heels became the fashion. The materials used included dyed leather in bright colours and metallic finishes could be found. Luxury materials such as satin, brocade and velvet were also popular. The heel of the shoe was also decorated, often in lace or rhinestones.

Unfortunately, the 1930s brought a depression and this meant that clothes and shoes had to last longer. Sensible, low-heeled footwear became the order of the day. However, strappy evening sandals were popular with those who could afford luxury items. Platform shoes were again introduced, this time made of cork or wood.

The war years meant that yet again people needed to cut back. Because of a leather shortage, other materials needed to be found. Reptile skins and mesh proved to be the most suitable. Decorations were rare, although many women made their own.

In the United States, rules were introduced limiting the height of shoe heels to one inch and shoes were restricted to six colour choices.

Eventually the war ended and rationing gradually finished. In the fashion world extravagance became a keyword and shoes were available in every shape, size and colour. Designers urged people to have a different pair of shoes to match every outfit. The stiletto heel was introduced during the 1950s.

In the 1960s teenagers took over fashion and experimented with every style, textile, shape and colour imaginable. Footwear reflected this trend and anything and everything was possible. Knee length boots in vinyl or plastic were immensely popular and became something of a symbol for the 1960s.

Although the 1970s saw a return of economic depression, the pop culture of this decade saw people tottering around on shoes and boots with huge platform soles. These could be as high as 7–8 inches and were often lavishly embellished.

By the end of the 70s, however, a more conservative approach was taken, with simple footwear. Some designers looked back in time for inspiration with Roman and Edwardian influences showing through. Running shoes became a popular item during this decade, but as a functional item.

The early 1980s brought a strange mixture of glamour and business. Power dressed women were very serious about their careers and in order to be taken seriously adopted a flat or low-heeled mode of footwear. The styles were classic and the colours muted – anything in fact to ensure they were not seen as frivolous women. However, the style of casual footwear compensated for this. Bright and colourful sandals, moccasins and espadrilles were popular with all.

At the beginning of the 21st century it appears that almost anything goes. People are no longer slavishly devoted to fashion. Comfort, it appears, has won the day.

Sharon Spencer

Cookery Article

COOKING TODAY

The Aga

Many people dream of living in a picturesque cottage deep in the heart of the country. In their dream cottage the kitchen features strongly. A large, sunny room with a huge pine kitchen table and an Aga is often featured.

Dr Gustaf Dalen invented the Aga or Aktiebolaget Gas Accumulator in 1924. The physicist and Nobel prize winner had lost his sight in an accident and it was while recovering at home that he decided to invent a multi-purpose, labour-saving cooker for his wife.

The original design was heavily insulated, with a small fire heating a large cast iron barrel. This barrel was kept at a specific constant temperature by means of an automatic draught control. Through conduction and radiation, the heat from the barrel was diverted to the key cooking areas of the appliance.

When first introduced, the Aga was said to be sufficient for a household of 16 people. In fact, early promotional literature stated that in intelligent hands a simple menu for 20 or 30 people could be prepared.

The range comprises a boiling plate, a simmering plate, a quick oven and a slow oven. It is capable of holding 10 gallons of hot water.

The Aga was first introduced to the UK in 1929. Despite the rising popularity of gas and electric cookers it quickly found a market in this country. The reason for its popularity must be because of its versatility. At the time of its introduction, traditional cooking facilities comprised a cast iron range. These were labour-intensive and required a great deal of cleaning and maintenance. The Aga is capable of all forms of cooking such as frying, grilling, roasting and baking. It requires only a minimum of cleaning and maintenance and is economical to run. Who could have asked for more?

The only real drawback to the early Agas was the price. In the early 1930s an Aga cost £57. 10s plus £5 for delivery and assembly. To justify the outlay of such a large sum the manufacturers boasted that the fuel bill for an Aga for one whole year would not exceed £4. However, £57. 10s was a substantial sum in those days and therefore only the affluent middle classes could afford them. The appliances were also popular with farm owners, hoteliers, innkeepers and other caterers who used them in a professional capacity.

In 1931 Bell's Heat Appliances, a newly formed company, began manufacturing Agas in this country. This widened their popularly and they could often be found in more professional catering establishments such as hospitals, factories and school canteens as well as army messes. These places received the benefits of using an appliance that was convenient, economical, efficient and simple to use.

Modern Agas

The popularity of large range type cookers has grown tremendously in recent years, with many people aspiring to own an Aga. The

6

What's new in the kitchen?

As home cooking rises in popularity, there is an increasing number of sophisticated gadgets available to assist the busy cook. This week we will look at two of the new appliances that will help you save time in the kitchen.

Breadmaker

Who doesn't enjoy the taste of freshly-baked homemade bread? A breadmaker will produce a freshly-baked loaf without any of the time consuming processes that have to be performed by hand. All you do is weigh the ingredients, place them in the machine and switch it on. A few hours later you will have a loaf of bread that tastes fantastic and has *no artificial preservatives*.

Many modern breadmakers have a timer facility that can be used so that you can wake to a just-baked loaf for breakfast. However, if you plan to do this you will need the loaf to finish approximately half an hour before you want to eat it. This is because the loaf needs to rest for a while to allow it to cool sufficiently to be cut.

As well as plain white or wholemeal loaves, you can bake a variety of different breads. Olive, sun-dried tomato and cheese and onion are all simple to make. Other uses for the breadmaker, depending on the model, can include:

- Cake making. Some models will bake large cakes, but it is important to follow the given recipe carefully.
- Jam and marmalade. These can be made in the appliance with relative ease, however, they can be a little runny.
- Pizzas. The breadmaker makes excellent pizza dough. All you need do is roll out, top and bake.
- Rolls and fancy breads. Depending on the model and recipe you can make any number of different breads and rolls. As with pizza dough, you must remove the dough from the machine, shape and then bake.

We have tried a number of appliances and have had excellent results from all. We highly recommend these machines to our readers.

Coffee Grinder

Although these are not new appliances we feel it is worth drawing attention to these handy gadgets. One quick blast from the coffee grinder and you have freshly ground coffee that tastes wonderful. Just the thing to go with the freshly baked bread!

The majority of grinders have a control that will allow you to choose how finely the coffee will be ground. This means they are suitable for both percolators and cafetières.

Coffee beans are readily available in supermarkets and delicatessens. Many enthusiasts combine beans of different types until they have created their 'own blend'. The only drawback we encountered is that cleaning around the blades can be difficult. Care should be taken as the blades are sharp.

Sharon Spencer Cookery Special

Sharon Spencer

Cookery Article

COOKING TODAY

The Aga

Many people dream of living in a picturesque cottage deep in the heart of the country. In their dream cottage the kitchen features strongly. A large, sunny room with a huge pine kitchen table and an Aga is often featured.

Dr Gustaf Dalen invented the Aga or Aktiebolaget Gas Accumulator in 1924. The physicist and Nobel prize winner had lost his sight in an accident and it was while recovering at home that he decided to invent a multi-purpose, labour-saving cooker for his wife.

The original design was heavily insulated, with a small fire heating a large cast iron barrel. This barrel was kept at a specific constant temperature by means of an automatic draught control. Through conduction and radiation, the heat from the barrel was diverted to the key cooking areas of the appliance.

When first introduced, the Aga was said to be sufficient for a household of 16 people. In fact, early promotional literature stated that in intelligent hands a simple menu for 20 or 30 people could be prepared.

The range comprises a boiling plate, a simmering plate, a quick oven and a slow oven. It is capable of holding 10 gallons of hot water.

The Aga was first introduced to the UK in 1929. Despite the rising popularity of gas and electric cookers it quickly found a market in this country. The reason for its popularity must be because of its versatility. At the time of its introduction, traditional cooking facilities comprised a cast iron range. These were labour-intensive and required a great deal of cleaning and maintenance. The Aga is capable of all forms of cooking such as frying, grilling, roasting and baking. It requires only a minimum of cleaning and maintenance and is economical to run. Who could have asked for more?

The only real drawback to the early Agas was the price. In the early 1930s an Aga cost £57. 10s plus £5 for delivery and assembly. To justify the outlay of such a large sum the manufacturers boasted that the fuel bill for an Aga for one whole year would not exceed £4. However, £57. 10s was a substantial sum in those days and therefore only the affluent middle classes could afford them. The appliances were also popular with farm owners, hoteliers, innkeepers and other caterers who used them in a professional capacity.

In 1931 Bell's Heat Appliances, a newly formed company, began manufacturing Agas in this country. This widened their popularly and they could often be found in more professional catering establishments such as hospitals, factories and school canteens as well as army messes. These places received the benefits of using an appliance that was convenient, economical, efficient and simple to use.

Modern Agas

The popularity of large range type cookers has grown tremendously in recent years, with many people aspiring to own an Aga. The cost of a double oven cooker starts at around £5,000 and so is still owned primarily by the more affluent in our society.

6

Sharon Spencer

Cookery Article

cost of a double oven cooker starts at around £5,000 and so is still owned primarily by the more affluent in our society.

Agas have the capacity to run a complete central heating system and, as new models have been designed to run on electricity, gas and oil as well as solid fuel, everyone can have one. Many self-builders choose to install an Aga as both a cooking appliance and a central heating boiler. The initial outlay does not seem so large when you add together the cost of a top of the range cooker and a central heating boiler which would otherwise need to be installed.

Apart from the initial cost, there are three main drawbacks. The first is that the temperature of the two ovens cannot be altered. The ovens are set at different temperatures to provide a hot oven and a slow oven, but you cannot regulate these as with modern cooking appliances. This problem can

be easily overcome but first you must take a whole new approach to cookery. In recent years, a number of cookery books specifically for Aga cookery have been published.

The second drawback is the heat that it produces. If you are using your appliance to supply hot water, then it must be kept on at all times. In warm weather, particularly in smaller kitchens, the heat can be rather intense. However, many owners feel this is a small price to pay for such a wonderful piece of equipment.

The third drawback is the sheer size and weight of the cooker. The Aga weighs in at around 12 cwt. Apart from needing a large space to put the cooker, the floor must be able to support its substantial weight.

However, those who own Agas feel that the benefits of having such a magnificent piece of equipment far outweigh the small drawbacks. The popularity of these cookers has risen in the last few years with an Aga being seen as a status symbol. 'Aga sagas' is a common term used to describe novels that feature usually middle-aged, middle class women who live in country properties. Recently a programme devoted to Agas, their history and the people who own them, was screened on television. This programme featured an owner who had the floors of his flat strengthened at considerable cost in order to install an Aga.

New Range

The range of Agas has been extended considerably in recent years. As well as the traditional double oven model, you can now purchase larger models with 3 or 4 ovens. A smaller version is also available for those who do not have the space for the traditional model.

The Aga also comes in a range of colours. As well as the traditional cream, they are now available in red, orange, black, blue and green to match any fashionable kitchen. They are as much a focal point of the home in the 21st century as they were when they were first invented over 70 years ago. There are not many other appliances that have proved to be so enduring over the years.

7

Guide to Property Buying

Choosing a New Home

Obviously one of the biggest restrictions on your choice of new home is your budget. The first thing you need to do is find out how much you will be able to borrow from a mortgage lender. As a rough guide, most lenders will allow around three times the joint salaries, although some will allow three and three quarters. Remember, you will probably have to find a deposit, around five to ten percent of the purchase price of the property.

Once you have worked out how much you can afford then you can start to look for your dream home. Before you start, think about the following points. Do you have a particular type of property in mind, such as a Victorian home or a brand new property? Are you willing to compromise on this? Is a garage or off-road parking a must? What about the size of the garden? Are you willing to carry out repair or redecoration works? These decisions will help you in your search.

Visit as many estate agents as possible. Discuss your requirements thoroughly with each so that they understand the type of property you are looking for. The more information you can give them, the more chance they have of finding something suitable.

View as many different houses as you can. Be prepared to look at some properties that may not seem immediately suitable. You may be surprised to find that your tastes can change as you look at different properties.

If you can, be prepared to spend several weeks finding a property. *Don't forget, properties are placed on the market every day.* Do not feel as though you have to buy the first house that comes along. Your new home will probably be the biggest single purchase you will ever make. You will want to get it right first time.

Choosing a Mortgage

The mortgage market can be a minefield to many of us. The range of products available is huge and it changes rapidly. However, this should not deter you from shopping around to ensure you obtain the best deal available at the time. Given below is a brief description of some of the types of mortgage you may encounter.

- Variable rate loan. This is the most common type of loan and the interest rate moves up or down according to the Bank of England base rates. With this type of loan you must be prepared for the possibility of your mortgage payments increasing. In the late 1980s mortgage rates almost doubled in a matter of a year or so. Conversely, if the base rate falls then so will your mortgage repayments.

- Fixed rate loan. This type of loan has a fixed interest rate for a specified period. It may be for as little a time as one year or could be for as long as ten years. The advantage of this

type of loan is that you know how much your monthly repayments will be for the fixed period. This can be very useful.

- Discount rate loan. These loans offer a discount on the variable rate offered at the time. Some are guaranteed to be at least a certain percentage lower than the base rate for a specified period of time. Your mortgage payments can rise or fall as with the variable rate, albeit at a lower rate.

- Capped rate loan. With a capped rate, the interest rate will not rise above a certain specified amount during the period for which it is capped. This means that if interest rates rise sharply, your mortgage will be protected at a certain level, usually around one or two percent lower. However, if mortgage rates fall, then your monthly payments will decrease in line.

- Flexible loans. These have become more popular in recent years with a large number of new products being developed by mortgage lenders. With this type of loan you have the flexibility of paying larger or smaller amounts than usual, depending on your circumstances. Some products will allow you to take a 'payment break' or even withdraw some of your payments.

Whichever type of mortgage loan you are interested in, it is advisable to seek advice from a financial advisor or mortgage expert.

Cookery Article

New Range

The range of Agas has been extended considerably in recent years. As well as the traditional double oven model, you can now purchase larger models with 3 or 4 ovens. A smaller version is also available for those who do not have the space for the traditional model. The Aga also comes in a range of colours. As well as the traditional cream, they are now available in red, orange, black, blue and green to match any fashionable kitchen. They are as much a focal point of the home in the 21st century as they were when they were first invented over 70 years ago. There are not many other appliances that have proved to be so enduring over the years.

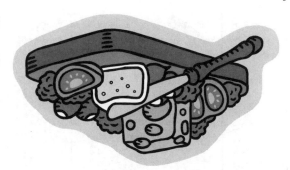

around 12 cwt. Apart from needing a large space to put the cooker, the floor must be able to support its substantial weight.

However, those who own Agas feel that the benefits of having such a magnificent piece of equipment far outweigh the small drawbacks. The popularity of these cookers has risen in the last few years with an Aga being seen as a status symbol. 'Aga sagas' is a common term used to describe novels that feature usually middle-aged, middle class women who live in country properties. Recently a programme devoted to Agas, their history and the people who own them, was screened on television. This programme featured an owner who had the floors of his flat strengthened at considerable cost in order to install an Aga.

Sharon Spencer

Agas have the capacity to run a complete central heating system and, as new models have been designed to run on electricity, gas and oil as well as solid fuel, everyone can have one. Many self-builders choose to install an Aga as both a cooking appliance and a central heating boiler. The initial outlay does not seem so large when you add together the cost of a top of the range cooker and a central heating boiler which would otherwise need to be installed.

Apart from the initial cost, there are three main drawbacks. The first is that the temperature of the two ovens cannot be altered. The ovens are set at different temperatures to provide a hot oven and a slow

oven, but you cannot regulate these as with modern cooking appliances. This problem can be easily overcome but first you must take a whole new approach to cookery. In recent years, a number of cookery books specifically for Aga cookery have been published.

The second drawback is the heat that it produces. If you are using your appliance to supply hot water, then it must be kept on at all times. In warm weather, particularly in smaller kitchens, the heat can be rather intense. However, many owners feel this is a small price to pay for such a wonderful piece of equipment.

The third drawback is the sheer size and weight of the cooker. The Aga weighs in at

Exercise 20

PARKER SECONDARY SCHOOL FILM CLUB

About Us

The Parker Secondary School Film Club was set up two years ago by Ralph Jameson and Penny Lamb, both of whom were sixth formers at the time. The club started with a membership of 12 students. The club meets once a month on Thursdays at 3.30 pm in the sixth form common room.

A film is shown followed by a discussion – usually stimulating and sometimes heated. Members pay a small subscription fee of £2 each month, however, there is no obligation to remain a member for any length of time. A list of films is circulated to all members at the beginning of each month and members vote for which film they would like to view. A wide range of films to suit all tastes is offered and can range from the latest cartoon to a horror story or thriller.

We are always on the look-out for new members. If you would like to join please contact Sarah Lipton, the club secretary.

Coming Soon ...

We are changing the rules next month and will not be giving our members a vote! We will be showing a film that has often been requested but has never been made it to the final selection. We won't tell you which one it is, but can tell you that it was only released last year and is an action movie. The film will be shown next month at the usual time of 3.30 pm. New members are very welcome.

Trips Out

As well as showing films at school each month we often organise other events with the film club run by Bertram School. The advantage of this is that we can share the cost of hiring the films and of course have a drink afterwards! Bertram School also visits our club on a regular basis.

Next term we hope to arrange the following 007 season with Bertram School. This should be an exciting series for fans of James Bond. These events are in addition to our monthly viewings. In order for people to travel to the school these films are shown at 4.30 pm. If you have an idea for a series of films that we can show, please let us know.

Date	Film	Location
13/1	Live and Let Die	Bertram School
31/1	Diamonds are Forever	Parker School
4/2	The Spy who Loved Me	Parker School
18/2	A View to a Kill	Bertram School

Christmas Viewing

The club has received a number of suggestions for our Christmas film this year. All are old favourites and whichever is selected, we are sure it will be very entertaining. The films that have been suggested this season include White Christmas – a well-loved favourite starring Bing Crosby – A Nightmare before Christmas – an animated film with wonderful characters and interesting story line – and It's a Wonderful Life – a fabulous classic weepie starring James Stewart. It is not too late to make a suggestion if there is a film you would particularly like to see. Final suggestions should reach Sarah by the end of the month.

It is customary to have refreshments after the Christmas film and this year is no exception. Poppy is in charge of organising this and feels that a payment of £2 per person will be sufficient to cover the cost. If you would like to join in please ensure you give your money by 8 December.

A raffle is held at this event. Tickets are 20p and the first prize is a £20 cinema voucher for the local multiplex. Poppy will be selling tickets outside the dining hall at lunchtime each day from 1 December.

The raffle is open to non-members. The proceeds are divided in two with half going to a local charity. The rest of the profits are put towards the cost of running the film club.

Exercise 19.8 – CLOTHES

CAREER CLOTHING COMPANY AUTUMN NEWSLETTER

Autumn/Winter Range

Our Autumn/Winter range hits the shops next month and we hope you will agree that it's our best yet. The range comprises many new styles and colours and comes with the quality and value-for-money guarantee our customers expect from Career Clothing Company.

This season we have introduced a new range of casual clothes for both men and women. This has been in response to requests from many of our customers. Cotton jersey separates, sweatshirts and fleeces are included in the range. Prices start from as little as £18 for a sweatshirt and £35 for a polar fleece. We feel sure you will love the casual designs in easy-to-wear fabrics. All designs come in a choice of colours and, of course, our usual wide variety of sizes.

The Classic range has been extended this season and now includes wool mix suits for both men and women. Smart, stylish and beautifully made, these are suitable for any occasion. Prices for these high-quality garments start from £180 for a skirt suit. Men's suits start at £240. We have also included a selection of carefully chosen accessories to match our new range. Belts, bags and shoes have been specially designed to complement our Classic range. They are made from high-quality leather and are manufactured to a high specification. Both the Classic and Casual ranges an be seen at any of our stores, in our mail-order catalogue and on our website.

Loyalty Card

Career Clothing Company is delighted to announce its new loyalty card. This card will entitle holders to a minimum of 5% discount on all purchases. The discount rises the more you spend. Customers who spend over £250 in any one transaction will receive a discount of 15%. There is no membership or application fee and you can use your card immediately. The card can be used at any of our retail stores, by mail order or at our Internet store.

To obtain your loyalty card please call our Freephone number on 0800 426791. An application form will be sent by return. Just complete and return it to us and we will process your application immediately. Don't delay – you could be saving pounds!

Warehouse Sale

In order to make way for our new autumn/winter range we are having a warehouse clearance. Many of our summer lines will be reduced by up to 50% of the full price. The sale is by mail order only and a leaflet will be sent to everyone who is registered on our mailing list. The sale is for a limited period only and some items have very limited availability.

If you are not currently registered on our list, don't despair. Call us on 0800 426791 and order your sale leaflet, quoting reference SA14. Our usual postage rates are also reduced for the sale period and are as follows:

Order value	Postage and packing
Up to £25	£2.00
£25-£75	£2.80
£75-£150	£3.20
Over £150	Post free

Career Clothing Goes Online!

If you like our garments, but don't enjoy shopping, visit our new website at careerclothes.co.uk for the latest ranges and sales information. The website shows the full range of styles and gives detailed descriptions of all garments in our range. You can even shop online.

We offer a full ordering service and can provide you with up-to-date information on stock availability. The ordering service is a secure site so you can have complete peace of mind. Delivery is usually within 7 to 10 days.

We welcome feedback on our site. If you have any comments to make regarding our website, or our service, please e-mail us on feedback@careerclothes.co.uk. We look forward to hearing from you.

Exercise 22 – FILM1

PARKER SECONDARY SCHOOL FILM CLUB

About Us

The Parker Secondary School Film Club was set up two years ago by Ralph Jameson and Penny Lang, both of whom were sixth formers at the time. The club started with a membership of 12 students, and it has now grown to just over 50. The club meets once a month on Thursdays at 3.30 pm in the sixth form common room.

A film is shown followed by a discussion – usually stimulating and sometimes heated. Members pay a small subscription fee of £2 each month, however, there is no obligation to remain a member for any length of time.

A list of films is circulated to all members at the beginning of each month and members vote for which film they would like to view. A wide range of films is offered and can range from the latest cartoon to a horror story or thriller.

We are always on the look-out for new members. If you would like to join please contact Sarah Lipton, the club secretary.

Christmas Viewing

The club has received a number of suggestions for our Christmas film this year. All are old favourites and whichever is selected, we are sure it will be very entertaining. The films that have been suggested this season include White Christmas – a well-loved favourite starring Bing Crosby – A Nightmare before Christmas – an animated film with wonderful characters and interesting story line – and It's a Wonderful Life – a fabulous classic weepie starring James Stewart. It is not too late to make a suggestion if there is a film you would particularly like to see. Final suggestions should reach Sarah by the end of the month.

A raffle is held at this event. Tickets are 20p and the first prize is a £20 cinema voucher for the local multiplex. Poppy will be selling tickets outside the dining hall at lunchtime each day from 1 December. The raffle is open to non-members. The proceeds are divided in two with half going to a local charity. The rest of the profits are put towards the cost of running the film club.

Coming Soon ...

We are changing the rules next month and will not be giving our members a vote! We will be showing a film that has often been requested but has never made it to the final selection. We won't tell you which one it is, but can tell you that it was only released last year and is an action movie. The film will be shown next month at the usual time of 3.30 pm. New members are very welcome.

Trips Out

As well as showing films at school each month we often organise other events with the film club run by Bertram School. The advantage of this is that we can share the cost of hiring the films and of course have a drink afterwards! Bertram School also visits our club on a regular basis.

Next term we hope to arrange the following 007 season with Bertram School. This should be an exciting series for fans of James Bond. These events are in addition to our monthly viewings. In order for people to travel to the school these films are shown at 4.30 pm. If you have an idea for a series of films that we can show, please let us know.

Date	Film	Location
13/1	Live and Let Die	Bertram School
31/1	Diamonds are Forever	Parker School
4/2	The Spy who Loved Me	Parker School
18/2	A View to a Kill	Bertram School

Exercise 21.9 – CLOTHES1

CAREER CLOTHING COMPANY AUTUMN NEWSLETTER

Autumn/Winter Range

Our Autumn/Winter range hits the shops next month and we hope you will agree that it's our best yet. The range comprises many new styles and colours and comes with the quality and value-for-money guarantee our customers expect from Career Clothing Company.

This season we have introduced a new range of casual clothes for both men and women. This has been in response to requests from many of our customers. Cotton jersey separates, sweatshirts and fleeces are included in the range. Prices start from as little as £18 for a sweatshirt and £35 for a polar fleece. We feel sure you will love the casual designs in easy-to-wear fabrics. All designs come in a choice of colours and, of course, our usual wide variety of sizes.

The Classic range has been extended this season and now includes wool mix that suits for both men and women. Smart, stylish and beautifully made, these are suitable for any occasion. Prices for these high-quality garments start from £180 for a skirt and £240 for a suit. Men's suits start at £240. We have also included a selection of carefully chosen accessories to match our new range. Belts, bags and shoes have been specially designed to complement our Classic range. They are made from high-quality leather and are manufactured to a high specification. Both the Classic and Casual ranges an be seen at any of our stores, in our mail-order catalogue and on our website.

Loyalty Card

Career Clothing Company is delighted to announce its new loyalty card. This card will entitle holders to a minimum of 5% discount on all purchases. The discount rises the more you spend. Customers who spend over £250 in any one transaction will receive a discount of 15%. There is no membership or application fee and you can use your card immediately. The card can be used at any of our retail stores, by mail order or at our Internet store.

To obtain your loyalty card please call our freephone number on 0800 426791. An application form will be sent by return. Just complete and return it to us and we will process your application immediately. Don't delay – you could be saving pounds!

Warehouse Sale

In order to make way for our new autumn/winter range we are having a warehouse clearance. Many of our summer lines will be reduced by up to 50% of the full price. The sale is by mail order only and a leaflet will be sent to everyone who is registered on our mailing list. The sale is for a limited period only and some items have very limited availability.

If you are not currently registered on our list, don't despair. Call us on 0800 426791 and order your sale leaflet, quoting reference SA14.

Career Clothing Goes Online!

If you like our garments, but don't enjoy shopping, visit our new website at careerclothes.co.uk for the latest ranges and sales information. The website shows the full range of styles and gives detailed descriptions of all garments in our range. You can even shop online.

We offer a full ordering service and can provide you with up-to-date information on stock availability. The ordering service is a secure site so you can have complete peace of mind. Delivery is usually within 7 to 10 days.

We welcome feedback on our site. If you have any comments regarding our service, or our website, please e-mail us on feedback@careerclothes.co.uk. We look forward to hearing from you.

Exercise 23.6 – FORM – Page 2

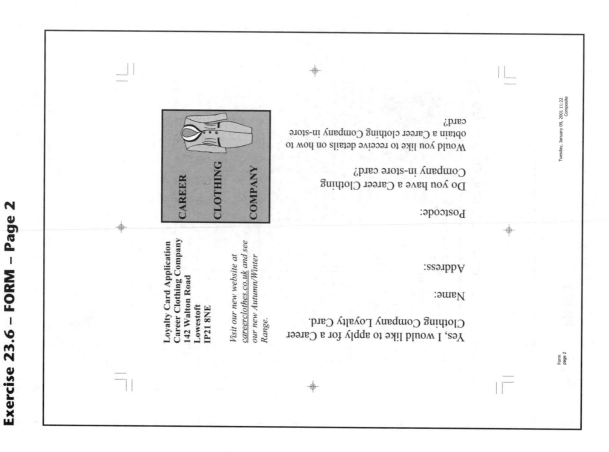

(Content shown upside-down/mirrored as a composite printer's form proof)

CAREER

CLOTHING

COMPANY

Would you like to receive details on how to obtain a Career clothing Company in-store card?

Do you have a Career Clothing Company in-store card?

Postcode:

Address:

Name:

Yes, I would like to apply for a Career Clothing Company Loyalty Card.

Loyalty Card Application
Career Clothing Company
142 Walton Road
Lowestoft
IP21 8NE

Visit our new website at careerclothes.co.uk and see our new Autumn/Winter Range.

Tuesday, January 09, 2001 11:22
Composite

Form
page 2

Exercise 23.6 – FORM – Page 1

LOYALTY
CARD

Application Form

CAREER

CLOTHING

COMPANY

Our new Loyalty Card could be saving you money. You will receive a minimum of 5% discount on all your purchases. However, the more you spend, the more you save. If you spend over £250 in any one transaction you will receive a massive 15%.

To apply to join our Loyalty Scheme, fill in the details overleaf and return the card to us at
142 Walton Road
Lowestoft
IP21 8NE

Tuesday, January 09, 2001 11:22
Composite

Form
page 1

Exercise 23.6 – FORM – Page 1 Spot 1

Exercise 23.6 – FORM – Page 1 Black

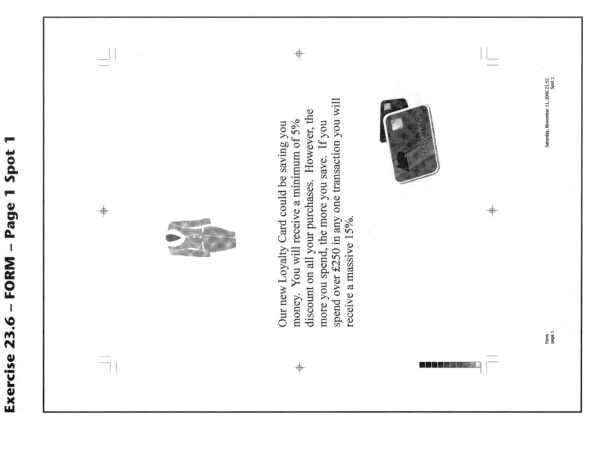

Exercise 23.6 – FORM – Page 2 Spot 1

Exercise 23.6 – FORM – Page 2 Black

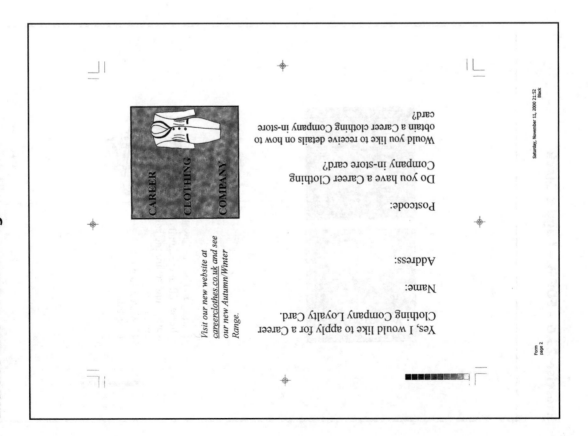

Exercise 24 – TICKET – Page 2

PARKER SECONDARY SCHOOL FILM CLUB

This year the film nominations are:

- White Christmas
- A Nightmare Before Christmas
- It's a Wonderful Life

If you can help with refreshments please let Poppy know

Raffle tickets are available at 20p each.
First prize: £20 voucher for multiplex cinema
Second prize: £10 voucher for multiplex cinema
Third prize: Box of chocolates

Exercise 24 – TICKET – Page 1

PARKER SECONDARY SCHOOL

REFRESHMENTS!
RAFFLE!
SEASONAL FILM!

CHRISTMAS PARTY TICKET
12 December
Sixth Form Common Room
3.30 pm

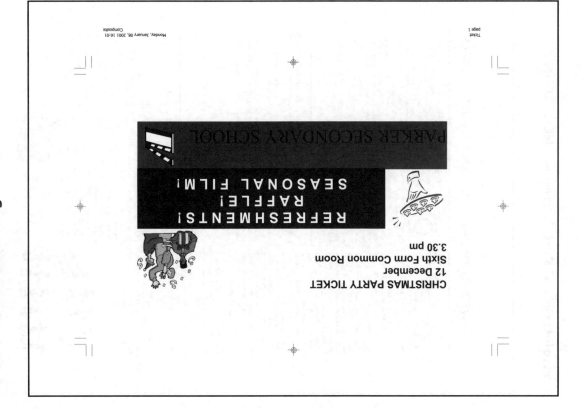

Consolidation 5, Part 2, Step 7 – NEWTOWN1

NEWTOWN PRIMARY SCHOOL PTA NEWSLETTER

The PTA

All parents of Newtown Primary School are members of the PTA. The committee, elected by members, consists of 8 parents and 1 teacher representative. Committee members can serve for a maximum of 4 years. Meetings are held every 4 weeks and all members are welcome. The details of these meetings are displayed on the PTA noticeboard in the main school corridor.

The committee's officers comprise a chairperson, vice chairperson, treasurer and secretary. These posts are for a 2-year period. The officers must be serving on the committee and are elected by the committee members.

The main function of the PTA is to raise funds for the school. These monies help provide the more luxurious items such as IT equipment, musical instruments, library books and play equipment. It also subsidises school trips which means that trips are affordable by all. Funds are raised by 3 or 4 main events each year. These usually include a Christmas Bazaar, Summer Fete and Sponsored Spell. The children are actively involved in these events which prove to be educational and enjoyable.

As well as fund-raising the PTA also organises social events. Discos, barn dances, barbecues and quiz nights are a few of the events that have been held in the last few years. These are well supported and great fun.

If you would like to be involved in the PTA but haven't the time to join the committee don't worry! We are always looking for willing helpers to man stalls, make refreshments and, of course, wash up.

During the coming year we will need to replace 3 committee members as their children will be leaving the school. If you are interested in joining please contact Marge Lovell, the committee secretary.

Auction of Promises

Our next main fund-raising event should prove to be a great night out for parents and supporters of the school. We are holding an Auction of Promises on 23 March at 7.30 pm in the school hall.

The auction lots will consist of 'promises' made or donated by parents and local businesses. A promise can be anything from a pair of theatre tickets to receiving a freshly baked cake for a birthday party.

We have been given a number of promises but we could do with lots more. You can promise almost anything. Ideas include doing the ironing, walking the dog, looking after a pet hamster for a week, digging the garden, an evening's babysitting – whatever you can do. If you can persuade your company to give a fee for the proceedings, giving his services free of charge, an evening's babysitting – whatever you can do. If you can't help, please attend the meeting as it should be lots of fun. Philip Malcolm, a local auctioneer, has kindly agreed to run the proceedings, giving his services free of charge. Refreshments will be available and there will also be a raffle.

Tickets will be available at the end of next week and will cost £1.50 per person.

School Clothing

We have been asked by the Headteacher to remind parents that we sell school clothing on Tuesdays in the dining hall.

From 3.30 pm to 4.15 pm you can purchase any of the school garments including sweatshirts, gym kit and polo shirts. These items are all embroidered with the school logo.

The garments are made from 100% cotton and we feel they represent excellent value for money. They are machine washable and can be tumble dried. These garments do not shrink and are very hard wearing.

We usually have all sizes in stock. Given below are examples of the low cost of these garments.

Item	Price
Sweatshirt	£9.50
Polo shirt	£5.00
Gym shirt	£4.50
Gym shorts	£4.00

Dates for your Diary

As well as the Auction of Promises we have some more events lined up for this term. On March 17 we will be helping with the annual Sponsored Spell. About a week beforehand your child will be given 20 words to learn and a test will be given on the day. Prizes are given for children who get all 20 words correct. Please help your child by sponsoring them per word. Last year we raised over £700.

A cake sale will be held on Friday 3 April. This is to tie in with the children's charity day. As you are aware, children are encouraged to raise money for a local charity and can help to do this by paying a fee to wear 'civilian' clothes on Charity Day. The proceeds from the cake sale will go to our local charity, the Homeless Shelter. Please send in cakes on Friday morning and come and buy after school at 3.30 pm.

Book week is another important event in our school calendar. This will be held the week beginning March 10. The PTA will be holding a book sale each day after school in the main hall. Please support this event by coming along and buying a book. The proceeds from the sale will enable us to purchase more books for the school library.

Consolidation 5, Part 1, Step 8 – NEWTOWN

NEWTOWN PRIMARY SCHOOL PTA NEWSLETTER

The PTA

All parents of Newtown Primary School are members of the PTA. The committee, elected by members, consists of 8 parents and 1 teacher representative. Committee members can serve for a maximum of 4 years. Meetings are held every 4 weeks and all members are welcome. The details of these meetings are displayed on the PTA noticeboard in the main school corridor.

The committee's officers comprise a chairperson, vice chairperson, treasurer and secretary. These posts are for a 2-year period. The officers must be serving on the committee and are elected by the committee members.

The main function of the PTA is to raise funds for the school. These monies help provide the more luxurious items such as IT equipment, musical instruments, library books and play equipment. It also subsidises school trips which means that trips are affordable by all. Funds are raised by 3 or 4 main events each year. These usually include a Christmas Bazaar, Summer Fete and Sponsored Spell. The children are actively involved in these events which prove to be educational and enjoyable.

As well as fund-raising the PTA also organises social events. Discos, barn dances, barbecues and quiz nights are a few of the events that have been held in the last few years. These are well supported and great fun.

If you would like to be involved in the PTA but haven't the time to join the committee don't worry! We are always looking for willing helpers to man stalls, make refreshments and, of course, wash up.

During the coming year we will need to replace 3 committee members as their children will be leaving the school. If you are interested in joining please contact Marge Lovell, the committee secretary.

Auction of Promises

Our next main fund-raising event should prove to be a great night out for parents and supporters of the school. We are holding an Auction of Promises on 23 March at 7.30 pm in the school hall.

The auction lots will consist of 'promises' made or donated by parents and local businesses. A promise can be anything from a pair of theatre tickets to receiving a freshly baked cake for a birthday party.

We have been given a number of promises but we could do with lots more. You can promise almost anything. Ideas include doing the ironing, walking the dog, looking after a pet hamster for a week, digging the garden, an evening's babysitting – whatever you can do. If you can persuade your company to give a fee for this item, so much the better.

We need to have your promise by the end of February as catalogues need to be collated. Please contact Jenny Riseman as soon as possible.

If you can't help, please attend the meeting as it should be lots of fun. Philip Malcolm, a local auctioneer, has kindly agreed to run the proceedings, giving his services free of charge. Refreshments will be available and there will also be a raffle.

Tickets will be available at the end of next week and will cost £1.50 per person.

School Clothing

We have been asked by the Headteacher to remind parents that we sell school clothing on Tuesdays in the dining hall.

From 3.30 pm to 4.15 pm you can purchase any of the school garments including sweatshirts, gym kit and polo shirts. These items are all embroidered with the school logo.

The garments are made from 100% cotton and we feel they represent excellent value for money. They are machine washable and can be tumble dried. These garments do not shrink and are very hard wearing.

We usually have all sizes in stock. Given below are examples of the low cost of these garments.

Item	Price
Sweatshirt	£9.50
Polo shirt	£5.00
Gym shirt	£4.50
Gym shorts	£4.00

Dates for your Diary

As well as the Auction of Promises we have some more events lined up for this term. On March 17 we will be helping with the annual Sponsored Spell. About a week beforehand your child will be given 20 words to learn and a test will be given on the day. Prizes are given for children who get all 20 words correct. Please help your child by sponsoring them per word. Last year we raised over £700.

A cake sale will be held on Friday 3 April. This is to tie in with the children's charity day. As you are aware, children are encouraged to raise money for a local charity and can help to do this by paying a fee to wear 'civilian' clothes on Charity Day. The proceeds from the cake sale will go to our local charity, the Homeless Shelter. Please send in cakes on Friday morning and come and buy after school at 3.30 pm.

Book week is another important event in our school calendar. This will be held the week beginning March 10. The PTA will be holding a book sale each day after school in the main hall. Please support this event by coming along and buying a book. The proceeds from the sale will enable us to purchase more books for the school library.

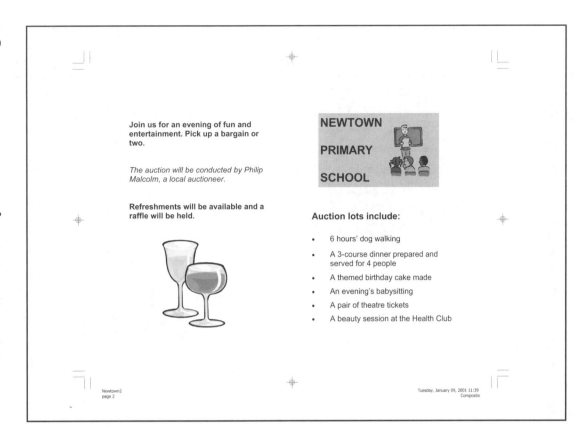

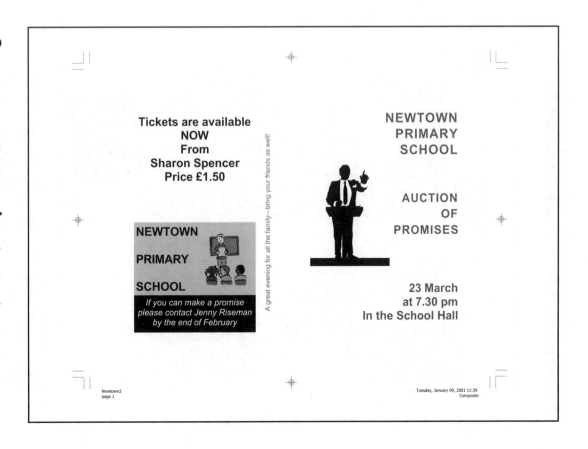

WEDDING BELLES

About Us

Wedding Belles is a brand new store supplying everything you need to plan and organise a wedding under one roof. From organising and booking the ceremony to supplying and serving the champagne on the day, we can help with every aspect of your special occasion.

Our staff have been specially trained to provide you with an expert, first-class service. If you have any questions regarding the organisation of your wedding then do pop in and see if we can help. We are sure we will be able to!

Wedding Belles aims to stock all your wedding requirements from invitation and stationery, through outfits for the bride, groom and bridesmaids to gifts and household items for your new home. Call in to see us or visit our website at www.weddingbelles.co.uk.

Watch Out For …

Our two-day exhibition events that are to be held at various venues across the country. On show will be displays of all our goods and services. A fashion show of the latest designs in gowns and accessories will be held twice daily. There will also be competitions with fabulous prizes including a two-week, all-expenses-paid honeymoon in Cyprus.

Entrance will be by ticket only. We recommend that you apply for tickets as soon as possible as demand is sure to be high.

Wedding Gowns

We think you will be amazed when you see our selection of over 300 wedding gowns. Whatever your taste and budget, we are confident that we will be able to supply the dress of your dreams.

Our range includes exclusive designs from famous names such as Caroline Sullivan, Marie Hendy and Ralph Langdon to name just 3. However, if your budget won't stretch to a designer dress then don't despair. We have beautiful gowns costing from as little as £300.

If you have set your heart on a particular style of dress then talk to us. We can commission the dress of your dreams to be custom made.

As well as gowns we stock a complete range of matching accessories such as veils, shoes and headdresses.

Did You Know …

Changes in the law mean that you can now have a much greater choice of where to hold your wedding ceremony. Country hotels, places of historic interest, theatres and even castles can now be hired as wedding venues. For those who would like a wedding with a difference there are thousands of venues to choose from all over the country.

Although the choice is much greater, there are still legal requirements that have to be met. The premises must be approved by the local authority for marriages. If, however, the venue you have in mind does not currently have this status, it may be possible for approval to be obtained.

There are a number of advantages to holding your civil ceremony at a hotel or other location. You may be able to choose a venue that has special significance for you and your partner. It can be very convenient to hold the ceremony at the same venue as the reception. Many Registry Offices are rather sombre venues and do not have the romantic setting that a wedding requires.

If you do decide to hold your wedding ceremony at an approved venue then obviously you will have to book the date and time directly with the manager of the venue. However, you will still have to give formal notice to the Superintendent Registrar of the district in which you live. Under normal circumstances a period of 21 days' notice should be given. It is possible to obtain a special licence which reduces this period. Your local Superintendent Registrar will be able to give you full details on how to apply for a special licence.

We recently attended a wedding in a theatre. The ceremony took place on stage and the guests formed the 'audience' and sat in the stalls. The bride was led onto the stage by a piper and it was a very exciting occasion. The bride and groom enjoyed putting together 'wedding programmes' for their guests. These contained a brief history of themselves, the best man, bridesmaids and other principal guests. The order of ceremony was included and they made a great souvenir of a very romantic day.

Your local authority will be able to supply you with a list of approved venues in your district or you can look at the listings on our website.

WEDDING BELLES

About Us

Wedding Belles is a brand new store supplying everything you need to plan and organise a wedding under one roof. From organising and booking the ceremony to supplying and serving the champagne on the day, we can help with every aspect of your special occasion.

Our staff have been specially trained to provide you with an expert, first-class service. If you have any questions regarding the organisation of your wedding then do pop in and see if we can help. We are sure we will be able to!

Wedding Belles aims to stock all your wedding requirements from invitation and stationery, through outfits for the bride, groom and bridesmaids to gifts and household items for your new home. Call in to see us or visit our website at www.weddingbelles.co.uk.

Wedding Gowns

We think you will be amazed when you see our selection of over 300 wedding gowns. Whatever your taste and budget, we are confident that we will be able to supply the dress of your dreams.

Our range includes exclusive designs from famous names such as Caroline Sullivan, Marie Hendy and Ralph Langdon to name just 3. However, if your budget won't stretch to a designer dress then don't despair. We have beautiful gowns costing from as little as £300.

If you have set your heart on a particular style of dress then talk to us. We can commission the dress of your dreams to be custom made.

As well as gowns we stock a complete range of matching accessories such as veils, shoes and headdresses.

Given below are a few of our favourite gowns for this season.

Dress	Price
White satin	£490
Cream silk	£680
Blue velvet	£875
Red velvet	£950

Did You Know …

Changes in the law mean that you can now have a much greater choice of where to hold your wedding ceremony. Country hotels, places of historic interest, theatres and even castles can now be hired as wedding venues. For those who would like a wedding with a difference there are thousands of venues to choose from all over the country.

Although the choice is much greater, there are still legal requirements that have to be met. The premises must be approved by the local authority for marriages. If, however, the venue you have in mind does not currently have this status, it may be possible for approval to be obtained.

There are a number of advantages to holding your civil ceremony at a hotel or other location. You may be able to choose a venue that has special significance for you and your partner. It can be very convenient to hold the ceremony at the same venue as the reception. Many Registry Offices are rather sombre venues and do not have the romantic setting that a wedding requires.

If you do decide to hold your wedding ceremony at an approved venue then obviously you will have to book the date and time directly with the manager of the venue. However, you will still have to give formal notice to the Superintendent Registrar of the district in which you live. Under normal circumstances a period of 21 days' notice should be given. It is possible to obtain a special licence which reduces this period. Your local Superintendent Registrar will be able to give you full details on how to apply for a special licence.

We recently attended a wedding in a theatre. The ceremony took place on stage and the guests formed the 'audience' and sat in the stalls. The bride was led onto the stage by a piper and it was a very exciting occasion. The bride and groom enjoyed putting together 'wedding programmes' for their guests. These contained a brief history of themselves, the best man, bridesmaids and other principal guests. The order of ceremony was included and they made a great souvenir of a very romantic day.

Your local authority will be able to supply you with a list of approved venues in your district or you can look at the listings on our website.

Watch Out For …

Our two-day exhibition events that are to be held at various venues across the country. On show will be displays of all our goods and services. A fashion show of the latest designs in gowns and accessories will be held twice daily. There will also be competitions with fabulous prizes including a two-week, all-expenses-paid honeymoon in Cyprus. Entrance will be by ticket only. We recommend that you apply for tickets as soon as possible as demand is sure to be high.

Consolidation 6, Part 3, Step 6 – WEDDING3 – Page 2

Don't miss the fashion show, held twice daily at 11.00 am and 3.00 pm.

Admittance by Ticket only.

Tickets are available from:

**Wedding Belles
129 Havelock Road
LONDON
WC1 2QB**

Visit our website: www.weddingbelles.co.uk

Everything you need for a fabulous wedding will be found at our two-day exhibition. There will also be many trade stands including:

- Jewellery
- Gowns
- Gifts
- Stationery
- Cakes
- Flowers

Wedding Belles

Monday, January 08, 2001 16:03
Composite

WEDDING 3
page 2

Consolidation 6, Part 3, Step 6 – WEDDING3 – Page 1

Enter our Free Draw to win fabulous prizes including:

First Prize –
Two-week honeymoon in Cyprus

Second Prize –
Bridal gown to the value of £1000

Third Prize –
Jewellery voucher to the value of £750

Wedding Belles

has pleasure in inviting
Sharon Spencer
to a

WEDDING EXHIBITION

**Saturday and Sunday
1 and 2 June
At the Bristol Exhibition Centre**

Refreshments will be served

Monday, January 08, 2001 16:03
Composite

WEDDING 3
page 1

GRANNY'S GARDEN CENTRE

This Month

This month we are having a special feature on water gardens. Come along to the centre and see our magnificent display of equipment and plants. \These will help you make a wonderful water feature in your own garden. Our friendly and experienced staff would be delighted to answer any of your questions, or you can pick up one of our free guides to designing and building a pond.

Most people like to have a water feature in their garden. From large ponds to small containers, you can always find room in your garden for one. They don't have to be expensive either. Good quality liners do not cost a great deal and if you visit Granny's Garden Centre this month you will find many special offers on selected liners, plants and equipment.

We feel now is the right time to plan your garden so that it can be in place by the summer. Imagine sitting in your deckchair, basking in the warmth of the sun and watching the reflections in your newly finished pond or container. Sounds appealing? Pay us a visit soon. We look forward to seeing you.

One-Day Workshops

These are back by popular demand! We held a few workshops last autumn and were astounded by the response we received from our customers. As they were so popular we have decided to make these a regular feature of the centre. We are therefore pleased to announce that we have enlisted several well-known names in the gardening world to host these events.

This month, to tie in with our special feature, we will be holding workshops on water gardens. These will be led by Peter Walters, who is an expert in this area.

The first is entitled Planning and Building a Water Garden and aims to tell you all you need to know in order to build a feature in your own garden. The second, Planting a Water Garden will give you masses of ideas on how to turn your water garden into a stunning display.

Date	Title
31 May	Planning and Building a Water Garden
2 April	Planning a Water Garden
5 April	Planning and Building a Water Garden
11 April	Planning a Water Garden

Garden Furniture

We have managed to source a wonderful new supplier of quality garden furniture. We will soon be taking delivery of the new ranges and we are sure you will agree that these are superb items.

There are two main ranges, the Chatsworth and the Kensington. The Chatsworth is made from best quality Indonesian teak. The wood has come from renewable sources. The designs are traditional and the furniture has been hand-crafted to the highest possible standard. These items will last for many years with only a minimum of maintenance. The range includes tables, chairs, benches and parasols.

The Kensington range is of the same excellent quality and also made from best quality Indonesian teak. The designs, however, are modern and very striking. They will be a real talking point among your friends and family. This range also includes tables, chairs, benches and parasols.

We have samples of both ranges at the centre and would be pleased to reserve stock for you. We are expecting our full stock to be delivered by the end of the month.

Your Summer Garden

We are now building up our stocks of bedding plants for the summer season. Start planning your requirements now as our stocks won't last for ever! If you have any special requirements let us know. We keep stocks of a wide variety of plants and can supply almost anything. However, if your requirements are not part of our usual stock we would be pleased to make a special order on your behalf.

GRANNY'S GARDEN CENTRE

This Month

This month we are having a special feature on water gardens. Come along to the centre and see our magnificent display of equipment and plants. These will help you make a wonderful water feature in your own garden. Our friendly and experienced staff would be delighted to answer any of your questions, or you can pick up one of our free guides to designing and building a pond.

Most people like to have a water feature in their garden. From large ponds to small containers, you can always find room in your garden for one. They don't have to be expensive either. Good quality liners do not cost a great deal and if you visit Granny's Garden Centre this month you will find many special offers on selected liners, plants and equipment.

We feel now is the right time to plan your garden so that it can be in place by the summer. Imagine sitting in your deckchair, basking in the warmth of the sun and watching the reflections in your newly finished pond or container. Sounds appealing? Pay us a visit soon. We look forward to seeing you.

Your Summer Garden

We are now building up our stocks of bedding plants for the summer season. Start planning your requirements now as our stocks won't last for ever! If you have any special requirements let us know. We keep stocks of a wide variety of plants and can supply almost anything. However, if your requirements are not part of our usual stock we would be pleased to make a special order on your behalf.

If you would like help in designing your summer flower beds then pop into the centre. We can design a garden for you using our new landscape garden software. All you need to do is bring measurements of your garden plus a small sample of your garden soil. Discuss you requirements with one of our garden designers and they will plan a garden layout for you.

Plant suggestions, colour schemes and features are all included in the plan. A small charge of £15 is made for this service. We are confident that you will be delighted with the results.

Garden Furniture

We have managed to source a wonderful new supplier of quality garden furniture. We will soon be taking delivery of the new ranges and we are sure you will agree that these are superb items.

There are two main ranges, the Chatsworth and the Kensington. The Chatsworth is made from the best quality Indonesian teak. The wood has come from renewable sources.

The designs are traditional and the furniture has been hand-crafted to the highest possible standard. These items will last for many years with only a minimum of maintenance. The range includes tables, chairs, benches and parasols.

The Kensington range is of the same excellent quality and also made from best quality Indonesian teak. The designs, however, are modern and very striking. They will be a real talking point among your friends and family. This range also includes tables, chairs, benches and parasols.

We have samples of both ranges at the centre and would be pleased to reserve stock for you. We are expecting our full stock for you. We are expecting our full stock to be delivered by the end of the month.

One-Day Workshops

These are back by popular demand! We held a few workshops last autumn and were astounded by the response we received from our customers. As they were so popular we have decided to make these a regular feature of the centre. We are therefore pleased to announce that we have enlisted several well-known names in the gardening world to host these events.

This month, to tie in with our special feature, we will be holding workshops on water gardens. These will be led by Peter Walters, who is an expert in this area.

The first is entitled Planning and Building a Water Garden and aims to tell you all you need to know in order to build a feature in your own garden. The second, Planting a Water Garden will give you masses of ideas on how to turn your water garden into a stunning display.

The fee for each day is £20 and includes lunch and refreshments. The day starts at 10.30 am and will finish at 4.30 pm. These are sure to be very popular and so it is advisable to book early. Telephone 01262 238998 to secure your place.

Date	Title
31 May	Planning and Building a Water Garden
2 April	Planning a Water Garden
5 April	Planning and Building a Water Garden
11 April	Planning a Water Garden

Exam Practice 5, Element 3, Step 5 – GARDEN3 – Page 2

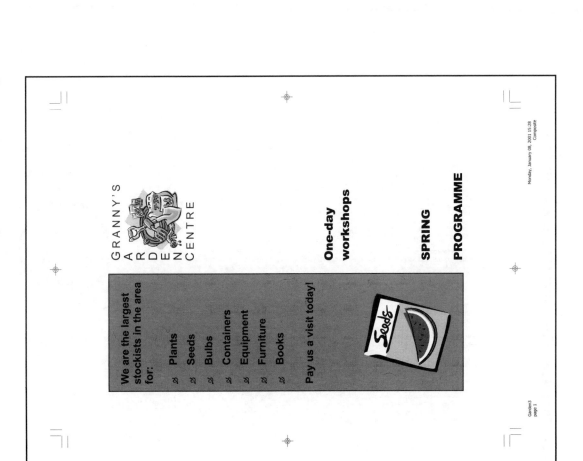

Visit our website at GrannysGardens.co.uk

Tickets are available
From

Sharon Spencer
Granny's Garden Centre
ANYTOWN
AN1 9NO

Phone:
01262 238998
E-mail
Granny@Anytown.co.uk

Price £20 to include lunch
and refreshments

GRANNY'S
GARDEN
CENTRE

Our workshops this spring concentrate on water features. We feel sure you will enjoy the two workshops which will help you plan, build and plant a water feature in your garden.

Each workshop starts at 10.30 am and finishes at 4.30 pm.

It is advisable to book early as places are limited and demand is sure to be high.

31 May
Planning and Building
a Water Garden

2 April
Planting a Water
Garden

5 April
Planning and Building
a Water Garden

11 April
Planting a Water

Monday, January 08, 2001 15:28
Composite

Garden3
page 2

Exam Practice 5, Element 3, Step 5 – GARDEN3 – Page 1

GRANNY'S
GARDEN
CENTRE

We are the largest
stockists in the area
for:

✿ **Plants**
✿ **Seeds**
✿ **Bulbs**
✿ **Containers**
✿ **Equipment**
✿ **Furniture**
✿ **Books**

Pay us a visit today!

**One-day
workshops**

SPRING

PROGRAMME

Seeds

Monday, January 08, 2001 15:28
Composite

Garden3
page 1

Exam Practice 6, Element 2, Step 7 – SPORT2

SPORT FOR ALL

Try a New Sport

If you feel you are not a 'sporty' person, nor do you enjoy organised or team games, you may miss out on a great deal of fun and healthy exercise. Not all sports are organised games and there are many that do not involve joining a team or club.

Some sports that can be enjoyed include archery, windsurfing, sub aqua and tobogganing. The centre is holding a display of many types of solo sport. Why not pay us a visit and investigate further? You may be missing out.

Focus on Fencing

Fencing is a fast and athletic sport. The object of the game, or 'bout' as it is officially called, is to score 15 points on your opponent. As the play is so fast, scoring is carried out electronically with points being gained when a 'touch' is scored. A touch is when your weapon hits your opponent in the target area. The fencers bout in an area (called a piste) that measures 6 x 40 feet. A match is made up of 3 bouts, each lasting 3 minutes.

There are 3 different weapons used in fencing; the foil, épée or sabre. All 3 are point thrusting weapons, however the sabre is also a cutting weapon. The target area differs according to the weapon being used and obviously weapons are not mixed during a game. Therefore participants generally become skilled using one type of weapon, although some like to master all 3.

The foil is approximately 35 inches long and has a flexible, rectangular blade. It weighs less than one pound and is therefore light to handle. To score a point, the tip of the blade must be used and it should land within the torso of the body.

The torso is the target area of the foil, from the shoulders to the groin, front and back. The arms, head, neck and legs are not included in the target area. In order for points to register, the fencer's uniform includes a metallic vest, called a lamé, which covers the valid target area. A small spring-loaded tip is attached to the point of the foil and is connected to a wire inside the blade. The fencer wears a body cord inside the uniform which connects the foil to a reel wire, connected to the scoring machine.

There are 3 scoring lights on the machine. One shows a green light when the fencer is hit, one shows a red light for when the opponent is hit and one shows a white light for a hit off target.

The épée is similar in length to the foil but weighs approximately 27 ounces and has a larger guard and much stiffer blade. Touches are scored with the point of the blade only and the entire body is a valid target area. The fencer's uniform does not contain a lamé as the entire body is a valid target area.

The sabre is similar in length and weight to the foil. The main difference is that the sabre is a cutting weapon as well as a thrusting weapon. The target area is from the bend of the hips to the top of the head including the arms, simulating a cavalry rider on a horse. The uniform consists of a lamé and a metal mask as the head is also a valid target area.

As with the foil, there are three scoring lights, a green, a red and a white, on the machine.

If you are new to this sport, it can be difficult to follow the speed of the action. It is a good idea to follow just one of the fencers to start with. Watch out for the 'parry', which is a motion used to deflect an opponent's blade and the 'riposte' which is the answering attack. Players change between attack and defence throughout the bout. Whenever a hit is made, the referee will stop the bout, describe the actions and decide whether or not to award the touch.

As you become accustomed to the speed of the game, the tactics and strategies become more apparent and you will begin to understand the fascination of this sport.

Fee Information

Unfortunately the cost of running the sports centre has risen substantially over the past few months. It has been decided that in order to meet these costs, fees will be increased with effect from next month.

Exam Practice 6, Element 1, Step 8 – SPORT1

SPORT FOR ALL

Focus on Fencing

Fencing is a fast and athletic sport. The object of the game, or 'bout' as it is officially called, is to score 15 points on your opponent. As the play is so fast, scoring is carried out electronically with points being gained when a 'touch' is scored. A touch is when your weapon hits your opponent in the target area. The fencers bout in an area (called a piste) that measures 6 x 40 feet. A match is made up of 3 bouts, each lasting 3 minutes.

There are 3 different weapons used in fencing; the foil, épée or sabre. All 3 are point thrusting weapons, however the sabre is also a cutting weapon. The target area differs according to the weapon being used and obviously weapons are not mixed during a game. Therefore participants generally become skilled using one type of weapon, although some like to master all 3.

The foil is approximately 35 inches long and has a flexible, rectangular blade. It weighs less than one pound and is therefore light to handle. To score a point, the tip of the blade must be used and it should land within the torso of the body.

The torso is the target area of the foil, from the shoulders to the groin, front and back. The arms, head, neck and legs are not included in the target area. In order for points to register, the fencer's uniform includes a metallic vest, called a lamé, which covers the valid target area. A small spring-loaded tip is attached to the point of the foil and is connected to a wire inside the blade. The fencer wears a body cord inside the uniform which connects the foil to a reel wire, connected to the scoring machine.

There are 3 scoring lights on the machine. One shows a green light when the fencer is hit, one shows a red light for when the opponent is hit and one shows a white light for a hit off target.

The épée is similar in length to the foil but weighs approximately 27 ounces and has a larger guard and much stiffer blade. Touches are scored with the point of the blade only and the entire body is a valid target area. The fencer's uniform does not contain a lamé as the entire body is a valid target area.

The sabre is similar in length and weight to the foil. The main difference is that the sabre is a cutting weapon as well as a thrusting weapon. The target area is from the bend of the hips to the top of the head including the arms, simulating a cavalry rider on a horse. The uniform consists of a lamé and a metal mask as the head is also a valid target area.

As with the foil, there are three scoring lights, a green, a red and a white, on the machine.

If you are new to this sport, it can be difficult to follow the speed of the action. It is a good idea to follow just one of the fencers to start with. Watch out for the 'parry', which is a motion used to deflect an opponent's blade and the 'riposte' which is the answering attack. Players change between attack and defence throughout the bout. Whenever a hit is made, the referee will stop the bout, describe the actions and decide whether or not to award the touch.

As you become accustomed to the speed of the game, the tactics and strategies become more apparent and you will begin to understand the fascination of this sport.

Try a New Sport

If you feel you are not a 'sporty' person, nor do you enjoy organised or team games, you may miss out on a great deal of fun and healthy exercise. Not all sports are organised games and there are many that do not involve joining a team or club.

Some sports that can be enjoyed include archery, windsurfing, sub aqua and tobogganing. The centre is holding a display of many types of solo sport. Why not pay us a visit and investigate further? You may be missing out.

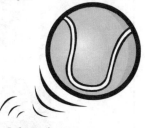

Fee Information

Unfortunately the cost of running the sports centre has risen substantially over the past few months. It has been decided that in order to meet these costs, fees will be increased with effect from next month.

The new fee structure will be as follows:

Activity	Cost
Swimming	£2.50 per session
Squash Court	£4.80 per half hour
Badminton Court	£10 per hour
Gym	£4.50 per session

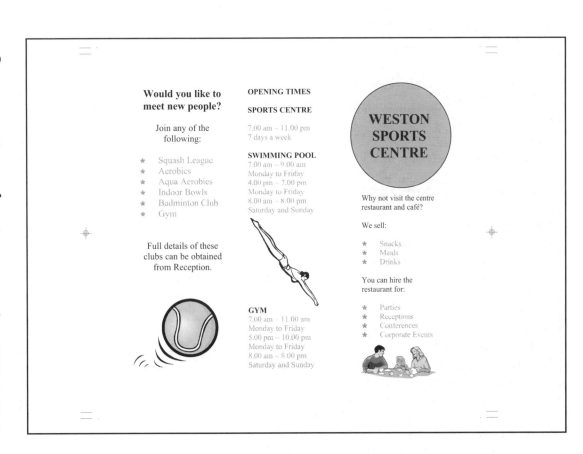

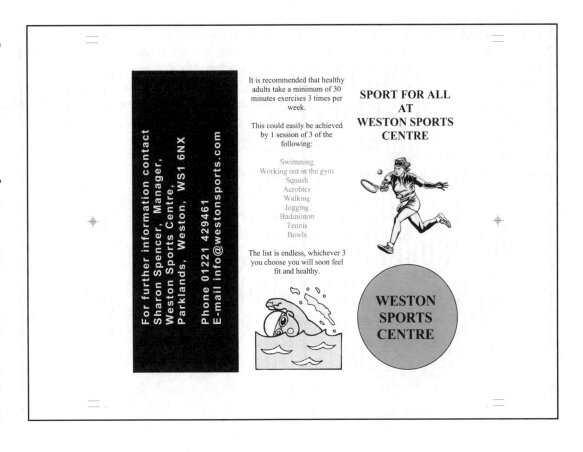

Appendix

Terminology

Bold darker, thicker version of a font or typeface

Bullet symbol that is used to highlight points instead of numbers; often takes form of full stop that sits in middle of typing line

Character letters, numbers and other symbols

Clip Art graphic images that are non-copyright

Crop to cut a graphic image

Font typeface

Footer text printed outside bottom margin

Graphic picture, line or drawing

Guide non-printing lines that allow you to place text and images accurately

Gutter space between columns on a page

Header text printed outside top margin

Indent text moved in from left margin

Italic sloping version of a typeface

Justification alignment of text flush to both margins

Kerning spaces between letters

Landscape page orientation – longer edge at top

Leading spacing between lines of text

Lower case small letters

Master page/template templates set for each page in a document or publication; items placed on master pages will print on each page of document

Monospaced type each character takes up same amount of space on page regardless of size

Orphan line of text that appears on own at top of page

Point unit of measurement for type sizes

Portrait page orientation – shorter edge at top

Proofreading checking a document for errors

Proportional spacing each character uses only amount of space it needs on page

Sans serif typeface that does not have strokes on bottom of letters such as **m**, **n** and **k**

Serif typeface that does have strokes on bottom of letters such as **m**, **n** and **k**

Style sheet set of formatting details set to be applied to sections of text in a document

Text wrap invisible border of space around graphic image that acts as barrier between text and graphics

Typeface family of type characters – e.g. Times New Roman or Gill Sans

Upper case capital letters

Widow line of text that appears on own at bottom of page, or column

Keyboard Shortcuts

Keyboard	Menu
F1	Help
F5	Go to Page (enables you to go to a specified page in a multi-page document)
F6	Arrange: Bring to Front
Shift + F6	Arrange: Send to Back
F7	Spell Check
F9	Toggle view from page view to 100%
Ctrl + N	File: New document
Ctrl + O	File: Open an existing document
Ctrl + S	File: Save a document
Ctrl + P	File: Print document
Ctrl + X	Edit: Close
Ctrl + C	Edit: Copy
Ctrl + V	Edit: Paste
Ctrl + A	Edit: Highlight entire story
Ctrl + F	Edit: Find
Ctrl + H	Edit: Replace
Ctrl + G	View: Go to Page
Ctrl + M	View: Go to Background (or to Foreground)
Ctrl + Shift + Y	View: Show special characters
Ctrl + Shift + O	View: Hide boundaries and guides
Ctrl + Shift + N	Insert: New page
Ctrl + D	Format: Shadow
Ctrl + W	Tools: Snap to Guides
Alt + F4	Exit Publisher

Right Mouse Clicks

Clicking on the right mouse button will bring up a variety of menus, depending on what you are doing. For example, if you have selected an image so that the handles are showing and you right-click, then the following menu will appear:

You can then move the pointer up the menu and choose any of the functions listed. Note that there are two items with submenus: **Change Picture** and **Change Frame**.

If you then decided to click on the **Change Picture** option the following submenu will appear:

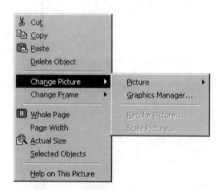

If you have selected a text frame and then right-click, the following menu will appear:

As you can see, the options that this menu gives are slightly different.

The functions of the right-mouse click are too numerous to list here as the menu that appears differs according to what you are doing. However, you can test them out yourself. Try right-clicking when you are manipulating text or images and see what functions appear on the menu. These can be very useful and save you considerable time.

Glossary

The menu and mouse actions change depending on what you are doing in Publisher. For example, if you have clicked on some text or a text frame, then the menus will relate to text manipulation such as enhancements, alignment, spacing etc. If you have selected a graphic or image frame then the menus will relate to graphics and images. Ensure that you have selected the correct type of item – graphic or text before you use this guide.

Action	Keyboard	Mouse	Menu
Alignment of text		Click on: one of the alignment buttons: ≡ ≡ ≡ ≡	**Format: Indents and Lists**
Autofit			**Format: Autofit: Best Fit**
Bold text	**Ctrl + B**	Click on: **B Bold**	**Format: Font**
Boxes		Click on: ☐ **Rectangle Tool**	
Bring to Front	**Shift + F6**	Click on: **⤢ Bring to Front**	**Arrange: Bring to Front**
Bulleted lists		Click on: ≔ **Bullets**	**Format: Indents and Lists**
Centre Text		Click on: ≡ **Center**	**Format: Indents and Lists**
Clip Art		Click on: ▣ **Clip Art**	**Insert: Clip Art**
Close a file			**File: Close**
Columns – Guides			**Arrange: Layout guides**
Columns – Insert			**Arrange: Layout guides**
Connecting Text Boxes		Click on: ⬭ **Connect Text Frames**	**Tools: Connect Text Frames**
Copying text or images	Select text or image to be copied		
	Ctrl + C	Click on: ▤ **Copy**	**Edit: Copy**
Cropping Graphics		Click on: ⌗ **Crop Picture**	
Crop Marks (printer's marks)			**File: Print: Advanced Print Settings: Printer's Marks: Crop Marks**
Colour separations *to set up in document*			**Tools: Commercial Printing Tools: Colour Separation**
to print			**File: Print: Print Separations**
Cursor Movement *to required position*	Use arrow keys:		
to top of document	**Ctrl + Home**		
to end of document	**Ctrl + End**		
left word by word	**Ctrl + ←**		
right word by word	**Ctrl + →**		
to end of line	**End**		
to start of line	**Home**		
to top/bottom of paragraph	**Ctrl +** or **Ctrl +**		
up/down one screen	**PgUp** or **Pg Dn**		

Action	Keyboard	Mouse	Menu
Custom Shapes		Click on: 🔲 **Custom Shapes**	
Cut text	**Ctrl + X**	Click on: ✂ **Cut**	**Edit: Cut**
Disconnect Text Frames		Click on: ✄ **Disconnect Text Frames**	
Dropped Capitals			**Format: Drop Cap**
Enumeration		Click on: ▤ **Numbering**	**Format: Indents and lists**
Exit the program	**Alt + F4**	Click Control Button at right of title bar	**File: Exit**
Facing Pages			**Arrange: Layout Guides; Create two backgrounds with mirrored pages**
Fill colour (Text or picture frame)		Click on: 🪣 **Fill Color**	**Format: Fill Color**
Find text	**Ctrl + F**		**Edit: Find**
Font colour		Click on: ⬛ **Font Color**	
Font size		Key in value in ⬚ the **Font Size** box	**Format: Font**
to increase	**Ctrl +]**	Click on: **A** **Increase Font Size**	
to decrease	**Ctrl + [**	Click on: **A** **Decrease Font Size**	
Font typeface	**Ctrl + Shift + F** Select font	Select font from ⬚ the **Font** box	**Format: Font**
Format Painter (to copy formats)	**Ctrl + Shift + C**	Click on: 🖌 **Format Painter**	
Full page borders		Click on: ▤ **Line/Border Style**	**Format: Lines/borders**
Go to (a specified page)	**Ctrl + G** *or* **F5**		
Go to Background (master pages)	**Ctrl + M**		**View: Go to Background**
Go to Foreground (master pages)	**Ctrl + M**		**View: Go to Foreground**
Go to Next Frame		Click on: ▣ **Go to Next Frame**	
Go to Previous Frame		Click on: ▣ **Go to Previous Frame**	
Gutter Space		Click on: ▣ **Text Frame Properties**	**Format: Text Frame Properties: Columns: Spacing**
Help function	**F1** (contents) *or* **Shift +F1** (What's this?)	Click on: ❓ **Help**	**Help**

Action	Keyboard	Mouse	Menu
Hyphenation	**Ctrl + Shift + H**		**Tools**: **Language**: **Hyphenation**
Indent text		Click on: **Increase Indent** *or* Click on: **Decrease Indent**	**Format**: **Indents and Lists**
Insert Page	**Ctrl + Shift + N**		**Insert**: **Page**
Insert Picture Frame		Click on: **Picture Frame**	**Insert**: **Picture**; **From file**
Insert text box		Click on: **A Text Frame**	
Insert text file			**Insert**: **Text file**
Irregular Text Wrap		Click on: **Wrap Text to Picture**	**Format**: **Picture Frame Properties**
Italics	**Ctrl + I**	Click on: **Italic**	**Format**: **Font**
Justified Right margin		Click on: **Justify**	**Format**: **Indents and Lists**
Kerning			**Format**: **Character Spacing**: **Kerning**
Landscape Orientation			**File**: **Page Setup**, **Paper Size**, **Landscape**
Leading			**Format**: **Line Spacing**
Left Aligned text		Click on: **Align Left**	**Format**: **Indents and Lists**
Lines (change colour)		Click on: **Line Color**	**Format**: **Line Style**: **More Styles**: **Line Colour**
Lines (drawing)		Click on: **Line Tool**	
Lines (dotted or dashed)		Click on: **Dash Style**	**Format**: **Line Style**: **More Styles**: **Dashed Style**
Lines (change weight)		Click on: **Line/Border Style**	**Format**: **Line/Border Style**
Line Spacing			**Format**: **Line Spacing**
Margin Guides (to change)			**Arrange**: **Layout Guides**
Margins (to change)			**Arrange**: **Layout guides**
Mirrored Pages			**Arrange**: **Layout Guides**: **Create two backgrounds with mirrored guides**
Non-Standard Page Size			**File**: **Page Setup**: **Choose a Publication Layout**: **Special Size** (then complete Width and Height Boxes)
Open an existing file	**Ctrl + O**	Click on: **Open**	**File**: **Open**
Open a New File	**Ctrl + N**	Click on: **New**	**File**: **New**
Page Numbering			**Insert**: **Page Numbers**
Page Numbering (from page other than 1)			**Tools**: **Options**

Action	Keyboard	Mouse	Menu
Page Setup			**File: Page Setup**
Paragraph Spacing			**Format: Line Spacing**
Print hard copy	**Ctrl + P**	Click on: 🖨 **Print**	**File: Print**
Print colour separations			**Tools: Commercial printing tools, Print spot colour** then **File: Print; Print Separations**
Regular text wrap		Click on: ▣ **Wrap Text to Frame**	**Format: Picture Frame Properties**
Remove text emphasis		Click on: **B** *I* U the appropriate button	**Format: Font**
Replace Text	**Ctrl + H**		**Edit: Replace**
Restore deleted text	**Ctrl + Z**	Click on: ↺ **Undo**	
Resize Image			**Format: Scale Picture**
Reverse Text		Highlight text Click on: ▲ **Font Color** and select white Click on: 🖌 **Fill Color** and select black	
Right Align Text		Click on: ☰ **Align Right**	**Format: Indents and Lists**
Rotate (Text or Image) Custom		Click on: 🔄 **Custom Rotate**	**Arrange: Rotate or Flip: Custom Rotate**
Rotate (Text or image) Left		Click on: ◤ **Rotate Left**	**Arrange: Rotate or Flip: Rotate Left**
Rotate (Text or Image) Right		Click on: ◥ **Rotate Right**	**Arrange: Rotate or Flip: Rotate Right**
Ruler (to display)			**View: Ruler**
Ruler Guides (to display)			**Arrange: Ruler Guides;** choose appropriate guide
Save work	**Ctrl + S**	Click on: 💾 **Save**	**File: Save**
Save work as			**File: Save as**
Send to Back	**Shift + F6**	Click on: ▣ **Send to Back**	**Arrange: Send to Back**
Shading (text)		Click on: 🖌 **Fill Color**	**Format: Fill Color**
Spellcheck	**F7**		**Tools: Spelling**
Tables (insert)		Click on: ▦ **Table Frame Tool**	**Table: Insert**
Tables (inserting rows or columns)			**Table: Insert rows or columns**
Tables (deleting rows or columns)			**Table: Delete rows or columns**
Tables (Autofit)			**Table: Autofit**

Action	Keyboard	Mouse	Menu
Tabs		∟ Left tab ⊥ Centre tab ⌐ Right tab ⊥ Decimal tab	**Format: Tabs**
Text Styles			**Format: Text Style**
Text Wrap		Click on: **Wrap Text to Picture**	**Format: Edit irregular text wrap**
Tracking			**Format: Character spacing**
Two-Page Spread			**View: Two page spread**
Underscore	**Ctrl + U**	Click on: U **Underline**	**Format: Font**
Units of Measurement			**Tools: Options: General: Measurement Units**
View		Click on: 100% and select zoom size	
Zoom		Click on: − **Zoom Out** Click on: + **Zoom In**	**View: Zoom**